London's *Bastille*

The only contemporary representation of a cell in Coldbath Fields, this etching from 1818 depicts Thomas Ranson (1784–1828), who had been arrested for forgery. His cell was probably one of those usually allocated to state prisoners. (Heritage Image Partnership Ltd/Alamy Stock Photo)

LONDON'S
Bastille

Mutineers, Radicals and Murder in COLDBATH FIELDS HOUSE OF CORRECTION

STEPHEN HADDELSEY

FOREWORD BY LORD KEN MACDONALD, KC

> Out of the way we went, and then we found
> What 'twas to tread upon forbidden ground:
> And let them that come after have a care,
> Lest heedlesness makes them, as we, to fare:
> Lest they, for trespassing, his prisoners are,
> Whose Castle's Doubting, and whose name's Despair.
>
> John Bunyan, *The Pilgrim's Progress* (1678)

Persons obnoxious to a minister or a magistrate, may be committed to such a prison, and never be heard of more. Like the prisoners of the late Bastille of France, they may disappear from among their friends, and be forgotten.

> Sir Richard Phillips, *A Letter to the Livery of London* (1808)

First published 2025

The History Press
97 St George's Place, Cheltenham,
Gloucestershire, GL50 3QB
www.thehistorypress.co.uk

© Stephen Haddelsey, 2025

The right of Stephen Haddelsey to be identified as the Author of this work has been asserted in accordance with the Copyright, Designs and Patents Act 1988.

All rights reserved. No part of this book may be reprinted or reproduced or utilised in any form or by any electronic, mechanical or other means, now known or hereafter invented, including photocopying and recording, or in any information storage or retrieval system, without the permission in writing from the Publishers.

British Library Cataloguing in Publication Data.
A catalogue record for this book is available from the British Library.

ISBN 978 1 80399 887 9

Typesetting and origination by The History Press
Printed and bound in Great Britain by TJ Books, Padstow, Cornwall.

The History Press proudly supports

Trees for Life

www.treesforlife.org.uk

EU Authorised Representative: Easy Access System Europe
Mustamäe tee 50, 10621 Tallinn, Estonia
gpst.request@easproject.com

Contents

	Foreword by Lord Ken Macdonald, KC	7
	Prologue	9
1	'The Cries of the Miserable': Howard's Call to Reform	13
2	'Some Alteration Should Be Made': Design and Build	26
3	'Diversified in Disposition and Pursuits': The Governor and His Wards	42
4	'Our Jacks Will Grumble': Naval Mutinies at Spithead and the Nore	56
5	'Disaffected Persons': The Advocates of Radical Reform	67
6	'The Heaviest Penalty': Radicals in the House of Correction	85
7	'Everybody Knows the Bastille': Burdett's Campaign	100
8	'Disgraceful to Humanity': Debates and Inquiries	123
9	'An Improper Place of Confinement': The Royal Commission	141
10	'The Ambition of an Honest Man': The Middlesex Elections	152
11	'He Never Did Feel Shame': The Fall of Thomas Aris	168
12	After Aris	189
	Notes	199
	Bibliography	226
	Acknowledgements	234
	Index	235

Foreword

After decades in which the UK's main political parties have shamelessly weaponised criminal justice for electoral gain, our prisons are full to bursting once more. Successive governments have created new offences, raised sentences, reduced remission and increased tariffs. Meanwhile, ministers, cowering before a full-throated media, use inflammatory language to pressure judges and the parole board – and always in one direction: heavier terms of imprisonment, and longer sentences to be served.

The result has been an epic failure of public policy. We have the largest prison population in Western Europe, combined with the worst recidivism rates. Emergency release schemes, which are regularly forced upon the government by prison overcrowding, surely put the public at risk as inmates who have received no rehabilitation or training are unceremoniously dumped back into the community, frequently to reoffend.

Conditions inside our gaols, too, are a dehumanising disgrace, and successive inspection reports, detailing the filth and squalor of much of the British prison estate, should be a source of national shame. Rather, as though they were operating a brewery without manufacturing any bottles, Labour and Conservative governments have drunkenly raised the flow of inmates without creating any new spaces to house them. Frightening the public for political gain is one thing, refusing to spend public money to meet the consequences of your fearmongering is quite another.

But we should not be surprised that building new prisons is low on any government's wish list. It is shockingly expensive, with each new cell in a newly created gaol requiring around £630,000 of capital expenditure.

And for legions of prisoners, those who are not dangerous, those who are addicts, mentally ill or just a nuisance, this huge cost is largely wasted. Studies show that 25 per cent of adult prisoners go on to reoffend after release. For young offenders the figure is closer to 30 per cent. And for adults released from sentences of less than two years, no less than 50 per cent reoffend.

On the other hand, those committing similar offences who are put on community sentences outside prison have lower recidivism rates than their gaoled counterparts. Why should this be surprising? As a notably right-wing Conservative home secretary said many years ago 'prison is an expensive way of making bad people worse'.

In this remarkable book, Stephen Haddelsey reminds us that none of this is new. Just as we clash bitterly over social policy in the twenty-first century, so the years of 'London's Bastille' raged with debate between those disgusted by the appalling conditions which inmates suffered in that terrible place, and those inclined through self-interest, venality or political convenience to condone or to conceal the barbarism within its walls. Then, too, Parliament rang with arguments about diet, violence, dirt and overcrowding.

But this illuminating work is about more than a single prison in nineteenth-century London. Rather, through the lens of a contested penal policy, Dr Haddelsey paints a wonderfully compelling portrait of the great, centuries-long struggle in British public life between reformers and reactionaries, between the desire for social progress and a concomitant drive to protect the present. The cast of characters could not be more vivid: the repulsive warden of the gaol, Thomas Aris, the great reformers John Howard and Francis Burdett who fought for years to mitigate its brutality, the incurious and complicit magistracy of Middlesex, the callous and imperious High Court judges who consistently beat back improvements in the lives of the inmates, and the politicians more invested in stability and the maintenance of social hierarchy than in justice for the poor.

It is to be hoped that this timely reminder that penal reform has a long and stony history will not deter reformers of the future from emulating the great radical heroes, surely now vindicated, of this colourful, and frequently cruel, past.

Lord Ken Macdonald, KC
President, The Howard League for Penal Reform
London, March 2025

Prologue

On the morning of Wednesday 28 November 1798, two gentlemen might have been observed mounting the steps of a richly accoutred four-in-hand standing before the fashionable frontage of No. 76 Welbeck Street, Westminster. Once they were safely aboard and rugs placed across their knees by an attentive footman, the liveried coachman whipped up the horses and expertly guided the equipage into the busy streets of the capital.[1]

Although his destination lay some 2 miles to the north-east, keen to avoid scratching the coach's paintwork or becoming hopelessly entangled among the wagons, handcarts and pedestrians in the narrower thoroughfares, he headed south, following the course of the old River Tyburn (its murky waters now safely culverted), down Mary Le Bone Lane to turn east along Oxford Street, with its gleaming shopfronts and wide pavements, and then Camden High Street. Passing St Giles's church on the right, the coachman and his passengers would have been uncomfortably aware that for all the grandeur of Henry Flitcroft's Palladian-style edifice they were venturing dangerously close to the noisome alleys and lanes of the St Giles rookery, known, according to one contemporary commentator, as the haunt of 'the lowest of rogues, the lowest of harlots, and, in a word, the worst of mankind',[2] and where murder, prostitution, thievery and grinding poverty were rife.

Fortunately, no footpads or highwaymen barred their way – deterred perhaps by the biting cold – and the coach very quickly entered Broad Street and then climbed High Holborn, passing Lincoln's Inn and

Chancery Lane on the right. At the Holborn Bars – two substantial wooden posts set upright beside the road to mark the western boundary of the City of London – they turned left to head due north up the famously dirty Gray's Inn Lane, skirting the ancient walls of Gray's Inn and its rather more salubrious gardens so beloved of Sir Francis Bacon, who had planted many of its elm trees during his period of residence. Speeding past the few remaining dwellings dating from the reign of Elizabeth I, 'looking like houses built of cards, one storey projecting over another',[3] the coach finally turned right along narrow Elm Lane before crossing Mount Pleasant to reach Coldbath Square, where the coachman reined in his horses.

He had drawn up in front of an intimidating stone gateway, its reinforced wooden gates painted green and embellished by a pair of door-knockers 'large as pantomime masks', a letter box and a grated Judas hole, no bigger than a domestic gridiron. The stone quoins on either side of the gate displayed great sculpted fetters, impressive enough, according to one observer, 'to frighten any sinful passer-by back into the paths of rectitude',[4] and overhead, like the sword of Damocles, hung the three seaxes of the County of Middlesex. On either side stretched tall brick walls, high enough to prevent all possibility of seeing what lay behind them, and topped by a vicious-looking *chevaux de frize* resembling 'some giant hundred-bladed penknife'. Having arrived at this gloomy spot, the footman clambered down from his perch beside the coachman and announced to the passengers within that they had arrived at Clerkenwell, a down-at-heel neighbourhood known for its poor housing – much of it inhabited by men and women scratching a living manufacturing components for the City's booming watchmaking industry[5] – for the now-redundant smallpox hospital and for the Coldbath Fields House of Correction, at whose entrance they had stopped.

Ordering the footman to summon the prison's porter and to show him an admission pass obtained from the Middlesex magistrates, the coach's occupants descended to the street, where they shook hands with a third well-wrapped gentleman who had been awaiting their arrival, stamping his feet and clapping his gloved hands in a vain attempt to keep warm. Gentlemen of rank, leading lights in Georgian society, two possessed of immense wealth, and two of them sitting MPs, these men could expect that their guide around the prison would be no less a person than its governor, Thomas Aris. What they would find within its walls – neglect, starvation, vicious beatings and sexual exploitation – would horrify them, and their attempts to publicise and remedy the injustices and crimes not only countenanced but actively defended by the government itself would become the cause célèbre of the last years of the eighteenth century, and make Coldbath Fields notorious for its cruelty and injustice. Little wonder, then, that the prison had already come to be known locally as 'the Bastille', after the infamous Parisian fortress, or, in the prisoners' parlance, 'the Steel'.

I

'The Cries of the Miserable'
Howard's Call to Reform

Unlike England's other infamous prisons, such as the Marshalsea and Newgate, or the original Bastille in Paris, London's Bastille was not an ancient structure, its origins lost in the mists of time, and some, at least, of its flaws the product of long years of neglect and decay; in fact, at the time of its greatest notoriety, it had been standing for less than a decade. Moreover, its design did not proceed from the 'heat oppress'd brain' of a latter-day Torquemada, but came into being as a direct result of the work of one of the most enlightened and dedicated campaigners for prison reform in English history, John Howard.

Born in Enfield in 1726, Howard was the son of a wealthy upholsterer and warehouseman. The elder Howard intended that his son and namesake should follow him into business and apprenticed him to a grocer in Watling Street; but the young Howard had other ideas, and on his father's death in 1742 he immediately bought up his indentures and thereby freed himself from what he saw as a lifetime of drudgery. While he may have disagreed with his father's plans for his future, he had, however, inherited his unbending Calvinist faith and despite being a wealthy man at sixteen, and free from strict parental oversight, he showed no inclination to live a wild, dissolute life; instead he spent two years on the Grand Tour and then settled down to a life of quiet reflection and study in an attempt to fill the gaps in an education rendered wholly inadequate by his father's insistence on tutors more remarkable for their faith than for their learning or abilities as teachers.

In January 1756, Howard decided to visit Portugal and the seeds of his interest in prison reform are perhaps to be found in his first-hand experience of a French gaol which he obtained when a French privateer overhauled the Lisbon packet in which he had sailed from England. Transferred to the French ship at the point of a cutlass, the packet's passengers and crew reached Brest two days later, where they spent a week in a filthy dungeon of the Château de Brest, sleeping on vermin-ridden straw and surviving on a meagre allowance of water and on a joint of mutton which they gnawed in turns as their captors refused to permit them the use of a knife.

As a wealthy man clearly able to pay a ransom, Howard's situation improved when his captors moved him to lodgings in Carhaix, some 30 miles inland, and allowed him out on parole, but it was not until March that he returned to England, having been exchanged for a French officer. Home at last, his first act was to visit the Commissioners for Sick and Wounded Seamen to whom he reported all that he had seen and endured while a prisoner in France. The commissioners promptly despatched a strongly worded protest to the French court and Howard's fellow captives were swiftly released. With this success, Howard probably believed that his association with prisons had come to an end, and for the next sixteen years he dedicated himself to improving his estate in the Bedfordshire village of Cardington, to marriage and fatherhood, to charitable works and to travelling both at home and abroad. Then, in the autumn of 1772, he was appointed to the post of High Sheriff of Bedfordshire – and his life's work could begin at last.

A part of Howard's duties as High Sheriff was to greet and entertain the peripatetic judges of the courts of assize on their entry into the county town of Bedford, 4 miles from his home in Cardington. But, not satisfied with merely wining and dining the judges, he chose also to attend their hearings in the stone Sessions House on the south side of St Paul's Square, and here he first became aware of the injustice being meted out on a routine basis. In particular, and according to his own account, 'the circumstance which excited me to activity' was:

> the seeing some, who by the verdict of juries were declared *not guilty*; some, on whom the grand jury did not find such an appearance of guilt as subjected them to trial; and some, whose prosecutors did not appear against them; after having been confined for months, dragged back to gaol, and locked up again till they should pay *sundry fees* to the gaoler, the clerk of assize, &c.[1]

In other words, what most shocked him was that individuals who had been found guilty of no crime or misdemeanour were routinely confined until they paid off debts they had incurred while being held in prison awaiting their trials: debts made up solely of the charges levied by gaolers for providing the very necessaries of life, including rent for rooms and bedding, the provision of cleaning materials, and the sale of food and alcohol. In Bedfordshire, at the very least each prisoner would be required to pay 15s 4d to the gaoler, and a further 2s to the turnkey in order to obtain their liberty, no matter what the result of their trial.

To Howard it seemed obvious that the most effective method to end such a travesty was to pay gaolers and turnkeys a suitable salary, thereby eradicating their reliance for a substantial portion of their income upon commercial transactions conducted within the prison. He wrote to the county's Justices of the Peace suggesting this approach, only to be told that while the bench 'were properly affected with the grievance, and willing to grant the relief desired',[2] they must first be satisfied that a precedent existed for making ratepayers liable for such costs. At this juncture, Howard might have written to the magistrates of other counties to obtain the required information but he chose, instead, to embark upon a fact-finding tour, his interest no doubt spurred by the knowledge that in the eyes of the law as High Sheriff he was ultimately responsible for the conduct of the county's gaolers, who were deemed to be his servants.[3]

During the course of the following months, he travelled far and wide and entirely at his own expense, touring the prisons of Great Britain and no doubt causing great consternation to many a gaoler as he poked his great beak of a nose into every murky corner of their hitherto sacrosanct fiefdoms. Because, inevitably, his researches quickly expanded far beyond the establishment of a precedent for the salarying of gaolers, Howard himself admitted that 'the work grew upon me insensibly'[4] until it swelled to cover every aspect of prison life: from fees to food, from security to sewerage and from punishments to prayer times. 'Hearing the cries of the miserable,' he later wrote, 'I devoted my time to their relief. In order to procure it, I made it my business to collect materials, the authenticity of which could not be disputed.'[5]

Of course, Howard was not alone in advocating prison reform and during his year as High Sheriff of Bedfordshire, MPs laid a Bill before the House of Commons which sought to provide 'Clergymen to officiate in the Gaols and Places of Confinement for Debt, within that Part of Great Britain called England'; the Bill passed both houses of Parliament and received royal assent in June 1773.[6] But what differentiated Howard from other reformers was his conviction that his work was 'God-given': that it would be criminal for him to enjoy his 'ease and leisure in the neglect of an opportunity offered me by Providence'.[7] This belief led him, despite a history of physical weakness and ill health, to travel thousands of miles, mostly in a post-chaise but often on horseback, criss-crossing the country from Newgate to Newcastle, Penzance to Preston, Canterbury to Cardiff, Bristol to Berwick, inspecting every Bridewell, county gaol and debtors' prison, from large, if antiquated, complexes like the Marshalsea, to castle dungeons and to squalid single rooms such as the Bridewell at Horsham in Sussex, where multiple prisoners spent all day and all night locked in a space just 10ft by 6½ft by 6¼ft.

Howard admitted that it was not 'without some apprehensions of danger' that he undertook his crusade,[8] and he had very good cause to be anxious. Chief among the risks he faced was epidemic typhus – known as 'gaol-fever' or 'gaol distemper' – which had been endemic in Britain's prisons for centuries. The first reported outbreak was that of 1414 which claimed, according to John Stowe, 'the Gaylers of Newgate and Ludgate ... and prisoners in Newgate to the number of 64'.[9] Writing in 1548, the chronicler Edward Hall describes another eruption at the assizes held in Cambridge in 1522 that spread like wildfire through the packed court so that not only prisoners, but justices, lawyers, bailiffs and witnesses 'toke such an infeccion, whether it wer of the sauor of the prisoners, or of the filthe of the house, that many gentlemen ... and many other honest yomen thereof died, and all most all whiche were there present, were sore sicke and narrowly escaped with their liues'.[10]

But this death toll was as nothing when compared with that at Oxford's 'Black Assizes' of 1577. In *The Haven of Health*, the physician Thomas Cogan tells us that between 6 July and 12 August over 500 died, including two judges, the Lord Chief Baron, a sergeant-at-law, the High Sheriff, five justices, four councillors-at-law, an attorney, plus 300 townsmen and upwards of 200 people in the country around: all infected, according to Cogan, 'in a manner at one instant, by reason of a dampe or mist which arose among the people within the Castle yard and court house'.[11] For his part, the antiquarian John Hooker inserted into Raphael Holinshed's chronicle a description of the serious outbreak at Exeter assizes in 1586 – an account made particularly interesting because it is clearly based upon first-hand observation and offers perhaps the best early attempt to analyse the disease's pathology. The fever, Hooker writes:

> was contagious and infectious, but not so violent as commonlie the pestilence [plague] is; neither dooth there appeare anie outward vlcer or sore.

> The origen and cause thereof diuerse men are of diuerse iudgements. Some did impute it, and were of the mind, that it proceeded from the contagion of the gaole, which by reason of the close aire, and filthie stinke, the prisoners newlie come out of a fresh aire into the same, are in short time for the most part infected therewith.[12]

Of equal importance is the fact that this outbreak among the prisoners 'mooued manie a mans hart' and caused the Lord Chief Justice not only to demand an improvement in conditions within the gaol, but also to introduce more frequent trials in order to reduce the prison population.

It was not just the gaols that the more forward-thinking sought to remedy. When the Old Bailey was rebuilt in 1673 to replace the medieval courthouse destroyed in the Great Fire, the architect left one side of the courtroom open to the elements in order to increase the flow of air and thereby reduce the risk of contagion. The good sense of this measure was amply demonstrated in 1750 when, after the building had again been remodelled and the draughty courtroom fully enclosed, fever ripped through the Court killing sixty people, including the Lord Mayor and two judges. Though this event did not result in the wall's demolition, other measures were introduced, such as fumigating the Court several times a day by means of plunging a hot iron into a bucket filled with vinegar and sweet-smelling herbs in an attempt to keep the air fresh – a practice maintained, with some modifications, until well into the twentieth century.[13]

Howard's investigations convinced him that gaol-fever remained as prevalent in the second half of the eighteenth century as at any previous time, and his outrage that any prisoner should die in such circumstances drove him to remind his countrymen in impassioned prose that:

> Gaol is not designed for the final punishment ... but for the *safe custody* of the accused to the time of trial; and of convicts till a legal sentence be executed upon them. The laws of England do not suffer private executions. No condemned malefactor may be secretly put to death; nor murdered in a prison directly or indirectly: much less ought those to be destroyed whose sentence does not affect their life.[14]

As to the number of fatalities caused by infection, he felt convinced that 'many more were destroyed by it, than were put to death by all the public executions in the kingdom'[15] – a startling claim given that he wrote at the height of the 'Bloody Code', with some 35,000 individuals being condemned to death in England and Wales between 1770 and 1830, with roughly 7,000 being executed.[16]

Although eighteenth-century physicians recognised that squalor and overcrowding were the conditions most likely to give rise to typhus, they remained ignorant of the exact mechanisms by which it incubated and spread, with the miasma theory first propounded by the fifth-century Greek physician Hippocrates being the commonly accepted explanation for all contagious disease. Sir John Pringle, the 'father of military medicine', who wrote extensively on the subject in the middle years of the century, observed, for instance, that the disease should be expected when 'the air is confined, especially in hot weather' and that it 'is incident to every place ill-aired and kept dirty, that is filled with animal steams from foul or diseased bodies'.[17] Dr William Grant, meanwhile, in his 1775 *Essay on the Pestilential Fever of Sydenham, Commonly Called the Gaol, Hospital, Ship, and Camp-Fever*, noted that:

> If a number of people are long confined ... in any close place, not properly ventilated, so as to inspire, and swallow with their spittle, the vapours of each other, they must soon feel the bad effects, particularly if any of them should be sickly ... warm weather, bad provisions, nastiness, and gloomy thoughts will add to their misery, and soon breed the *seminium* [seed] of a pestilential fever, dangerous not only to themselves, but also to every person who visits them.[18]

To intelligent observers such as these, the record of outbreaks proved beyond a shadow of a doubt that insanitary living conditions contributed to the spread of the disease, but they did not appreciate that the primary medium of transmission was not foul air but the excreta of lice infected with the bacteria *Rickettsia prowazekii*, which prisoners, when scratching themselves, unknowingly rubbed into their irritated skin. Where conditions encouraged the breeding and spread of lice, epidemic typhus would surely follow – as would again be proved in the First World War, when the disease acquired a new name: trench fever.

Of suggested treatments there was, of course, no shortage, with emphasis being placed, as always, on a combination of bleeding, vomiting, purging and sweating, though most reputable physicians accepted that none of these offered a miracle cure and mortality rates would remain obstinately high. As to means of prevention, beyond cleanliness and a free flow of fresh air, these were limited to a reliance upon vinegar, which might be sprinkled in rooms, applied to handkerchiefs and even used for cleaning teeth and gums. In fact, vinegar would prove an effective means by which to kill lice, and would be employed to delouse troops on the Western Front,[19] but the limited application upon which Howard and others relied – the 'smelling to vinegar'[20] as a means by which to shield oneself against noxious miasma – offered no meaningful protection. Of course, other preventatives had their champions. In one parliamentary discussion on the subject an MP who delighted in the nickname of 'Little Cocking' George Onslow, suggested that plugging one's nostrils with tobacco might be effective, though he was put somewhat out of countenance when the eminent physician John Fothergill tersely pointed out that 'unless you could likewise stop your mouth and ears, it would be of no service'.[21]

Though the conditions which gave rise to typhus were well understood, it might perhaps be argued that ignorance regarding the disease's pathology offered some kind of excuse for its prevalence. The same could not be said for another common characteristic of prison life: hunger. 'There are several Bridewells,' wrote Howard, 'in which prisoners have no allowance of FOOD at all':

> The same complaint, want of food, is to be found in many COUNTY-GAOLS. In about half these, debtors have no bread; although it is granted to the highwayman, the house-breaker, and the murderer ... I have often seen those prisoners eating their water-soup (bread boiled in mere water) and heard them say, 'We are locked up and almost starved to death.'[22]

Various reasons could be found for this want: the insistence by some authorities that prisoners should work for their bread – but without the tools or even the space for work being made available; the peculation of gaolers intent on supplementing their often derisory incomes; and, in other cases, the statutes of particular gaols not being updated, so that the stipulated allowance for the provision of bread and meat to a certain value had not been adjusted to keep pace with inflation, meaning that prisoners sometimes found themselves expected to live on half the quantities consumed by their predecessors. The result, Howard noted, was that many who entered a gaol in a state of rude health 'come out almost famished, scarce able to move, and for weeks incapable of any labour'.[23] Water, too, was often in shockingly poor supply – sometimes because prisons had been built, or expanded in a piecemeal fashion, without due consideration being given to this most basic of requirements, and sometimes because a lack of space or poor security made it necessary to keep prisoners confined indoors, rendering the outdoor pumps inaccessible and leaving them wholly dependent upon the attentiveness of the turnkeys.

Drainage and sewerage were all too often altogether absent or, if present, neglected to such a degree that the air became tainted and 'offensive beyond description'.[24] So all-pervading did the stench become that it impregnated not only Howard's clothes, but also the pages of the notebook in which he recorded his observations, often obliging him to ride on horseback rather than be confined within a post-chaise and to air his book by a fire before consulting it between inspections. Many prisons possessed subterranean cells, and in these the floors were often damp, or even submerged, meaning that the prisoners' bedding – which often consisted of nothing but straw – quickly rotted. Even if their cells remained dry, the gaolers changed the straw so infrequently that it turned to dust before being replaced, their excuse being that the authorities made no provision for straw, so either the prisoners or the gaolers must pay for it: the former being unable, and the latter unwilling, to do so.

If Howard felt appalled by the physical neglect of inmates, he was no less horrified by the effect of the prevailing conditions upon prisoners' morals. Broadly speaking, under English law prisoners were divided into three categories: firstly, debtors; secondly, vagrants, rogues, vagabonds and misdemeanants – meaning those imprisoned for terms of from seven days to two years for relatively minor offences such as prostitution and petty theft – who were incarcerated in houses of correction, or 'Bridewells';* and, thirdly, felons – those whose crimes warranted sentences of penal servitude or transportation – who were committed to the convict prisons or, worse still, to rotting hulks on the Thames. In addition, there were those held prior to trial, who might eventually be sentenced or set free depending upon the decision of the Court.

Crucially, the administrative and physical boundaries separating these different types of inmate were all too often porous, with debtors, in particular, often living cheek by jowl with misdemeanants despite a law enacted during the reign of Charles II which dictated that the two types of prisoner should be 'put, kept, and lodged separate and apart from one

---

* The term 'Bridewell' was derived from the first such institution having been established in Henry VIII's old home of Bridewell Palace in the City of London.

another, in distinct rooms'.[25] Instead, whether as a result of the inadequacies of the prisons, of the gaolers who ran them or of the authorities who inspected them, all too often hardened criminals and petty offenders, the incorrigible and the redeemable, mixed together – with the corruption of the latter being the inevitable result. Most depressing of all, Howard thought, was to see 'boys of twelve or fourteen eagerly listening to the stories told by practised and experienced criminals, of their adventures, successes, stratagems, and escapes'.[26] 'What is this,' he asked, 'but devoting them to destruction?'[27]

In many prisons, at least during the daytime, male and female prisoners of all ages mingled together, making both debauchery and sexual exploitation all too common. And then there was the plight of the insane. According to the medical historian Roy Porter, during the whole of the eighteenth century Parliament passed only two Acts that dealt specifically – though not exclusively – with the policing of the mad.[28] The Vagrancy Act of 1714 authorised two or more magistrates to arrest any person considered to be 'furiously Mad and dangerous', and to confine him 'locked up or chained ... for and during such time only as such Lunacy or Madness shall continue'.[29] The provisions of the new Vagrancy Act of 1744, thirty years later, developed the definition of the furiously mad to include 'those who by Lunacy or otherwise are so far disordered in their Senses that they may be dangerous to be permitted to go Abroad'.[30] By the terms of the 1714 Act the destitute insane were placed in the same category as vagrants, vagabonds, rogues, beggars, gypsies, mountebanks and players, with one important exception: though liable to arrest, and subject to being chained, the insane were not to be whipped. With the country possessing only a tiny number of asylums for pauper lunatics, the fate of the majority was to be immured in prisons, houses of correction or workhouses, none of which possessed either the staff or the facilities to care for them properly and where, according to Howard, they not only served as 'sport' for the idle, but also disturbed and terrified other prisoners. 'No care is taken of them,' he complained, 'although it is probable that by medicines, and proper regimen, some of them might be restored to their senses, and to usefulness in life.'[31] Another slightly later reformer put it even more strongly: the incarcerated insane, Charles Williams-Wynn, the MP for Montgomeryshire, told the Commons, 'were precluded from all possible chance of recovery ... [and] doomed to irremediable misery'.[32]

In 1774 Howard at last had an opportunity to share publicly at least some of his discoveries. Following the passing of the legislation relating to the provision of clergymen to officiate in gaols the previous year, in February the

House of Commons ordered that leave be given to bring in a Bill that sought to address two issues: firstly, the relief of prisoners 'charged with Felony, or other Crimes, who shall be acquitted or discharged by Proclamation, respecting the Payment of Fees to Gaolers', and secondly, the establishment of means 'for more effectually securing the Health of Prisoners in Gaol, during their Confinement'.[33] One of the sponsors of this Bill was Howard's friend, the wealthy brewer and MP for Bedford, Samuel Whitbread, and it seems certain that the two had discussed their shared interest in prison reform and that Whitbread had encouraged Howard in his crusade. It might even be the case that Whitbread had helped to secure the post of High Sheriff for Howard who, as a dissenter, would not normally have been eligible. In order to discuss the Bill, the House formed a special committee of enquiry, and Howard met with its members between 10 and 17 February, then, on 4 March, he was asked to share his findings with the whole House.

Although his attendance was widely reported in the newspapers, Howard felt that some of the published accounts contained inaccuracies; he therefore wrote to the editor of the *London Chronicle* to set the matter straight and, no doubt, to keep the issue before the public gaze:

> I informed the House that I had travelled and seen 38 out of the 42 gaols in the Lent circuit, besides others, as Bristol, Ely, Litchfield, &c ... That I released a person out of Norwich city gaol who had been confined five weeks for the Gaoler's fee of 13s. 4d. That at Launceston the Keeper, Deputy Keeper, and ten out of eleven prisoners were ill; at Oxford eleven died last year of the small-pox ... That the gaols were generally close and confined, the felons' wards nasty, dirty, confined, and unhealthy: That even York Castle, which to a superficial viewer might be thought a very fine gaol, I thought quite otherwise; with regard to felons their wards were dark, dirty, and small, no way proportioned to the number of unhappy persons confined there. Many others are the same; as Gloucester, Warwick, Hereford, Sussex, &c. The latter had not for felons, or even for debtors, at their county gaol at Horsham, the least outlet, but the poor unhappy creatures were ever confined within doors without the least breath of fresh air.
>
> I was asked my reasons for visiting the gaols? I answered I had seen and heard the distress of gaols, and had an earnest desire to relieve it in my own district as well as others.[34]

Having listened to this testimony, delivered calmly, eloquently and with absolute conviction, the House asked Howard to return to the bar so that he might be publicly thanked for his humanity and zeal. No matter how gratified he might have felt at this highly unusual acknowledgement, he was no doubt even more delighted when the House subsequently passed not one, but two pieces of wide-reaching legislation: the 'Discharged Prisoners Act', which abolished fees for acquitted prisoners, and an 'Act for Preserving the Health of Prisoners in Gaol, and Preventing the Gaol Distemper', the former on 31 March, the latter on 2 June.

Howard published his research and recommendations in *The State of the Prisons in England and Wales* three years later. Continuing his campaign to improve both the physical conditions and the moral wellbeing of prisoners, he now advocated a systematic programme of refurbishment and replacement. Prisons, he argued, must not be located in the middle of towns or cities, but 'should be built on a spot that is *airy*, and if possible near a river, or brook'[35] to ensure a fresh supply of water for drinking and washing and to improve sewerage. Proximity to a river would also discourage the construction of dank subterranean dungeons, which the physician and reformer John Roberton believed to 'have been destructive to thousands'.[36] By placing prisoners' wards in free-standing buildings and on top of arcades, a triple benefit would be obtained: air would circulate more freely, a dry walkway would be created for use in inclement weather and security improved, as inmates would not be able to tunnel their way to liberty. Male and female prisoners should be segregated at all times and, on the basis that 'Solitude and silence are favourable to reflection; and may possibly lead them to repentance',[37] each individual should have a separate cell. Given the high levels of sickness in the dilapidated old prisons, each must have an infirmary, a bath and an oven, since 'nothing so effectually destroys vermin in cloaths [sic] and bedding, nor purifies them so thoroughly when tainted with infection, as being a few hours in an oven moderately heated'.[38] These, Howard contended, were basic requirements, not luxuries. Glass in cell windows, on the other hand, he deemed an unjustifiable extravagance for any but the ill or pregnant — an opinion that would prove highly contentious in the years to come.

Howard was equally clear on the critical importance of differentiating between convict prisons and the houses of correction: while the former were designed for the long-term incarceration of those found guilty of serious crimes and were directly controlled by the government, the latter were intended to house only misdemeanants sentenced to short terms and were under the management of the local magistracy. Though housed separately, convicts sentenced to penal servitude and misdemeanants must both be made to undertake hard labour, the labour often taking the form of dredging or canal construction for convicts, with misdemeanants expected to beat hemp for the manufacture of rope, the prisoners 'twisting, rolling, rubbing, until their soft, thievish fingers grow red and sore, and afterwards hard by their contact with those stiff chunks of tarry hemp'.[39] Like many reformers before and after, Howard believed that such labour would have a salutary effect, convincing the prisoners of the error of their ways, and thereby encouraging them to turn from future wrongdoing.[40]

In terms of the regulations that should govern conduct within the prisons, some of Howard's recommendations now seem truly extraordinary – not because they are in any way absurd, but because he found it necessary to articulate what, today, seems blindingly obvious. That he had to make such suggestions serves to highlight the kind of abuses that were rife in the prison system of the late eighteenth century. A gaoler, he argued, should be sober; moreover, he and his turnkeys should not 'be suffered to hold the *Tap*; or to have any connexion, concern, or interest whatever in the sale of liquors of any kind'.[41] Gaolers should be fit and healthy and be expected to conduct personally daily inspections of the prison. Each gaol should have its own chaplain, surgeon and apothecary – and, crucially, each of these should be 'a man of repute in his profession'. No fighting, abusive language or gaming – 'the frequent occasion of them' – should be tolerated. Finally, Howard believed, to 'every prison there should be an Inspector appointed; either by his colleagues in the magistracy, or by Parliament'.[42]

In January 1777, nearly three years after he presented his evidence to the House of Commons, Howard visited for the first time the old Clerkenwell Bridewell, which stood just to the north of Clerkenwell Green.* Built during the reign of James I (1603–25), by the time of Howard's inspection it exhibited many, though not all, of the shortcomings that had first provoked his ire:

> The Prison is much out of repair. It has not been so much as whitewashed for years ... one person sick; a woman who lay on the floor. No straw. No Infirmary.

---

* Carrington Bowles's 'New pocket plan of the cities of London & Westminster with the borough of Southwark; comprehending the new buildings and other alterations to the year 1783' shows the Bridewell to have been located in the crook of the elbow formed by the junction of Clerkenwell Green and St John's Street, between Rosoman's Row to the north and New Prison Walk to the south. The old Bridewell was demolished in 1804.

Of the one hundred and eight in January last, above thirty were Fines, that is, Criminals committed for a term of years, five or six. Some of these, and of the others, were sick. They complained to me of sore feet, which the Turnkey said were quite black.[43]

One of the male prisoners' dormitories he found 'so crowded, that some Prisoners spent the nights in hammocks hung to the ceiling', while the women slept in 'dark unwholesome night-rooms'.[44] In addition to the mixing of prisoner types, the prison's poor state of repair and its high levels of sickness, the gaoler's salary was little more than a pittance, making him reliant upon the money that he could extort from the inmates, his income being supplemented, according to one inmate, 'By letting Men and Women lie together in his Beds'.[45] Overall then, few would disagree with the contention that the condition of Clerkenwell Bridewell offered a perfect opportunity to apply the principles of construction and management that lay at the heart of Howard's proposed new model.

2

'Some Alteration Should Be Made'
Design and Build

Surprisingly, perhaps, so far as the inadequacies of the Clerkenwell Bridewell were concerned, Howard, the champion of reform, and the Middlesex magistrates, those responsible for its maintenance and for the security and health of its inmates, found themselves in complete agreement. The only real difference lay in their sense of urgency when it came to remedying the prison's flaws.

As early as 1757 one inmate had addressed an account of the prison to the sheriffs and magistrates of the county, describing it as 'one of the greatest, the most notorious ... and most horrid Sinks of Debauchery, Fornication, Licentiousness and Drunkenness, and also of the most horrible Distress, Poverty and Oppression to be found in the World',[1] but it was not until the beginning of 1783 – six years after Howard's first visit – that the magistrates ordered a detailed inspection. The resulting report was read to them in April at a meeting in their imposing new classical Sessions House on Clerkenwell Green. The buildings of the seventeenth-century prison were, the inspectors noted, 'in a deplorable state ... being very inconvenient and much decayed'.[2] That part of the prison set apart for male prisoners they considered 'very much crowded ... whereby the health of the prisoners was endangered'.[3] Security was risible, with no fewer than thirty-one prisoners having recently escaped in a single day,[4] and the male prisoners were not, as the law required, engaged in hard labour.[5] Finally, neither the Bridewell, the nearby felons' prison, nor – most embarrassing of all – the Sessions House, which had been completed only the year before at a cost of £13,000, were 'well supplied with water'.[6] All in all, the report concluded with masterly understatement, 'it is necessary some alteration should be made'.[7]

The key problem of overcrowding, from which many of the other issues stemmed, was certainly not unique to Clerkenwell. With the American War of Independence causing an interruption to convict transportation that would last until the settling of New South Wales from 1788, overcrowding had become commonplace throughout Britain's prisons. The Penitentiary Act of 1779 had been designed in part to address this problem, its provisions including the erection of two centrally funded houses of hard labour somewhere in Middlesex, Surrey, Kent or Essex, one to hold 600 men and the other 300 women. But these aspirations would not be realised for decades and, as one historian of the Act has observed, 'No government-funded "penitentiary" of a scale commensurate with the scheme of 1779 came into being until Millbank was opened in 1816'.[8] In the meantime, with the demands for reform becoming irresistible, the ratepayers of Middlesex would become some of the first to foot the bill for improved prisoner accommodation at a local rather than the planned national level.

Initially, the Middlesex magistrates hoped that the existing Bridewell on the south side of Corporation Row might be expanded and improved: a proposal that appeared viable, so long as they were able to acquire the garden belonging to the adjacent Quaker's workhouse, the garden and the workhouse itself being on a long lease 'from His Majesty's Justices of the Peace for this County'.[9] Upon further consideration, however, the magistrates decided that it would be more sensible to future-proof their plans by acquiring not just the garden but the whole site, thereby facilitating substantial alterations. They therefore pursued negotiations with the Society of Friends, while at the same time keeping their options open by placing in the local press advertisements for any alternative and suitable tract of ground in the vicinity. By June the Quakers had obtained professional advice which suggested that £1,600 might be deemed a reasonable sum for the surrender of the remaining thirty-five years of their lease – that sum having been generously discounted against commercial rates on the basis that the magistrates' proposals were 'for a publick good and not for any private Benefit'.[10] They stipulated just one condition: that they should be given a term of no less than two years in which to find alternative accommodation, making it unlikely that ground would be broken before the middle of 1785, at the earliest.

In reality, like so many projects both before and since, the plan to construct a new house of correction would be plagued by changes to the scope of the works to be completed. Over time, the magistrates' vision for the new prison grew ever more ambitious, primarily because they came to recognise that they could now embrace an opportunity not merely to remedy the worst defects of the old Bridewell, but to create a new model institution that would place Middlesex at the forefront of prison reform and include the features so vocally championed by John Howard, whose opinion they obtained.

In February 1784, the committee appointed to manage the project outlined what they deemed to be the minimum requirements for the new prison. It must be able to accommodate up to 500 prisoners, with male and female inmates separated at all times, and felons, debtors and misdemeanants 'in the night lodged separately and kept in the day as distinctly as the nature of their several employments will admit'.[11] There should be punishment cells for solitary confinement, a dedicated chapel and two infirmaries: one for the men and another for the women, each capable of accommodating twelve patients – a hospital capacity of less than 5 per cent of the prison population underscoring the belief that improved facilities would massively reduce sickness. The governor's house should be located close to the prison's main entrance, and the turnkeys' lodges at its centre, so that all areas would be equally accessible to them. Finally, the whole institution should be encompassed by a suitably high free-standing wall, with none of the buildings abutting against it. Unfortunately, as the building committee informed their fellow magistrates, while these features would ensure that the new prison met the exacting expectations of the reformers, it would be quite impossible to squeeze them all into the combined footprint of the old Bridewell, the Quakers' workhouse and its garden. A new site must be found.

Meanwhile, the publicity arising from the magistrates' decision to advertise for suitable plots had naturally attracted the interest of entrepreneurial architects, and in July 1784 Robert Brettingham and James Burton both submitted unsolicited proposals for the new prison, the latter modestly noting that, should his plan meet with their approval, 'I shall be extremely happy in having filled up some vacant hours to a good purpose'.[12] Ultimately, neither man would receive the sought-for commission, but their interest did prompt the magistrates to launch a public competition inviting 'any person or persons desirous to offer a Plan or Plans for such a Building, with all necessary apartments and conveniences'[13] to submit an application by 9 December.

The advertisements went on to note that 'a premium of thirty guineas will be given for that plan which shall be adjudged to be the best; twenty guineas for that which shall be adjudged to be the second in merit; and ten guineas for that which shall be adjudged to be the third in merit'.[14] The eventual winner was a young and little-known architect named Aaron Henry Hurst, who would shortly go on to design the Palladian chapel of St James on nearby Pentonville Road. But following his victory, Hurst would play no further part in the construction of the new prison, with the role of supervising architect being awarded instead to Jacob Leroux, himself a magistrate for the county and an experienced property developer in his own right. This award Leroux might well have considered his by right since he had submitted plans for the redevelopment of the now abandoned workhouse site long before the idea of a competition had been mooted.

Leroux was not the only architect to base his plans on the workhouse site — so, too, had Hurst and the other competitors. Inevitably, this meant that the newly appointed supervising architect would be obliged to adapt the approved plans to fit onto a new plot of ground. And by the time the competition had been decided that plot had at last been identified. Known as Gardiner's Field, it lay just a few hundred yards from the old Bridewell, at Coldbath Fields, a point roughly midway between the Quakers' workhouse in the east and the Foundling Hospital in the west, and on the east bank of the River Fleet. The name of the locality was derived from a privately run hydropathic establishment opened in 1697 by an entrepreneurial lawyer named Walter Baynes, who claimed, with the support of Dr Edward Baynard, a leading advocate of hot and cold bathing, that the local salt- and mineral-impregnated waters could ease a vast array of illnesses, including 'Dissiness, Drowsiness, and heavyness of the head, Lethargies, Palsies, Convulsions, all Hectical creeping Fevers, heats and flushings … disorders of the spleen and womb, also stiffness of the limbs and Rheumatick pains, also shortness of breath, weakness of the joints, as Rickets, etc'.[15]

Originally on the periphery of the City, during the eighteenth century the fields surrounding Baynes's marble bath had been lost to rapid urban growth, with low-grade housing followed by a distillery in the 1730s and, in 1752, by the conversion of a property once owned by the Lollard leader Sir John Oldcastle into a smallpox hospital — a charitable institution much opposed by the local population who feared the spread of the disease. To the north lay the once fashionable spa of Bagnigge Wells, established on the site of Nell Gwynne's home, Bagnigge House,[16] while to the south the parish workhouse for all non-Quakers stood in Hockley-in-the-Hole, a notorious neighbourhood known as the haunt of thieves and highwaymen and celebrated as a local Mecca for the aficionados of blood sports, including cockfighting and bull- and bear-baiting. Not that the bears always had the worst of it: the historian of Clerkenwell, William J. Pinks, tells us that in 1709 'a most tragical occurrence took place' when Christopher Preston, proprietor of the Bear Garden, was attacked by one of his own animals 'and almost devoured before his friends were aware of his danger'.[17] To the modern reader's eye, surely a case of just desserts.*

Gardiner's Field stood immediately adjacent to Mount Pleasant, once a muddy slope running down to the River Fleet, which gained its ironic name and its physical elevation from its historic use as a laystall – a dumping ground for human waste which, contrary to popular belief, was not simply thrown into the street and onto the heads of unwary passers-by but collected in cesspits, which were emptied, usually on an annual basis, by nocturnal 'gong farmers', despised but well-paid labourers who carted the contents to designated sites outside the City's boundary. In Tudor times, the largest of these sites had been Mount Pleasant which, over the years it was in use, probably achieved an elevation of some 20ft to 30ft above the Fleet, which at this point flowed south-eastwards before disappearing beneath Fleet Market. By the eighteenth century, the river had become little more than an open sewer, with Alexander Pope writing of its 'large tribute of dead dogs',[18] and in the nineteenth century the journalist James Ewing Ritchie would observe that, 'On a dull, dreary morning, it is anything but pleasant, that Mount, in spite of its name'.[19]

Surely the Middlesex magistrates could hardly have found a location more in keeping with the letter, but at the same time more at variance with the spirit of Howard's suggestion that prisons should be situated 'on a spot that is *airy*, and ... near a river, or brook'.[20] All the more surprising, then, that the site seems to have first been brought to their attention by Howard himself, who told them it 'would be a much more proper place for such a Building than the Ground at present intended both on Account of its being a more Airy Situation and because it would admit of a more extensive Plan'.[21] Howard had become aware of the plot during his abortive efforts to find suitable locations for the Penitentiary Act's proposed two national prisons, and he might have been told of it by his friend and fellow campaigner Samuel Whitbread who sat with the majority landowner, Jervoise Clarke Jervoise, on the Opposition benches of the House of Commons. At 8 acres the site was double the size originally thought to be necessary for the new house of correction, but with Howard's recommendation ringing in their ears the magistrates nonetheless instructed the County Surveyor to make enquiries regarding its availability and likely price.[22]

---

* Pinks informs us that in 1709 the vicar of St James's, Clerkenwell, preached a no doubt edifying sermon 'On Mr Preston being torn to pieces by his own bears'.

Although some magistrates felt reluctant to abandon the original site chosen for the redevelopment of the house of correction, events on the national stage would prove that the majority who voted for its rejection had acted with commendable foresight. On 19 August 1784 the king signed into law two new Acts relating to the building of gaols and houses of correction. These Acts sought to 'amend and explain' legislation passed during the reign of William III (1689–1702), but whereas the earlier Acts had merely outlined the means by which magistrates would be allowed to fund the 'building finishing or repairing a publick Gaol or Gaols belonging to the Shire or County',[23] the new Acts went much further and, in the manner of the Penitentiary Act and 'in order to avoid the evils arising from unwholesome and inconvenient prisons', detailed the nature of the accommodation and facilities to be included in such builds and refurbishments. 'The Justices are directed,' the new legislation declared:

> as well in the choice of the ground, as in the building of the gaols, &c. to adopt such plans as shall provide separate and distinct places of confinement, and dry and airy cells, in which the several prisoners may be confined ... The males of each class to be separated from the females ... also separate infirmaries or sick wards for men and women; also a chapel and convenient warm and cold baths, or bathing tubs, for the use of the prisoners.[24]

Like their predecessors, these Acts authorised the funding of such projects through the county rates; crucially, however, in acknowledging that the costs 'may in some cases become very burdensome' to ratepayers, they went on to authorise magistrates to borrow money to pay for the new prisons – just as, forty-four years later, the 1828 County Asylums Act would enable magistrates to borrow money in order to build asylums for the care of pauper lunatics.

All in all, by the end of 1784 the Middlesex magistrates could congratulate themselves quite justifiably on having selected a design and a site for the new prison that would enable them to fully comply with the new legislation. Unfortunately, any complacency they might have felt took something of a knock when, at a Sessions meeting held on 21 February 1785, a 34-year-old Southwark-born architect named William Blackburn angrily asserted that Aaron Henry Hurst had plagiarised his work.

Blackburn had won first prize in a competition three years earlier to design a male prison for the Commissioners for Penitentiary Houses under the Act of 1779. Although this prison was never built – indeed, by 1785 no prison designed by Blackburn had been completed – his success in the competition had established him as the foremost penitentiary architect of the age and a man who enjoyed John Howard's full confidence; his accusation must, therefore, be taken seriously. The magistrates had little option but to agree to examine the matter further at a future meeting and they must have breathed a collective sigh of relief when Blackburn failed to appear to substantiate his claims, perhaps due to the influx of commissions he was now receiving to design new prisons across the country.* Whatever its cause, his absence left the magistrates free to adopt Hurst's proposals.

More embarrassing still, at their meeting in May, they learned that, acting on the agreement already reached regarding the surrender of the lease for their workhouse and garden, the Society of Friends had proceeded with the purchase of an alternative plot of ground for the continuation of their charitable work, and that 'they could not think of waiving the said Agreement'.[25] Now, as a result of their own administrative ineptitude or that of their agents, the magistrates found themselves obliged to pay £1,600** for a piece of land they had already dismissed as being entirely unsuited to their purposes.

At an earlier meeting, William Bleamire, a barrister and magistrate at the Hatton Street Police Court, who had been elected as chairman of the building committee, had presented to his fellow magistrates the specifications that he and the committee believed should inform the work to be undertaken by Leroux in adapting Hurst's plans to fit the new site – those specifications being subject, he acknowledged, 'to such alterations as to this Committee should appear to be most advisable in order to fully answer the purpose of establishing a proper and commodious and beneficial House of Correction'.[26] The committee, Bleamire assured his colleagues, had worked with three main objectives constantly in view: the security of the inmates, their health and their reformation.

The primary means of ensuring security would be the erection of a perimeter wall similar to that surrounding the King's Bench Prison in Southwark – though the committee believed that this wall need not be 'constructed to any extraordinary Thickness ... provided the Inclosure were circumscribed by a Wall of such an Height as to frustrate the Prisoner's Endeavours to Escape even supposing the Vigilance of his Keeper to have

---

* William Blackburn (1750–90) would go on to design prisons in Oxford, Liverpool, Gloucester, Northleach, Ipswich, Shrewsbury, Monmouth and Limerick.

** Roughly equivalent to £207,000 in 2024. Source: Bank of England inflation calculator.

been Eluded or his Cell to have been broken through'.[27] Reduction of the wall's thickness would, of course, save expense – as would surmounting it with a wooden, rather than an iron, *chevaux de frize*. So far as health was concerned, from a design perspective the main contributing factors would be the prevention of damp by raising the cell floors to a level that would 'best answer the purpose of keeping this Floor perfectly dry', the complete avoidance of subterraneous rooms – as recommended by Howard – and the guaranteeing that 'free and copious currents of air should be admitted and that ample Supplies of Fresh Water should be Secured'.[28] The provision of water, it was suggested, could even become part of the regime of hard labour if prisoners were made to work the pumps designed to raise the water into a reservoir, 'to be thence distributed by Leaden Pipes thro' the several parts of the Prison'.

So far as the prisoners' reformation was concerned, Bleamire assured his colleagues that:

> The Correction of the Prisoners not only by the Execution of the Sentence of Corporal Punishment but more especially by enforcing the sentence to hard Labour and also by the Closer Confinement of such Offenders as are of a Refractory or more than usually vicious Disposition has by no means escaped the Notice of this Committee.[29]

In order to address a problem highlighted by Howard, the prison would be furnished with both workrooms and cells sufficiently large to enable inmates to work even when they were kept in solitary confinement. A total of 236 single-occupancy cells would be provided (122 for men and 114 for women) each 8ft in length, 6ft in width and 10ft high, with a further 114 prisoners being accommodated in shared-occupancy rooms. This would mean that the prison's maximum capacity would be reduced to 350, rather than the 500 originally envisaged, but as the reformers believed the separation of prisoners to be a key means by which to prevent the dissemination of criminal knowledge and behaviours, the reduction seemed justifiable and, accordingly, Leroux was ordered to proceed with working up his detailed plans based upon the committee's recommendations.

The results of his labours were presented to the Court on 27 March and, after due consideration, the Middlesex magistrates agreed that, nearly three years after deciding that the old Bridewell should be modernised, they now had before them a proposal which constituted 'a proper and Convenient plan for a House of Correction for this County and that the same ought to be adopted and carried into Execution'.[33] Of course, the delivery of this proper and convenient plan would come at a price. Having accepted the need to build 'in the least expensive way' while at the same time ensuring that the materials 'should be of that Quality which is best suited to its purpose', Leroux estimated that the project would cost approximately £27,360.[31] When added to the £4,000 that Jervoise and the heirs of Walter Baynes wanted for their land, this meant that the ratepayers of the County of Middlesex now faced a bill totalling more than £31,000 for their new prison.* In reality, just like the time frame first suggested in April 1783, Leroux's estimate would prove wildly, even laughably, optimistic.

The first increase came when the proprietors of the cold bath sought indemnification for potential damage to their business should the building of the new prison interrupt the flow of the waters upon which they depended. After some haggling, the magistrates eventually agreed a compensation payment that pushed the total cost of the land to £4,350. Much worse was to come. In June 1787, the building committee reported that they now estimated that the total cost of construction would be in the region of £47,722 – an increase of over 57 per cent – though they attempted to soften the blow by suggesting that 'when Advertisements should be published for Workmen to Contract, it was their Opinion that Proposals would be delivered in at much lower Prices than those on which their Estimate had been formed'.[32] Acknowledging that the prison's design could not be altered substantially while at the same time remaining 'consistent with the necessary purposes of a House of Correction according to the present Laws', the assembled magistrates had no choice but to approve the increase – and hope for the best.

In the early stages of the build the key problem faced by the contractors was the nature of the ground itself, which – not surprisingly given its location next to the Fleet and its fame for healthy freshwater springs – was both marshy and steeply sloped, making levelling, draining and the laying of robust foundations both costly and time-consuming. According to one anonymous but apparently well-informed correspondent of the *Gentleman's Magazine*, 'it was found prudent to lay the foundation so deep, and pile it so securely, that it is supposed there are as many bricks laid underground in this vast building as appear in sight'.[33] Works above ground proved equally difficult and in April 1789 the Court heard that another £28,000 would be required if the project were to be 'carried on with all

---

*   Roughly equivalent to £4,136,000 in 2024. Source: Bank of England inflation calculator.

possible dispatch'.[34] In another year's time Thomas Rogers, the County Surveyor and architect who had designed the Sessions House, reported that the bricklayers could not proceed with their work because of delays in the completion of the stonework; the mason, William Hopcraft, blamed his stone merchant for not shipping the stone in a timely fashion, and the merchant, in turn, blamed the Royal Navy for impressing his workers in order to fight the French.[35]

Whoever was ultimately responsible, the build continued at a snail's pace, with a harassed Rogers telling the Court in June 1791 that there were only four masons at work on the site, 'that the Work is now almost standing still, and at the Rate it goes on at present it will be many Years before it can be completed'.[36] In the face of seemingly interminable delays and spiralling costs, the magistrates naturally sought to save money and Henry Holland, architect to the English nobility and erstwhile partner of Capability Brown, who sat on the building committee, suggested that 'a great saving might be made in Executing the remaining part of the Building and that a great part of the Stone Work might with propriety be omitted'.[37] Further discussions resulted in the removal from the plans of the stone galleries, from which it had been intended that the separate cells should be entered, and major alterations to the engine house, to the associated pump equipment, to the infirmaries and even to the total number of cells. Crucially, these economy-driven alterations would not affect the house of correction's compliance with legislative requirements; whether it would remain the model institution originally envisaged was a different matter entirely. And still the costs climbed ever higher, with Rogers announcing to the assembled Court on 8 December that a further £20,000 would be required to complete the build.[38]

In June 1793, nearly six years after the first spade had been driven into the clay of Gardiner's Field, an inspection of the still incomplete house of correction satisfied the Middlesex magistrates 'that a part of the Prison was perfectly dry and that Prisoners might be removed thither with great safety', though not before 'the great or principal Gates of the Prison be … put up and completed'.[39] After the erection of the imposing iron-strapped oak gates, priority was to be given to completion of the governor's apartments, and the ordering of oak bedsteads, straw mattresses, rugs and blankets for the first forty prisoners. Two freshwater butts would be placed in the courtyards for the prisoners' use and a specimen of the quaintly named 'poo poo tubs' – actually night soil boxes of the kind used on slave ships – submitted for the magistrates' inspection, so that they might approve their use in each of the individual cells.* Finally, two turnkeys from the old Bridewell, Messrs Harper and Harwood, were ordered to move to the new facility 'for the purpose of taking care of the Prisoners there confined'.[40] Accordingly, on Thursday 18 July, the first eighteen prisoners, some from Newgate and others from the old Clerkenwell Bridewell, were escorted to the new gaol, a reporter for the *Morning Chronicle* observing that 'As these were the first inhabitants of this large and much-talked-of prison, it was thought prudent to conduct them to their new habitation at five o'clock in the morning, in order to prevent the attendance of a mob which an idle curiosity might probably have assembled at a later hour'.[41]

If the magistrates believed that reaching this important milestone would mark the end of their trials and tribulations, they would be sadly disappointed. At the Sessions meeting on 27 September a woman described only as 'a poor widow' appeared to claim compensation for the death of her husband, who had been killed when he fell from a scaffold during the building work. Less tragic, but more embarrassing, was the report that a number of prisoners had escaped, apparently due to the laxity, incompetence or corruption of one of the turnkeys. One escapee, who made his exit on 7 August and was recaptured on 14 September, admitted to using a foot-long metal spike to break out of his cell, before employing the workmen's unguarded ladders and ropes to scale the prison wall. Faced with such humiliating evidence of failures in site safety and security, the Court had little option but to order that all prisoners then confined at Coldbath Fields should be immediately returned to the old Bridewell, where they would remain until such time as the new prison was finished. To pour yet more salt into their wounds, the following February, Rogers once again arrived cap-in-hand to request another £12,000 in order to complete the outstanding work – a request which the Court felt unable to refuse, meaning that they would be obliged to raise yet more cash by borrowing.

But, at last, after more than seven years of construction work and at a cost of nearly £80,000 – more than two-and-a-half times the original estimate – the new house of correction at Coldbath Fields was complete and at its meeting on 5 June 1794 the Court gave the long-anticipated instruction for the newly appointed prison governor to 'remove with the Prisoners in his Custody ... as soon as conveniently may be'.[42] Unsurprisingly given

---

* The term 'poo poo tub' appears to be derived from the Yoruba word *póò*, a name for a bucket serving as a traditional toilet or chamber pot, as used by enslaved members of the Yoruba people of Nigeria and Benin. See, for instance, *First Report from the Select Committee of the House of Commons on the Slave Trade* (1850), p. 167.

the history of the build, 'as soon as conveniently may be' turned out to be much later than hoped for due to a variety of last minute issues, including the need to consider whether more suitable beds could be found for the prisoners, 'some inconveniences being found to attend those at present made use of'.[43] But even these problems could not delay the opening forever, and in its edition of 8 October the *Whitehall Evening Post* reported that 'On Saturday, the 27th September, the Prisoners in the Old House of Correction at Clerkenwell were removed to the New Bridewell at Coldbath Fields'.[44]

Unfortunately, we have no record of the initial impressions of the first prisoners to enter the new house of correction. Probably the features that most struck them as the iron-studded gates clanged shut were the immense brick walls that surrounded the whole site – far more substantial and far less porous than those of the crumbling old Bridewell they had just vacated. Then there were the looming masses of the three-storey prison buildings with their tiers of arched and grated windows, the main block consisting of four long galleries which formed a parallelogram by their junction, on the sides of which were ranged the 232 cells. As they were led into the interior, they must have been struck, too, by 'the thick walls, numerous and massy doors and gates, and winding passages',[45] which, as one well-informed observer immediately recognised, had been designed specifically 'to render a sudden outburst of prisoners impracticable'.[46]

In 1813, Leigh Hunt and his brother, John, would each be sentenced to a fine of £500 and two years' imprisonment for writing and printing an article in which they lambasted the Prince Regent as 'a violator of his word, a libertine over head and ears in debt and disgrace ... a man who had just closed half a century without one single claim on the gratitude of his country'.[47] Leigh spent his two-year term in Horsemonger Lane Prison, which closely followed the pattern of Coldbath Fields, where John was incarcerated, and he later commented on the prisons' design not as a visitor, but as an inmate:

> At night-time the door was locked; then another on the top of the staircase, then another on the middle of the staircase, then a fourth at the bottom, a fifth that shut up the little yard belonging to that quarter, and how many more, before you got out of the gates, I forget: but I do not

exaggerate when I say there were ten or eleven. The first night I slept there, I listened to them, one after the other, till the weaker part of my heart died within me.[48]

Lying in their cells that first night, most of the newly transferred prisoners probably felt much the same.

The following day, the Reverend Samuel Glasse, himself a Middlesex magistrate and a man actively engaged in the project, preached a sermon in the prison chapel before the chairman of the Sessions, William Mainwaring, a committee of Middlesex magistrates, guests from the Surrey magistracy, invited journalists and, of course, the prisoners themselves. An enthusiastic author of sermons with such titles as *The Beneficial Effects of Harmony*, *Fear God, Honour the King* and *A Word of Comfort to the Poor*, Glasse had also compiled a helpful guide for his fellow magistrates entitled *The Magistrate's Assistant* and, according to one admiring contemporary, he had long since established himself as 'a divine, as a magistrate, and as a teacher and tutor of the first eminence ... of whose useful labors, the Gospel, the law, the church, the bar, the schools of learning, the rich and the poor, have long felt and confessed the benefit'.[49]

In 1764, Glasse had been elected a Fellow of the Royal Society on the basis of his being a 'Gentleman of Merit & Learning, & a great Enquirer into Natural History';[50] eight years later he had been further honoured with an appointment as one of the Chaplains in Ordinary to King George III, a sinecure that required nothing more of him than that he preach once a year in the Chapel Royal. Now he stood in powdered clerical wig and black silk cassock, the very epitome of the well-fed and affluent pluralist Anglican clergyman, short of stature, rotund of form and florid of complexion, preparing to explain to the men, women and children before him the error of their ways, and the means of their salvation. He took as his text the Gospel of St Matthew, chapter XXV, verse 36, 'I was in Prison, and ye came unto me', and, turning a blind eye to the incredulous faces of his captive audience, began by telling them of his temptation 'to congratulate my hearers' on becoming the first residents of the completed prison, and of how being transferred there would prove 'better for them, because, in this place, better means will be applied, for the purpose of producing their reformation and amendment'.[51]

Early in 1786, when the members of the Middlesex bench reviewed the building plans as adapted for the Gardiner's Field site, they had considered the adoption of 'an ingenious Contrivance'[52] whereby prisoners would be kept in isolation even when attending chapel, the contrivance perhaps presaging the cubicle model later adopted at Lincoln Prison and elsewhere as part of the 'Separate System'. But, with the magistrates keen to encourage chapel-going among the inmates, 'the habitual Neglect whereof was probably the Principal Cause of their being reduced to their present unhappy situation', the design had been rejected as potentially off-putting.[53] Instead, Glasse's congregation had been divided according to their offences, with misdemeanants, debtors and those awaiting trial corralled in separate areas of the chapel, partitioned by iron gratings and 'with Benches only and no Pews'.[54]

Glasse would later be described as 'a popular and eloquent preacher',[55] and the assembled magistrates were so impressed by his sermon, *The Sinner Encouraged to Repentance*,[56] that they later printed 500 copies at the expense of the county so that it might be 'from time to time distributed amongst the Prisoners'.[57] A reporter for the *Oracle* also declared it 'an excellent and pertinent discourse',[58] and, fully imbibing the evident satisfaction – to say nothing of the relief – of Mainwaring and his colleagues, went on to wax lyrical about the prison's facilities and the aspirations that had resulted in its construction:

> From the previous attention which the Magistrates ... have bestowed upon this important object, the most sanguine hopes are entertained of its being productive of the most salutary effects in reforming and restoring to society, and rendering useful, many individuals who, under the old system, by living in idleness and mixing with the most profligate of the human species, were ultimately returned upon the public infinitely more depraved than when their confinement commenced.
>
> The leading feature of this new establishment is to effect *reformation, by combining useful industry with solitary confinement*, and to preserve health by cleanliness and good air ... While the solitude which is attached to the situation of every prisoner, joined to a weekly attendance upon religious duties and moral instruction, applicable to their particular condition, holds out a reasonable prospect of reformation, the habits of industry and sobriety (for unless for the sick, nothing but water is allowed to enter the gates of the prison) which they are to acquire in this dreary abode, must (if anything will) give their minds a cast exceedingly different from what has been heretofore experienced by prisoners committed to Houses of Correction.[59]

Those magistrates who read this account might, perhaps, have been disappointed that it contained no suggestion that Coldbath Fields House of

Correction could, or should, be a model for other counties. To balance this oversight, however, they were no doubt immensely relieved that, with either a singular lack of journalistic acumen or an excess of diplomacy, the reporter uttered not one word about the lengthy delays in construction, the massive overspend, the bitter quarrels or the county's astonishing, if not absolutely crippling, level of indebtedness.

Regrettably, there is no record as to whether the assembled thieves, prostitutes and vagabonds who made up the majority of Glasse's congregation 'felt and confessed the benefit' of his sermon as he assured them of 'the *Humanity* of our Courts of Justice' in sentencing them, and of their prospects of becoming '*wiser*, and *better*, and *happier*' as a result of their incarceration. On one subject, though, if on no other, they were likely to find themselves in complete agreement with the Doctor of Divinity and his colleagues on the bench: the critical importance of the individuals chosen as the governor and his turnkeys in setting the tone of the prison. Those individuals, it had been observed in 1786, must be 'Men of Integrity and Sobriety, Men of Prudence and Firmness with Humanity ... ever anxious to secure the Persons, to preserve the Health, to inforce the Correction and (as far as occasional good Advice and a constant good Example can Effect it) to promote the Reformation of the Prisoners'.[60]

John Harwood, the governor of the old Bridewell who had died the previous year, had not always lived up to these exacting standards. Not long before his death he had been obliged to make an abject apology for his inadequacies, throwing himself 'very contritely on the mercy of this Committee', admitting that he 'trusted too much to my servants', and assuring the Court that 'if they will be so indulgent to forgive the neglect they shall never have cause again for Complaint'.[61] Whatever the extent of Harwood's reformation, his death had given the magistrates the opportunity to make a fresh start and, in the 51-year-old Thomas Aris, Glasse believed that he and his colleagues had found the perfect replacement:

> The person, to whose care the Court has thought proper to commit the prisoners, the Magistrates have great satisfaction in observing, seems well qualified for his arduous employment. He has entered on his office with great earnestness, and apparent purity of intention; desirous of executing his important trust with credit to himself, advantage to the prisoners, and satisfaction to the county. From that firmness and resolution which he seems to possess, from his great vigilance, his zeal and his integrity, they have every reason to expect from him a vigorous and faithful discharge of his duty.[62]

Glasse was undoubtedly sincere when he told the assembled inmates that 'the grand principle on which everything here is about to be conducted, is a principle of justice, tempered with mercy'.[63] Unfortunately, in Aris, he and his fellow magistrates had appointed a man who would, almost single-handedly, make the new Coldbath Fields House of Correction – a prison in which so much had been invested, and of which so much was hoped – a byword for brutality and degradation, and where he would exercise the kind of absolute power found nowhere else but on the quarterdeck of one of His Majesty's men-o'-war.

3

'Diversified in Disposition and Pursuits'
The Governor and His Wards

Nothing in his background or early career made Thomas Aris an obvious candidate for the role of governor of London's newest prison. Born in Brackley on the Northamptonshire–Buckinghamshire border in 1743, he had followed his father's trade as a baker, but after completing their apprenticeships he and his younger brother John had decided to establish their own business closer to London. Initially, Thomas settled in the village of Hornsey to the north of the City where he married Sarah Dyson in the summer of 1769, but shortly afterwards he moved again, to Rosoman Street, on the northernmost edge of Clerkenwell and just a short walk from the old Bridewell.

When the Arises took up residence at No. 5, Rosoman Street was a desirable new development built by the eponymous Thomas Rosoman, with the first houses – those on the west side – remarkable for the steep flights of steps leading to their front doors and for their views across the gardens and open countryside opposite, including Gardiner's Field where the Coldbath Fields House of Correction would later be built. Their new home stood on a portion of the site occupied until recently by the 'New Wells', an 'interlude house' or theatre erected in 1735 by Joseph Hooke, an entrepreneurial St Pancras physician looking to compete with the nearby Sadler's Wells theatre. Here patrons, no doubt fuelled by gin and ale from local hostelries like the Red Lion inn and the Merlin's Cave tavern, could enjoy a heady mixture of boisterous and often ribald entertainments that combined song, dance, acrobatics and satirical comedy. Alternatively, for 6*d*, they might choose to stroll in the adjacent gardens with their 'wonderful grotto' and 'enchanted fountain',[1] or gawp at the crocodile, rattlesnakes and other exotic creatures exhibited in the small zoo.[2] By the mid-1740s, however, and despite their attractively louche reputation for being 'places riotous, of great extravagance, luxury, idleness, and ill fame',[3] the appeal of the New Wells had begun to pall and Rosoman, an actor-manager who had taken over the struggling concern in 1744, moved on to the more resilient Sadler's Wells, closing the theatre altogether in 1747. It seems, though, that Rosoman shared his predecessor's entrepreneurial instincts because, in 1755, he purchased a ninety-nine-year lease for the site and having demolished the theatre, which had spent the last few years rather incongruously as a Wesleyan tabernacle, almost immediately he began to build.

According to William J. Pinks, initially Rosoman Street found particular favour with comfortably off retired tradesmen and artisans,[4] but as the development continued and the picturesque rural views became obscured by new housing more businesses located here, including book- and printsellers, engravers, and the ubiquitous watch- and clockmakers. It is possible, then, that Aris set up his bakery at No. 5, but it seems more likely that his premises were on the broader, busier and much more densely populated thoroughfare of nearby Compton Street, a little to the east, where his brother resided, perhaps living over their shop.

Shortly after moving to Clerkenwell, Thomas Aris became a father for the first time with the birth of his son, Samuel, who was baptised at the dilapidated old nunnery church of St James on Clerkenwell Green on 28 October 1770. But the birth was attended with complications and not long afterwards Sarah died, aged just 22, probably of either puerperal sepsis, post-natal haemorrhage or toxaemia, then the most common causes of maternal mortality.* With an infant son to care for, as well as a business to run, Aris wasted no time in marrying again, wedding the 20-year-old Priscilla Perkins in his old stamping ground of Hornsey on 11 August 1771. Thereafter, the Aris family grew swiftly, with the birth

---

*   In the eighteenth century only burials were registered; however, analysis of death-registration statistics for the period 1850–1935 tells us that, in this eighty-five-year period, the most common cause of maternal mortality was puerperal sepsis, accounting for roughly 50 per cent of fatalities, with ante- and post-natal haemorrhage and toxaemia responsible for another 25 per cent. Assuming that Sarah suffered from no underlying ailment, such as consumption, phthisis, typhoid or pneumonia, it seems fairly likely that one of these common complications caused her premature death. See Irvine Loudon, 'Deaths in Childbed from the Eighteenth Century to 1935', in *Medical History*, 1986, 30, pp. 1–41.

of two sons and three daughters over the next decade, and a further four children by 1790.

With a rapidly growing family to support, Aris clearly wished to supplement his income because, in 1780, he took on two additional roles, the first as collector of rates 'for the Use of the Commissioners, in Trust, for Paving, Lighting, Watching, and Cleansing' the parish of St James, a function that he fulfilled by meeting ratepayers each Thursday in the parlour of the Jerusalem Tavern on Rosoman Street, just a few steps from his own front door.[5] Of a similar nature, his second new job was as steward and collector to the Finsbury Dispensary. Also conveniently located on Rosoman Street, the dispensary, whose purpose was to administer advice and medicines to the poor of the surrounding parishes, had been opened on 12 August that year by a 'few Gentlemen, blessed with benevolent hearts, and liberal dispositions', who believed that since 'the wealth of nations springs from the production of labour; surely, then, poor industrious labourers have a just claim to, and merit, the care and assistance, not only of the affluent, but of all degrees not pinched with want'.[6] The new institution had been an instant success, with its physicians and apothecaries treating 685 individuals in its first six months of operation. By March 1792 it would have admitted 37,945, of whom it claimed to have cured or relieved 36,452.[7] Operating on a subscription model, the dispensary needed to employ a reliable man to receive the subscriptions and, no doubt, on occasion to politely jog the memories of those who had promised money but failed to contribute in a timely fashion. This was the role now filled by Aris.

Crucially, as well as increasing his income, these jobs introduced Aris to local men of influence, including Sir James Esdaile, alderman, banker, City magistrate, one-time Mayor of London and patron of Sir Joshua Reynolds, Dr Francis de Valangin, a Swiss émigré and author who would later become medical inspector of Bridewell prison and hospital, Dr John Coakley Lettsom, Quaker abolitionist, friend of Benjamin Franklin and founder of the Medical Society of London, and the Reverend Sir George Booth, one of the Middlesex magistrates, all of whom served as vice presidents of the dispensary. The establishment of such contacts would prove hugely beneficial in Aris's future career.

Aris took his next tentative step towards the governorship of Coldbath Fields in December 1782, when he submitted an application to the Middlesex magistrates 'praying to be appointed Baker to one of the prisons',[8] by which he meant either the Bridewell or the 'New Prison', in which prisoners committed for examination before the police magistrates, for trial at the sessions and for want of bail were held, and which stood just next door to its sister institution.* For some years the magistrates had contracted a number of local bakers to produce bread for the prisons and Aris succeeded in becoming one of them. But his employment in this role ended when the magistrates decided to adopt a new supply model which resulted in William Watherston becoming sole provider. However, when Watherston was dismissed in April 1786 following complaints regarding the quality of his bread (his loaves had been found to be occasionally underweight as early as September 1783), Aris seized his opportunity. The next month he submitted his application to become baker to the Bridewell and New Prison, describing his product as 'the best wheaten bread that can be made'.[9] The appointments committee, being 'satisfied with the character of the said Mr Aris', duly confirmed him as sole provider.

There can be little doubt that in making his regular deliveries to the prisons, and in hob-nobbing with the turnkeys who met him at the gates, Aris must have gained some familiarity with the workings of the two institutions, though it is difficult to imagine that this extended much beyond the routine security protocols surrounding access and egress. Nonetheless, when, in October 1793, the time came for the Middlesex magistrates to consider applications for the role of governor of their new house of correction, Aris's was among them and he exhibited no hesitation in asserting that he considered himself 'duly qualified to fill the office'.[10] He further assured them:

> That your Petitioner is fully aware of a rigid attention to cleanliness, Society, good Order, and due Labour in a House of Correction, and knowing how much it is the wish of the Magistrates to see the House of Correction Govern'd strictly according to Law, and their own Institutions, Solemnly pledges himself, that he will pay the most unremitting regard to those essential points of duty in such an Office …
>
> Your Petitioner begs leave to assure your Worships, that if he should be so happy, to be thought deserving of your Worships' favour, and be appointed, he will to the utmost of his Abilities, by a faithful, diligent, and Humane discharge of the Duties of the Office, endeavour to Deserve the Confidence reposed in him.[11]

He was also able to support his application with glowing testimonials from the Board of Commissioners for the parish of St James and from the

---

*   Clerkenwell's New Prison, originally built in the early years of the seventeenth century, was situated at the northern end of New Prison Walk, just to the south-east of the old Bridewell.

governors of the Finsbury Dispensary. The former confirmed that Aris had 'Conducted himself with Honesty and Propriety during the Thirteen Years that he has been the Collector to this Board' and that they believed him 'to be every way qualified and a fit Person to be appointed Governor'.[12] The latter, meanwhile, with 'great Chearfulness', opined that Aris was:

> highly qualified to fill such Situation of Keeper, the ... Governors having had an opportunity of judging fully of the character and abilities of the said Thomas Aris from the Institution of this Charity in the Year 1780 to the present period, during which time (now more than 13 years) he has been their Collector and Conducted himself with Fidelity, Honesty and Zeal.[13]

Of course, there is no reason to suppose that any of Aris's referees perjured themselves in making their fulsome recommendations; rather, it seems that he had genuinely impressed them with his abilities and integrity.

But Aris was not the only candidate to be considered, the others being Philip Chrystall, an apothecary temporarily employed at the Bridewell, Francis Tapp, the High Constable for Westminster, and William Wright, the High Constable for the Tower Division in the County of Middlesex. On paper, it might appear that a High Constable, an official responsible for suppressing riots and violent crime, and for arming the militia to enable him to do so, might be better qualified for the role of prison governor than either an apothecary or a baker, but only recently Tapp's reputation had been tarnished by his part in precipitating a minor riot in Mount Street following his unnecessary and high-handed arrest of a group of individuals who, according to the *Evening Mail*, 'had been employing themselves convivially in celebrating His Majesty's birthday, without any tumult, riot, or disorder whatever' – actions for which he himself had subsequently been arrested.[14] Chrystall appears never to have been considered a serious contender for the post, while Wright's candidacy seems to have been sunk by his admission that he wished his wife and children to accompany him into the governor's residence – in contrast with Aris, the death of whose second wife the previous month enabled him to state that he would 'go into the prison unincumbred'.[15] When the collected magistrates cast their votes, Aris was the clear winner receiving forty-one, against Wright's twelve and Chrystall's pitiful one; Tapp was disqualified due to non-attendance.

In selecting the baker and confirming his generous annual salary of £300, presumably none of the members of the board of magistrates recalled that, two decades earlier, this same Thomas Aris, then aged 30, had stood before them charged with having assaulted one Thomas Stone.[16] Nothing is known of Thomas Stone, or of the circumstances surrounding the alleged assault, and there is no reason to question the justice of the eventual verdict of 'not guilty'. Nonetheless, given Aris's subsequent career, it is impossible not to consider the incident as being distinctly ominous.

What of the prisoners consigned to Aris's care? William Lambard, an Elizabethan commentator on the English legal system and himself a Justice of the Peace, described misdemeanants as those who 'doe beat their braines for the finding out of shifts and subtilties, and doe for the most part lay Hookes, and make Traps as it were for the taking, intangling, and snaring of silly and simple folks'. From such individuals, he believed:

> spring those so many Cosenages, crafty reaches, undermining devices, subtile complots, counterfeit drifts, and fraudulent fetches, the Egges whereof be laid sometimes by desire of money, and sometime by thirst of revenge, but always, or for the most part hatched by Perjurie, Briberie, and Corruption, and are wholly addressed to the discredit of the good name of some, to the detriment of others in their Goods and Fortunes, and to the great danger, and hazard of the bodie and life of many a man.[17]

In fact, as Sir William Blackstone, the great eighteenth-century jurist and legal commentator, would remark, the number and range of misdemeanours was vast. It included, among many other crimes, affray, blasphemy, perjury, selling alcohol without a licence, assault, smuggling, poaching, mismanagement of gunpowder, prostitution and lewd behaviour, destruction of dykes or banks, bribery, desertion of a spouse (if that spouse was then forced onto the parish for relief), begging and overcharging for a sedan chair.[18] Little wonder then that, as a later governor of Coldbath Fields observed, the prison's occupants 'were as diversified in disposition and pursuits, as were their features and stature', and that 'it rarely happened that we could not number, amongst its heterogeneous inmates, some men of education, and erst of respectability; with others of high connexions, or of former position in society.[19] Despite this diversity, all the inmates had one thing in common: en route to the prison, each of them had first passed through a magistrate's court, with a large percentage appearing at the country's most famous on Bow Street.

Under British law, a magistrate could try cases on his own, and without a jury, meaning that he could determine guilt or innocence in the most summary fashion. Moreover, while Parliament had continually added to the number of offences that could be tried in this manner, it had failed to protect the rights of the accused by formulating strict procedures for the conduct of trials. Consequently, writes Anthony Babington, historian of Bow Street and himself a Bow Street magistrate, 'often what occurred was a travesty of justice from which the convicted person, be he a thief, vagrant, poacher or brawler, had little or no chance of appealing either against his conviction or against his sentence'.[20] So far as these sentences were concerned, Blackstone tells us that for first offences magistrates might inflict 'divers petty pecuniary mulcts, and corporal penalties',[21] such as whipping or being placed in the stocks, but terms of imprisonment within a house of correction were also routinely handed down, particularly for repeat offenders.

Typically, where a misdemeanant was sent to Coldbath Fields by a magistrate without reference to a higher court, we know almost nothing about them. Their names and a very brief summary of their offences might be recorded, but their histories and the minutiae of their crimes are almost invariably lost. For instance, of Daniel Howard, Ann Williams, Mary Clark, Elizabeth Vicus, Isaac Milan, Mary Davis and Sarah Conjuit, all we know is that they were imprisoned for disorderly behaviour, which almost certainly meant a suspicion of prostitution or other 'lewd behaviour'; Michael McDonald for assault; Gustavus Gordon for theft; and Margaret Brownlow, Ann Stamford, Richard Layton and John Noon for being rogues and vagabonds. Usually poor, often illiterate and, if not homeless, then dwelling in cheap rented accommodation, in most cases almost the only marks these individuals have left on history are to be found in parish registers and in the records of the magistrates' courts and in the prison's books of admission.

However, when a prisoner was only temporarily consigned to the house of correction prior to a jury trial, or when such a trial – held at either the Old Bailey or the Court of King's Bench in London, or at a county court of assize – resulted in their being found guilty of a misdemeanour rather than a felony, much more is recorded. A servant named John Lowrie, for example, was held at Coldbath Fields prior to his trial for stealing and then pawning a collection of napkins, bedsheets and other linen from a house rented by his mistress in Hans Place, Knightsbridge. Found guilty of larceny, he was sentenced to transportation for seven years.[22] Lowrie would go on to demonstrate an apparently genuine, if occasionally fragile, desire to reform. Remaining in Australia after his release, he would make and then lose a fortune in Sydney; later pardoned following a conviction for stealing a boat, he moved to New Zealand and ended his career managing the government's ferry service in Kawhia and Karaka.[23]

At his trial, Thomas Bucknell faced a phalanx of witnesses – including one who identified him during his preliminary detention at Coldbath Fields – all of whom swore that, on different occasions, in different places and using different names, he had paid for goods using forged £1 notes. Mr Justice Lawrence handed down a sentence of death by hanging, his public execution taking place outside Newgate Prison on 26 July 1804.[24] Augustus Seaton and Thomas Clifton received the same sentence for their audacious theft of gold and jewellery to a value of nearly £200* from John Nicholson, a jeweller in Cornhill, their haul carefully lifted through a hole they had cut in the shop's shutters using a centre-bit, and without their even setting foot in the building.[25] Various items were recovered, but it is impossible not to think Nicholson foolhardy in leaving such high-value and easily transportable merchandise literally within arm's reach of any thief willing to break through a wooden shutter and a pane of glass.

Lowrie, Bucknell, Seaton and Clifton all knew Coldbath Fields prior to their convictions. In contrast, others were more fortunate in that their experience of the gaol came after the verdict of guilty was passed, meaning that their term of imprisonment was highly unlikely to exceed two years: men like James Briscoe and John Denham who were indicted for the wilful murder of James Pamphlin. Despite ample evidence that they had stabbed their unarmed victim outside the Harrow public house on Compton Street – just yards from the bakery of Thomas and John Aris – the jury found the two men guilty of the lesser offence of manslaughter, probably because they considered that the pair had been provoked by the drunken Pamphlin's lewd suggestions to Briscoe's wife just moments earlier. Both men received sentences of twelve months in Coldbath Fields.[26]

The cases of John Kerr and Thomas Millar were both heard at the Court of King's Bench in the magnificent medieval surroundings of Westminster Hall, where Charles I had been tried nearly 150 years earlier. Fortunately for them, unlike the Stuart king, neither faced a charge that carried a capital penalty.

In November 1796, Kerr stood in the dock as proprietor of the Apollo Gardens in St George's Fields, Southwark. Like the larger and more famous New Spring Gardens at Vauxhall, upon which they were modelled, the Apollo Gardens were a place for music, dancing, eating and drinking, along with regular fireworks, operas, masquerades and assorted exhibitions. They

---

* Approximately £14,000 today.

were also designed as a place where the wealthy and fashionable might see and be seen as they promenaded among the shrubberies and Lilliputian waterways. The gardens had first been opened on 4 October 1788 by Walter Claggett, who took great pains to assure his prospective clientele among the nobility and gentry that the entertainments on offer, as well as 'the Wines, Confectionary, and other refreshments', would be 'the best of their respective kinds that can possibly be had in this kingdom without exception, and the attendance equal every way thereto'.[27] But even on the first night Claggett had cause to bemoan the disruption caused by 'the great number of improper persons that gained admission to all parts',[28] and over the coming years, as the gardens changed hands, their reputation grew ever more tarnished.

By the time of Kerr's trial, the Apollo Gardens were described as a scene of 'the most scandalous debauchery and immorality, frequented only by prostitutes and apprentices, who were guilty of every species of disorder and vice', and where 'no modest woman could possibly have appeared'.[29] What was the point of parents trying to instil in their children habits of industry, asked Lord Kenyon, the Lord Chief Justice, 'if places of this kind, where nothing was to be seen but dissipation and vice, were suffered'?[30] Worse still, this was not the first time that Kerr had fallen foul of the law. At the Surrey assizes the previous August, he had been found guilty of 'keeping a disorderly house, which was a public nuisance',[31] but instead of closing the venue or remedying its defects he had done nothing. With Kerr having been found guilty a second time, Kenyon determined that 'it would be better to delay passing judgement till it was seen whether the dread of it would be the means of having it effectually shut'.[32] He therefore remanded the impressario to Coldbath Fields in order to think on his sins and to demonstrate genuine repentance by organising the closure of the gardens. Brought back to Court more than five months later, on 7 May 1797, Kerr duly produced an affidavit showing that the gardens had indeed been closed and that the buildings were about to be demolished. 'The Court, taking into consideration the long imprisonment the defendant had suffered, ordered him to be discharged, on his entering into a recognizance of 1000l'.[33]

Like Kerr, Thomas Millar would spend months in prison between his conviction and sentencing. But, at last, after six months in gaol, at the beginning of November 1797 he was brought up to receive the judgement of the Court for keeping a gaming house in Leicester Fields, then transitioning from being a predominantly residential area to one renowned for the entertainments on offer, some reputable, others much less so. The defendant, Justice Sir William Ashhurst intoned, had been found guilty not only of keeping a gaming house, but also of 'causing divers idle and evil-disposed persons to frequent his house, and to play for large sums of money, at an unlawful game called Hazard'.[34] Again, like Kerr before him, so far Millar had shown not the slightest remorse. Instead, when first notified of the prosecution, he boasted that 'he did not mind the pillory', and that, so far as financial penalties were concerned, 'they might take 500l from his coffers without his missing it'.[35] Such bravado would serve Millar ill. 'These declarations,' observed Ashhurst:

> proved that the Defendant was very far gone in this trade of iniquity ... it was a crime of the greatest magnitude, and more destructive in its consequences than many that were declared Capital by the laws. What was the crime of sheep-stealing or picking pockets compared with gaming? Among the higher classes of Society it frequently led to self-murder and duelling; families were ruined by it, and innocent children reduced to beggary. Among those in lower life, it was notorious that its consequences were equally bad; they often betook themselves to shop-lifting and robbery to replenish their purses, and usually end their lives by the hand of Justice ... it extinguished every generous principle, destroyed friendship, and estranged the mind from the society even of their own families. Their whole attention was turned to the chance of a card or a die – a strange employment surely for a rational being.[36]

There is no record of whether Millar's previous sangfroid ebbed away as he listened to this tirade from the bench, nor of his reaction when he realised that his preliminary period of incarceration would not be taken into account, as it had been in Kerr's case. He had suggested that there would be no disgrace in the pillory and that 'vice could give dignity to any situation'; as a result he would spend another twelve months in Coldbath Fields and pay a fine of £500, plus another £500 as a surety for his future good behaviour.

Other prisoners placed in Aris's care, and about whom we know more than might usually be the case, are those who, for whatever reason, attracted the attention of the roving journalists who frequented London's magistrates' courts. Men like the so-called Vere Street Coterie, James Cooke, Philip Ilett, William Thompson, Richard Francis, James Done and Robert Aspinal, who were arrested at the White Swan, a notorious 'Molly house' on Vere Street, between Clare Market and Duke Street, and charged with offences under the Buggery Act of 1533.* Tried at the

---

*   An Acte for the punishment of the vice of Buggerie (25 Hen. 8. c. 6).

Middlesex Sessions for 'conspiring together ... for the purpose or exciting each other to commit a detestable offence',[37] the sextet were served very poorly by their barrister, John Gurney,* who declared in open Court that he had undertaken their defence 'because he felt himself bound to do so by his oath, and duty as an advocate', but that he found the prosecution's evidence 'so clear and uncontradicted, as to leave no ground of palliation upon which to make any appeal to the Jury, upon circumstances, which, if true, would go to excite an idea that the horrors of Sodom and Gomorrah were revived in London'.[38]

Not surprisingly, all six men were found guilty, but because they had not been found *in flagrante delicto*, they had escaped a capital charge – unlike their companions at the White Swan, the 16-year-old drummer boy Thomas White and John Newbold Hepburn, an ensign in a West India regiment, who were sentenced to death at the Old Bailey after White made a full confession of their 'detestable crime'. Nonetheless, they faced a terrifying ordeal even before they began their terms of imprisonment in Coldbath Fields.** Sentenced to be pilloried in the Haymarket, opposite Norris Street, the *Morning Chronicle* reported that, on their appearance:

> The concourse of people assembled was immense, even the tops of the houses in the Hay-market were covered with spectators. As soon as a convenient ring was formed, a number of women were admitted within side, who vigorously expressed their abhorrence of the miscreants, by a perpetual shower of mud, eggs, offal, and every kind of filth with which they had plentifully supplied themselves in baskets and buckets ... [They] were pelted till it was scarcely possible to distinguish the human shape.[39]

How they fared once they reached the house of correction is unknown but, placed in the yards with other misdemeanants, there seems little enough reason to hope that they escaped further abuse, as we know from the Royal Commission report of 1808 that another individual named Richards, who

---

* In 1835, Gurney became the last judge in England to impose a capital punishment for sodomy, after a jury convicted James Pratt and John Smith under the Offences Against the Person Act 1828, which had replaced the Buggery Act of 1533.

** Amos, having been twice before convicted of similar offences, was sentenced to three years' imprisonment, and to stand once in the pillory, in the Haymarket, opposite Panton Street; Cooke, the keeper of the house, Ilett, Thompson, Francis and Done, were each sentenced to two year's imprisonment, and the pillory in the same place. Aspinal, 'not having appeared so active as the others', was sentenced to one year's imprisonment, without being pilloried.

had been imprisoned 'for an attempt to commit an unnatural crime',[40] complained of being ill-treated by the other prisoners. Perhaps, though, for the Vere Street Coterie there was greater safety in numbers.

Another individual who would attract a great deal of press attention over the years, though for very different reasons, was John Bickerton.*** The son of a well-to-do Shropshire farmer, unusually for the time Bickerton had been educated at both Cambridge and Oxford, graduating from the latter in 1799. While at Oxford his behaviour seems to have raised concerns in the mind of the Reverend Isaac Crouch, the vice-principal of St Edmund Hall, who barred Bickerton's path to ordination. Crouch's doubts proved justified because after leaving the university Bickerton's behaviour became increasingly erratic, culminating on the afternoon of Wednesday 14 September 1803 when, 'decently dressed in black, with a large sword by his side', he attempted to gatecrash the king's levee in St James's Palace.[41]

According to the *St James's Chronicle*, Bickerton 'was proceeding upstairs towards the Levee, when the Yeoman of the Guard inquired of him where he was going, he not being in a court dress'.[42] When Bickerton replied that he wished to see William Cavendish-Bentinck, third Duke of Portland and Lord President of the Privy Council, the Yeoman naturally refused him admittance. But Bickerton persisted, stating that 'the Duke was to lay his claims to an estate which he was kept out of by Lord Cholmondeley'; he then claimed (spuriously) to be 'brother to Admiral Sir Richard Bickerton;**** and by virtue of the noble family to which he was allied he carried the sword by his side, which cut on both sides'.[43]

Of course, the grand staircase of St James's Palace was not the place, and a levee-day certainly not the time, to properly investigate any of Bickerton's claims. This was no doubt explained to him by the Yeomen of the Guard but, clearly in no mood to listen to reason, he refused to leave. With a risk of the situation getting out of hand, the Yeomen called the Bow Street Runners on royal protection duty that afternoon; they forced the sword from him and then took him into custody. The following day he was interviewed at the Bow Street magistrates' court by Sir Richard Ford, one of the Middlesex magistrates. The question to which Ford sought an

---

*** For a full account of Bickerton's extraordinary career see Stephen Haddelsey, *Poor Bickerton: A Journey to the Dark Heart of Georgian England* (Cheltenham: The History Press, 2024).

****Rear Admiral Sir Richard Hussey Bickerton (1759–1832) at that time commander-in-chief of the Mediterranean Fleet and soon to become Nelson's second in command.

answer was what had led Bickerton to attempt to force his way into a levee at St James's Palace – a levee hosted by the king himself, and attended by senior politicians, the nobility and foreign dignitaries? Were his intentions malevolent or harmless? And, if the latter, why had he felt it necessary to arm himself with a sword?

A few days later, Ford himself described the circumstances of the case and the outcome of Bickerton's examination in a letter to Thomas Stirling, the Deputy Clerk of the Peace at the Middlesex Sessions House, Clerkenwell:

> in regard to Mr Bickerton, he was taken up as he was going into the Anti Room [sic] at St James's on a levee day, his conduct & conversation denoted derangement & he had in his hand an old rusty sword. On his Exam'n he appeared deranged – talked of Claims he had from his ancestors on Estates in Cheshire, to recover which he wanted to see the king & the Duke of Portland – the sword, he said, he always carried because he was afraid a man who lodged in the house with him, wanted to murder him ... I wanted Bickerton to let me send to his relations, or to give me some good security for his future conduct, but he did neither.[44]

Bickerton's behaviour and language during his examination at Bow Street apparently satisfied Ford that his prisoner posed no immediate threat either to himself or to those around him. But he was equally satisfied that Bickerton was delusional and that, without a member of his family to provide sureties for his good conduct, or a credible undertaking from Bickerton himself, he could not be released. In normal circumstances this might not have been the case and as a man of education and some wealth he might, perhaps, have been released with an admonition to behave more reasonably in the future.* Unfortunately for Bickerton the prevailing circumstances were anything but normal. Revolution in France, a corresponding rise in radicalism in Britain, marked by increasingly vehement calls for political reform, and growing social unrest, even attempted insurrection – or the fear of it – had caused great anxiety in government, as had been revealed in its decision, in 1794, to suspend the Habeas Corpus Act of 1679. Successive poor harvests in 1795 and 1796 and a concomitant rise in

---

*   The exact duration of Bickerton's imprisonment is uncertain. All that can be said with confidence is that he was still being held 'at His Majesty's pleasure' on 27 October 1803, when Ford wrote to Thomas Stirling, and that he had been released by the beginning of May 1804 at the latest. Thus, his maximum term of imprisonment was some seven-and-a-half months.

the price of food had worsened matters still further, as had France's abortive invasion of Ireland in December 1796 – an invasion defeated not by the Royal Navy, but by the weather.

As a result of this combination of factors, prisons across the country had found themselves housing a growing number of individuals charged with offences relating to political campaigning, sedition and treason. It was this last category of prisoner, and rumours of their treatment by Thomas Aris, that resulted in the governor being called upon to provide a guided tour for his three unwelcome visitors towards the end of 1798.

4

'Our Jacks Will Grumble'
NAVAL MUTINIES AT SPITHEAD AND THE NORE

The three gentlemen who met at the gates of the house of correction on 28 November 1798 were markedly different in appearance and character. The owner of the elegant landau, 'Colonel' William Bosville – or 'Billy Bosville' as his cronies affectionately called him – was 53 years of age and noted for his insistence on wearing the single-breasted coat, powdered hair and other paraphernalia of a courtier of George II – a curious affectation given that Bosville had been just 15 when the old king died.[1] Although he had never attained a rank higher than lieutenant when serving with the Coldstream Guards,* his biographer tells us that 'the courtesy of the public assigned to him the brevet of a Colonel, by which appellation he was more generally designated, even by his friends, than any other'.[2]

During the American War of Independence, Bosville had served in the elite Brigade of Guards under General Edward Mathew, but his military career came to an abrupt end in 1784 when his father died, leaving him the bulk of his capital, investments and estates in Yorkshire. As a young man, Bosville had been a keen traveller, undertaking the Grand Tour through France and Italy, as well as serving on the staff of a British embassy sent to the court of Muhammad bin Abdallah, Emperor of Morocco, but aged 39 and in possession of a very substantial income, he decided that his travelling days were over: he resigned his commission and chose to settle in London, where he quickly established himself as a leading member of fashionable society, a *bon vivant* and raconteur. Indeed, Bosville became so inordinately

---

* Equivalent to a captaincy in a line regiment.

fond of the city that he could seldom be persuaded to leave it, even to visit his Yorkshire properties or the homes of his married sisters in Scotland, declaring that the capital was 'the best residence for winter, and he knew of no place to beat it in summer'.[3] Eccentric, sociable, kind-hearted, generous and politically radical, he loved to entertain his friends – on the condition that they complied with his unbending expectations regarding punctuality, with anyone arriving even a minute or two late likely to find themselves turned away by servants who lived by their master's maxim, 'Some say better late than never; I say, better never than late'.[4] As regular invitees to the old soldier's table, it was a stricture with which his fellow visitors to the prison were all too familiar.

He was followed from the coach by Sir Francis Burdett, a long-legged amateur philologist and, through the purchase of a rotten borough, MP for Boroughbridge in North Yorkshire. Bosville's junior by a full twenty-five years, Burdett had inherited his grandfather's baronetcy and estates in Derbyshire the previous year. Fashionably dressed in high collar, white stock and cut-way double-breasted coat, the 28-year-old was notable for his dark eyes, his rich curly hair, a nose of truly Wellingtonian proportions and, according to one enthusiastic admirer, for an 'elegant and manly figure' and a voice 'strong and musical'.[5]

He was also known for his mercurial character, which veered unpredictably between melancholia, self-reproach, pedantry and quickness of temper. This volatility, and his own infidelities, had recently come so close to ruining his marriage that earlier in the year Burdett had opined to the banker Thomas Coutts that 'marriage is ill calculated to realise the fleeting dream of happiness, much less those Ideas which youthful imagination creates: it is I think the worst bond and has with great truth been call'd the grave of love'.[6] Given that Coutts was his father-in-law, this statement must surely be taken as evidence of what the same admirer called Burdett's inclination to deliver his opinions with the rashness and 'energy of a man who speaks as he feels'. In the hope of finding for his son-in-law a useful occupation that might have the secondary benefit of distracting him from the pleasures to be found in the arms of the Countess of Oxford and others, it was Coutts who had engineered Burdett's election – and his plan seemed to be working, because the young baronet was already establishing for himself a reputation for energy, independence and what he himself described as 'a strong feeling of indignation at injustice and oppression, and a lively sympathy with the sufferings of my fellows'.[7]

Whatever the disparities in their appearance and personality, Bosville and Burdett were born aristocrats, supremely confident in their wealth and breeding. The same could not be said of the man waiting for them in the street. John Courtenay, MP for Appleby, had been born in Ireland in 1738, the son of a low-ranking revenue officer. Educated at Dundalk Grammar School rather than at Harrow or Westminster, he had joined the army as an ensign, but sold his commission in 1765 in order to purchase an appointment as a commissary of musters, responsible for mustering troops by regiment and checking their names against the muster roll in order to maintain detailed records of the army's strength. It was probably while fulfilling these duties that he came to the notice of the Lord Lieutenant of Ireland, Lord Townshend, who had introduced measures intended to increase the size of the Irish regiments. In 1769, Courtenay sold his office in order to meet at least some of his spiralling debts, and three years later he accompanied Townshend to England as his secretary.

In London, he turned his pen to literary as well as administrative work, publishing the elegiac *The Rape of Poloma* in 1773 and *A Poetical Review of the Literary and Moral Character of the Late Samuel Johnson* in 1785. These productions brought him to the attention of the circle of Johnson and Boswell, the latter describing his conversation as 'excellent; it has so much literature, wit, and at the same time manly sense in it'.[8] Through Lord Townshend's good graces, Courtenay also received the patronage of the Prime Minister Lord North, being returned as MP for his first constituency, Tamworth in the West Midlands, at the general election of 1780. A regular speaker in the Commons, he was described by his contemporary, Sir Nathaniel Wraxall, as being conspicuous for:

> a very uncommon and eccentric Species of Humour; original, classic, even Attic; allied to, and sustained by Learning; inexhaustible, and often irresistible in its Effect on the Muscles: but always coarse, frequently licentious, or at least, indecorous; and rarely under a becoming Restraint. His wit seemed indeed more adapted to a Tavern, or to a convivial Board, than to the grave Deliberations of such an Assembly as the House of Commons ... Ridicule constituted his never failing Arm, which he wielded with inconceivable Facility, though without Grace or Elegance.[9]

Nonetheless, few could doubt Courtenay's readiness to take an active part in the day-to-day cut and thrust of British democracy, nor, indeed, his loyalty to his friends, which he amply demonstrated when Lord North was forced from office following the British defeat at Yorktown in 1781, declaring, in the teeth of the opposition's jeers, that he 'could not form a more sanguine wish for the happiness of his country, than that ... an Administration might be formed, as able and disinterested, as upright in their intention but more fortunate in the event than the noble Lord's'.[10] This panegyric was all the more remarkable because Courtenay had consistently opposed the American war.

Upon North's resignation, Courtenay felt free to align himself with Charles James Fox, with whom his sympathies more naturally lay, and with the outbreak of the French Revolution in 1789, he again took up his pen, revealing his radical sympathies with his *Philosophical Reflections on the Late Revolution in France*, in which he lambasted any attempt to defend what Alexander Pope had called 'the right divine of kings to govern wrong'.[11] The horrors of the Terror might have caused him to amend his views somewhat, as articulated in his *The Present State of the Manners, Arts, and Politics, of France and Italy* (1794), but even here, in the words of one recent commentator, 'if he can't completely support the French Revolution, he can wholeheartedly attack those who are against it'.[12] Given these proclivities, it is not surprising that over the coming years Courtenay would become one of Burdett's most ardent supporters in his campaign against the abuses prevalent in Coldbath Fields.

Billy Bosville was famous for his lavish entertainments, reputedly spending an extraordinary £3,000 every year on dinners alone,[13] and it seems probable that the current expedition to Clerkenwell had originated at his table. Certainly, Burdett's biographer tells us that the young baronet was at dinner with a group of like-minded individuals when a series of letters were read purporting to be from prisoners within the Coldbath Fields House of Correction, the prisoners in question having taken part in the ill-fated mutiny aboard the ships of the Royal Navy at anchor in the Nore in May the previous year.

Writing to his wife in September 1793, Horatio Nelson had observed that 'If Parliament does not grant something to this Fleet, our Jacks will grumble ... all we get is honour and salt beef'.[14] Nelson knew his men; he knew, too, that they had very good cause for complaint. While the wages of the soldiers of the British Army had been increased as recently as 1795, sailors' pay had remained unchanged since the reign of Charles II, despite the fact that the cost of living had risen by approximately a third in the intervening decades. In addition, though custom dictated that they would be paid six months in arrears, in reality long periods at sea meant that many had not been paid for years. As a result, when in urgent need of cash, they became reliant upon 'slopsellers', who specialised in lending money to sailors, but at exorbitant rates of interest. When we take into account that sailors' wages were also subject to a number of compulsory deductions, including contributions to the Royal Naval Hospital at Greenwich, it hardly seems surprising that many claimed to be subsisting in 'indigence and extreme penury'.[15]

Provisions, too, were dreadful. With fruit and vegetables soon rotting, and badly stored flour becoming infested with weevils, crews at sea usually lived almost exclusively on hardtack and salted meat that was, itself, often years old due to the notorious inadequacies and peculations of the Victualling Board. To make matters even worse, ships' officers frequently reserved the best victuals for their own messes, and what remained was routinely served in quantities below those set by regulation. Drinking water and beer were commonly stored in casks polluted by previous usages, quickly rendering them unfit for consumption, making rum – and for higher ranking officers the wine they bought themselves – the only untainted drink on board. Living on such a diet, it was inevitable that sailors' health suffered.

A third important cause of unrest was the severity, even brutality, of some of the officers and non-commissioned officers. To function, a sailing ship relied entirely upon its crew and any man who failed in the performance of his duties could jeopardise the entire vessel and every one of his shipmates. Law and tradition furnished captains with an arsenal of tools with which to punish infractions: from denial of grog at one end of the spectrum, through 'starting' with a rope's end and the bloody business of flogging, to execution by hanging at the other. And the Articles of War of 1749 prescribed the death penalty for no fewer than fifteen crimes, including, among others, desertion, treason, sodomy, striking a superior officer, negligence, theft and murder.

In a well-run ship a captain would find the ideal balance between discipline and understanding, countenancing neither laxity nor undue harshness among his subordinates, and in so doing commanding not only the obedience and respect of his crew, but often their loyalty and admiration as well. But, whether through disposition, incompetence, neglect, illness or weakness, too few captains achieved this perfect balance and some ruled their ships with appalling, even sadistic, violence. The *Regulations and*

Instructions Relating to His Majesty's Service at Sea – the handbook that governed the sailors' daily lives and laid down the punishments for various offences – clearly stated that, without a court martial, 'No Commander shall inflict any Punishment upon a Seaman, beyond Twelve Lashes upon his bare Back',[16] but many captains ordered far more severe floggings for the most minor infringements; some even beat men with their own fists, or with whatever implement came most readily to hand, including speaking trumpets and telescopes. The crew of the frigate *Winchelsea* spoke for many when they declared in 1793 that 'our usage was more like Turks than of British seamen ... We are nockt about so that we do not know what to do. Every man in her would sooner be shot at like a taregaite by muskettree than remain any longer in her'.[17]

With such conditions and abuses so prevalent, it seems little short of a miracle that the Royal Navy performed so brilliantly throughout the French Revolutionary and Napoleonic Wars. Somehow thousands of men, the vast majority uneducated, many of their number being beggars and convicts, and perhaps half of them impressed, were forged into a fighting force without equal on the world's oceans. Just as surprising was the low incidence of organised resistance among its seamen. Indeed, it was this rarity, combined with their scale, that made the mutinies of 1797 so nightmarish both to the Royal Navy and to the government which, in the face of the repeated failures of both its own arms and those of its allies on land, relied upon the navy almost exclusively for the prosecution of its war with France.

The first mutiny broke out in April among the ships of the Channel Fleet anchored at Spithead, in the waters of the Solent, off Portsmouth. Angry that their numerous politely expressed petitions for an increase in pay had been ignored, on 16 April the crew of the 100-gun first-rate ship of the line, HMS *Royal Sovereign*, calmly but resolutely refused a direct order to prepare for sea. No guns were fired or flags hoisted, but leading mutineers put out in boats from *Royal Sovereign*'s sister ship, *Queen Charlotte*, and from Admiral Bridport's flagship, *Royal George*, in order to tour the other vessels, speak to their crews and arrange for the selection of spokesmen, or delegates, from each. In the meantime, officers continued to be treated courteously and their orders obeyed in all matters except that of putting to sea. As a highly experienced and respected officer, Bridport demonstrated great good sense in recognising that the scale of the mutiny rendered resistance futile, and that there was 'no method of checking the progress of this business but by complying in some measure with the prayer of the petitions'. He also opined that 'vigorous measures will not be necessary, as the men on board the *Royal George, Queen Charlotte* and several other ships have no objection to go to sea, provided an answer is given to their petitions'.[18]

Failing to appreciate the gravity of the situation, the Admiralty foolishly ordered Bridport to repeat the order to put to sea, the only attempt to placate the mutineers being a vague promise that their list of complaints would receive 'that serious consideration which its importance requires'.[19] Naturally, this response hardened the attitude of the mutineers, with every man in the fleet swearing an oath to support the mutiny on 17 April; at the same time the more unpopular officers were ordered ashore, though without any violence or disrespect being offered to them. Indeed, at all times the mutineers remained orderly, disciplined and moderate in their behaviour, mounting watches in the time-honoured fashion and performing all their routine duties without interruption, thereby maintaining the readiness of the fleet for action in the event of an emergency.

The following day a deputation from the Lords of the Admiralty arrived in Portsmouth, clearly signalling a new willingness on the part of the authorities to negotiate. And the concessions they made over the subsequent weeks were remarkable. The wages of petty officers and able seamen were raised by 5s 6d a month, and those of ordinary seamen by 4s 6d; wounded seamen would receive their wages in full and, if discharged as unfit, would receive pensions or become residents of the Greenwich Hospital; provisions were improved in both quality and quantity; and all participants in the mutiny were granted a royal pardon. Most astonishing of all, the Admiralty agreed to remove officers whose conduct had been objected to by the men under their command. Although delays in the passing of the necessary legislation caused some further unrest, by 15 May the Spithead mutiny was over and all concerned could breathe a sigh of relief that no blood had been spilt and that the French and Dutch had remained oblivious to the unrest.

The events at Spithead between 16 April and 15 May 1797 have been well described as a traditional work stoppage;[20] in contrast, those at the Nore between 12 May and 15 June appeared at the time – to the government at least – to be more in keeping with an altogether more dangerous republican uprising. And their consequences for the men involved were very different.

Whereas the ships at Spithead constituted a battle-ready fleet, those at the Nore – an anchorage at the mouth of the River Thames – were a heterogeneous collection of Royal Navy vessels gathered together more or less by happenchance. This fact, and the poor communications between the ships which resulted, almost certainly explains the lapse in time between the Spithead and Nore outbreaks. Nonetheless, the seamen at the Nore endured exactly the same conditions as the men of the Channel Fleet and incited by the latter's direct representations – made at a time when the government's response to the mutiny remained ambivalent – they rebelled on 12 May. Initially, the second mutiny followed the pattern of the first: officers continued to be treated with courtesy, delegates were selected from each ship, and routine duties were performed without interruption. In other respects, though, the mutineers in the Thames behaved differently from their comrades at Portsmouth. Perhaps most notable were their predilection for pomp and ceremony – a brass band played a conspicuous part in their every move – and their obvious desire to garner support from outside their own ranks, particularly among the population of Sheerness and the troops of the local garrison.

Another marked difference was the fact that whereas no single participant in the Spithead mutiny gained particular primacy among the mutineers or notoriety in the reports of their actions, at the Nore one man did come very much to the fore – however unwillingly. That man was the 31-year-old Richard Parker, an erstwhile schoolteacher and experienced mariner from Exeter who was elected President of the Delegates of the Fleet. Parker's history had been punctuated by instances of unruliness and rebellion, both at home and at sea, but it remains extremely doubtful that he exerted significant influence over the course of events or that he persuaded his fellows to convert the mutiny at the Nore from a rising in support of the Spithead mutineers into an attempt to use their grievances as a catalyst to achieve much wider reform of the Articles of War. In reality, Parker's election to the presidency appears to have been entirely involuntary and was probably founded upon his greater degree of literacy.

The Admiralty first became aware of the disparity in the aims of the two groups of mutineers when the agreement reached at Spithead failed to satisfy the men at the Nore. Apparently believing that more concessions could be squeezed from a supine government, on 20 May Parker and his followers issued a list of a further eight demands. The majority, relating to additional adjustments to pay and shore leave, were not unreasonable; two, however, were, in the words of one of the foremost historians of the mutinies, 'so aggressive and preposterous that they might well poison the minds of the Admiralty against the more moderate demands'.[21] The first suggested that officers evicted for undue severity should not be permitted to return without the consent of the crew. The second, that men who deserted should not only be allowed to return to the navy but be granted a free pardon to boot. The same historian has remarked that, 'If through some unimaginable folly or weakness the Admiralty had conceded these two demands, the one would have put the superior officers entirely at the mercy of the seamen, and would have paralysed their authority; the other would have turned the navy into a casual ward'.[22]

Of course, no such folly or weakness was demonstrated and the Admiralty refused the additional demands, limiting its response to a confirmation of a royal pardon to those who ended the mutiny and a reminder that the reasonable requests of the Spithead mutineers had been acceded to. In response, the Nore mutineers foolishly determined to extort their terms from the government through the use of violence, and what had begun as an attempt to obtain improvements in shipboard life teetered on the brink of outright treason. Having brought their ships into a better defensive position, using a combination of threats and entreaty they attempted, with some success, to persuade the crews of other nearby ships to rebel, and adopted a plan to blockade both the Thames and the Medway, thereby exerting direct control over the flow of goods to and from the capital. The courtesy that had typified negotiations between the mutineers and the senior officers of the navy was also abandoned and replaced with shows of increasing insolence. Crucially, in the process, the mutineers alienated public sympathy.

Broadly speaking, the mutiny at Spithead had been recognised as a justifiable, albeit shocking, attempt to remedy some of the abominable conditions experienced by Britain's sailors. Even the indignant *Annual Register* begrudgingly conceded that some of the complaints of the Channel Fleet seamen 'were not without cause',[23] while the *Evening Post*, another organ highly supportive of the administration, had described the mutiny in remarkably restrained terms, calling it an 'unpleasant business ... amicably settled'.[24] But there was no hint of sympathy with the Nore mutineers, whose actions, the *Annual Register* claimed, were 'looked upon in almost the same light that a treacherous stab would be from the hand of an old and cherished friend, in whom a boundless confidence had been placed'.[25]

The changes in strategy clearly made some of the rebelling seamen distinctly uncomfortable, and a number of the crews sought to secede from the mutiny, with the frigates *Clyde* and *San Fiorenzo* escaping on 30 May, despite the latter being fired upon by her brethren as she slipped away to Portsmouth. In the face of the Admiralty's outright refusal to enter into further negotiations, the mutiny seemed on the brink of collapse. However, at this critical juncture a development occurred which took both the mutineers and the Admiralty completely by surprise: a powerful squadron including eleven ships of the line, a frigate and two sloops previously under the command of Admiral Duncan at Yarmouth suddenly appeared in the mouth of the Thames, not to suppress the mutiny, but to join it. Riven by internal dispute and faced by the government's intransigence, suddenly it seemed that the mutiny had gained new life and the necessary strength to put in place the planned blockade of the Thames. But discipline was beginning to crumble. Gradually, the language of the mutineers took on the defiance of desperation, and the treatment of officers held hostage and of men whose loyalty was doubted became increasingly harsh, with some of the former being ducked or tarred and feathered, and the latter flogged and imprisoned.[26] Less harmful, but indicative of the mutineers' hardening political attitude, was their decision to hang from the rigging of HMS *Sandwich* effigies of the Prime Minister, William Pitt, and the Secretary of State for War, Henry Dundas, which they then riddled with musket balls.

These demonstrations revealed not strength but growing weakness and dismay as the government's tactics of non-negotiation, the stoppage of provisions and the prevention of ships' crewmen from landing, combined with the near-total loss of public sympathy, sapped the mutineers' morale. Towards the middle of June, they made one last attempt to negotiate, petitioning both the king and the Lords of the Admiralty. In addressing George III, they proclaimed themselves his 'loyal and faithful subjects', but at the same time hinted at how they might have committed 'some acts of Outrage and Revenge that might have shaken the very foundations of this Kingdom', cast aspersions on the competence of Pitt's ministry and threatened to sail their warships to another country 'if we are denounced as Outlaws in our own'[27] – an act capable of only one interpretation: treason.

When the Admiralty replied to these overtures with a demand for unconditional surrender, Parker hoisted a signal ordering the fleet to sea – but not a single ship's crew obeyed. Instead, recognising the futility of their position, but unwilling to commit the final act of defiance that their leaders had threatened, one by one, they surrendered. The sixty-four-gun third-rate *Repulse*, one of the first ships to abandon the mutiny, sustained a gruelling 90-minute barrage from her erstwhile comrades as she attempted to reach Sheerness, but the contagion quickly spread. The following day, 11 June, *Ardent* broke away, followed by another four ships on 13 June, and no fewer than thirteen on the 14th. As early as 12 June, the *London Packet* reported that 'every hour the Mutiny becomes less formidable' and by the 15th it was all over, with a much-relieved Admiral Keith able to write that the 'mutiny which prevailed among the ships at the Nore seems to be quite extinguished'.[28]

From the outset the government believed – or, perhaps, chose to believe – that the mutinies were the product of foreign influence or that of revolutionary organisations at home, rather than a consequence of their own, or the Royal Navy's, failings. This being the case, Pitt and his ministers must have been disappointed when, after a conscientious investigation, the agents they sent to investigate the extent of such influence reported that having 'unremittingly endeavoured to trace if there was any connexion or correspondence carried on between the mutineers and any private person or any society on shore ... they may with the greatest safety pronounce that no such connexion or correspondence ever did exist'.[29] In fact, while events like the American War of Independence and the French Revolution, along with the writings of Thomas Paine and others, had resulted in the spread of the concept of individual rights, there is no evidence that the mutineers' actions were directly influenced by Irish revolutionaries or by radical societies in London or elsewhere. And, as George E. Manwaring and Bonamy Dobrée have pointed out in their study of the mutinies, 'There can have been no connection with the French, otherwise Hoche* and Wolfe Tone** would have jumped at the golden opportunity'.[30]

Whatever the influences behind their actions, the leaders of the mutiny at the Nore could not expect to benefit from the all-encompassing royal pardon granted to their comrades at Spithead. Instead, a total of 412 men were court-martialled, of whom fifty-nine were sentenced to death. In the event, only twenty-nine, including Richard Parker, were executed, with nine receiving floggings of between forty and 380 lashes, and twenty-nine being imprisoned for terms of from one to eight years. In total, 355 were pardoned, including the entire crews of the *Comet* and the *Lancaster*. Of the men imprisoned, either while awaiting trial or following conviction, forty-two would spend time in Coldbath Fields House of Correction, where the treatment they received might well have been compared unfavourably with that which had caused them to mutiny in the first place.[31]

---

*   Louis Lazare Hoche (1768–97) was a highly respected general of the French Revolutionary Wars.

** Theobald Wolfe Tone (1763–98) was leader of the insurrectionary Society of United Irishmen. Following an attempt to land in Ireland with French troops in October 1798 he was captured and sentenced to hang, but committed suicide in prison.

5

'Disaffected Persons'
THE ADVOCATES OF RADICAL REFORM

As might perhaps have been expected of physically active men, many of whom had fought for their country, and all of whom had demonstrated courageous, if sometimes misguided and foolhardy, resistance to dehumanising conditions, the mutineers of the Nore did not placidly accept their internment in the Coldbath Fields House of Correction, and in the early hours of Sunday 1 April 1798, George Gainer, John Davis, Abraham Nelson, William Hooper, John Griffiths, John Wells and James Jones all contrived to escape over its walls. According to the *London Chronicle* of 3 May:

> The rope they used for scaling the wall was of their own making, from the oakum they were employed in picking. It is thought they must have been assisted by some persons who came over the wall, prepared with tools to force the locks off; a rope with loops to it, made to answer the purpose of a rope-ladder, was found hanging on the wall, and which, no doubt, had been thrown over by means of a grappling-iron.

The report goes on to state that, as well as their prison uniforms, the men left a note pinned to one of their cell doors, 'the purport of which was, that they were become quite desperate by the long state of dreadful suspence they had remained in, and were resolved to venture their lives in the attempt'. However, the contents of this note, as reported, do not quite ring true. Nor, indeed, do the details of the escape itself.

Would the escapees really have risked manufacturing a rope ladder under the eyes of the turnkeys if they had an accomplice who was willing to smuggle, or even to 'come over the wall' with, a grappling iron and a crowbar? In fact, it seems certain that all the elements of the plan, and every tool used in its execution, were of the mutineers' own contrivance and that the role of any accomplices was limited to waiting outside the prison's boundary wall with a change of clothes. This interpretation is supported by an official report written on the very day of the escape, but not shared with the press.[1] It confirms that one of the seven mutineers, John Davis, had rolled up his bedding to create the likeness of a sleeping man, carefully leaving his clothes and shoes by his bed, and stuffing his nightcap full of oakum to perfect the deception. Just before lock-up time he had then slipped out of his cell and hidden in the privy, 'there being no other place where he could secrete himself', where he waited until the turnkey had completed his evening rounds.[2] Sometime after midnight, when he felt confident that he would not be overheard, Davis used a holdfast previously wrenched from the 'poo poo tub' in his cell to prize off the locks of his companions' cell doors – a task that he must have performed with great care since the men in the adjoining cells claimed 'they did not hear the least of the transaction'.[3] Once released, all seven men had utilised their homemade rope and grappling iron, to say nothing of the agility so essential to their profession, to scale both the 14-ft inner yard wall with its topping of iron spikes and the 21-ft boundary wall, before disappearing into the dark alleys and lanes of Clerkenwell.*

As for the note, if the escapees had, as the newspaper article claimed, been sentenced to terms of three years for their part in the mutiny, what was the cause of their 'dreadful suspence'? Given that fifty-nine of their comrades had been condemned to hang at the yardarm and another nine to receive brutal floggings, they might have been expected to feel relief rather than suspense. And why, in the very act of escaping, had they felt it necessary to leave an explanation of their actions? In fact, the note survives and is to be found in the London Metropolitan Archives; scrawled on a scrap of paper, the mutineers' valediction was addressed not to the governor, the turnkeys, the magistrates or even to the public at large, but to their fellows, and it reads, quite simply:

---

*   The report's mention of iron spikes indicates that the earlier decision to use a wooden *chevaux de frize* in order to save money during construction had at some time been reversed.

Dear Shipmates, Let our Conduct turn out well or Ill for you, we hope you will not blame us, for we are always willing and ready to loose our Lives in the defence of our King and Countrey But are not permitted at present, So Hunger has drove us to gain our Liberty at the Risque of our Lives. God bless you all and a speedy Releasement to you, and we Trust you wish us the same. Adieu [4]

Little wonder, then, that the governor or the Middlesex magistrates, or both, had released a substantially doctored account of the escape: one that downplayed not only their own poor security and lack of vigilance, but also the appalling conditions that had persuaded the mutineers to make so desperate a bid for freedom.

When the embarrassed and furious Duke of Portland asked for an explanation and told William Mainwaring, the chairman of the Middlesex Sessions, that the Admiralty considered 'that great blame is to be attributed to the Person or Persons who were charged with the Custody of the Prisoners',[5] the magistrates remained economical with the truth, assuring the duke that 'upon a full Examination of the Governor and the several Officers and Servants belonging to the said Prison they have no reason to believe the Escape was effected by the wilful neglect or any Corrupt practice or Connivance of any Person entrusted with the Care of those prisoners'.[6] Understandably, they omitted any reference to the prisoners having manufactured ropes and tools under the very noses of the turnkeys and would even suggest, incredibly, that they had used 'Artifices which no Ordinary Sagacity could foresee or prevent'.[7]

For five of the seven mutineers, their freedom was short-lived. By Thursday 5 April they had travelled some 25 miles to Gravesend, where they volunteered for service on an outwardbound East Indiaman expected to sail the following day. Foolishly, when adverse winds prevented the ship departing they refused to come up on deck and thereby excited the suspicions of the captain, who told them that 'if they did not do their duty he would have them pressed'.[8] Reluctantly, they obeyed his command but moments later leapt into a jolly boat lying alongside and tried to cast off the rope that secured it. The ship's boatswain and one of its mates sought to prevent them, but after a vigorous struggle both men were overwhelmed and thrown overboard. The *Morning Herald* published the earliest and best account of the affray and tells us that 'The desperadoes then made the shore at Gravesend, from whence they immediately proceeded to Rochester, but the hue and cry overtaking them at that place, they were secured'.[9] Had the mutineers obeyed the captain without demur, they might well have escaped to India, confident that the authorities would never overtake them amid the teeming lanes and wild countryside of the subcontinent. Of the two men who appear to have separated from them after their prison break, nothing more was ever heard – at least by those who pursued them.

Of course, this daring escape was not the mutineers' last attempt to relieve the conditions they endured at Coldbath Fields. Some seven months later they at last managed to obtain more paper and, in the absence of ink or pens, described their plight using skewers as writing implements and tobacco juice and their own blood as ink.[10] It was the sensational and horrifying revelations contained in these letters that brought Burdett and his companions to the gate of the house of correction on 28 November.

The earliest description of the three campaigners' first visit to the prison is to be found in a speech made by John Courtenay in the House of Commons on 21 December. Having 'long made it a rule not to trust to rumours, but to ascertain facts',[11] he told the House, he and his companions had resolved to visit Coldbath Fields to learn whether there was any truth underpinning the stories of the mistreatment of state prisoners. They thought some of the claims exaggerated (an admission that brought roars of approval from the government benches), but had nonetheless 'found the prisoners in narrow cells, without fire or candle, with no other furniture than a truckle bed; and no other means of admitting light and air than iron gratings, thro' which ... the rain beat without interruption'.

The harsh conditions were not confined to the state prisoners; in one ordinary cell they discovered 'a disorderly woman in a state of wretchedness and disease which delicacy did not permit him to describe', while in the infirmary they met a man named John Smith, imprisoned in December 1796 for publishing a 'false, scandalous, and seditious libel' written by Edward Iliff and entitled *A Summary of the Duties of Citizenship!* Although it was claimed that Smith's name had been included on the pamphlet's colophon without his consent,[12] he was known to the government as the owner of one of the small bookshops that played such an important part in the distribution of radical literature and he and his co-defendants had been found guilty and sentenced to two years' hard labour. By the time Burdett, Courtenay and Bosville met him in November 1798, Smith had 'for nearly two years undergone hardships which had destroyed his health, and which would have been sufficient to drive many men into a state of insanity. He was treated in every respect worse than a felon'.[13] However, before they could open a proper conversation with the unfortunate man, Thomas Aris had intervened saying, 'Sir, you must excuse me; we never suffer anybody who visits the place to hold conversation with the Prisoners'. 'They would have been all day going round the Prison,' the governor is later recorded as saying, 'if I had let them ask questions as they were going on.'[14]

Undeterred by this prohibition, Burdett conducted further and much more rigorous inspections at the beginning and towards the end of December 1798. Although there is no detailed record of the second visit, Aris himself left a description of the third. According to the governor's account, Burdett and an unnamed companion arrived at the entrance lodge a little after midday on 29 December expecting to be shown over the prison. Given that the baronet had already made two visits in the course of the past month, Aris asked what part they wished to see. When Burdett replied 'the whole', but beginning with the mutineers, Aris escorted them to a yard where nine of the seamen were confined; here Burdett entered two of the cells, which he observed were 'very cold'.[15] Having inspected them, he then asked about the prisoners' provisions and was told that they received a pound of bread per day, with half a pound of meat and a quart of vegetable broth on four days each week. In addition, they might purchase further supplies or receive them from friends outside. Accepting the accuracy of these weights, it seems that the mutineers ate better as convicts than they ever had as sailors in His Majesty's navy.

Burdett next spoke to a mutineer named Wolfe who, despite being ill, remained in his cell. When the baronet observed 'that it was a very improper place for a sick person to be in', Aris replied that the prisoner had been examined by the medical attendant that morning and that 'if it had been an improper place, in his opinion, he would have had him removed to the infirmary'. The growing tension between the self-appointed inspector on the one hand and the prison governor on the other are further indicated by Aris's reaction to Burdett's comments on the condition of the recaptured John Davis. When asked how he fared, Davis replied 'Very badly, and short of provisions', leading Burdett to assert that the mutineer 'had very much fallen away, and weighed many stone less than he had done when he came to the Prison first'. Davis agreed, saying that he used to weigh 15 stone, but was now reduced to 11. Aris denied this and later claimed to have found that Davis actually weighed 13 stone, 3lb.

In the next cell lay James Jones, another of the mutineers who, like Davis, had escaped in April. In response to Burdett's enquiries regarding his health, Jones replied that his condition had improved somewhat. '"What,' said Sir Francis, "have you been ill?" Jones replied, he had been beaten by the Governor.' Keen to defend his actions, at this juncture Aris claimed that Jones 'had been very riotous, and had offered to strike him'; in self-defence he had given him 'a blow with a small stick he had in his hand; that Jones going to strike Deponent in return, he had again struck him with his fist'.

It seems probable that, in the presence of his assailant and fearful of reprisals, Jones felt reluctant to describe the incident in full. A few months later, however, he had an opportunity to speak more freely. According to the notes taken at this later interview:

> One evening in the month of August 1798, after he had gone to bed, a Turnkey opened his cell door, saying, 'Why do you make a noise?' He answered, 'I have not made a noise; but I suppose the noise was occasioned by some of the prisoners closing the window-shutters of their cells.' The Turnkey said, 'You are a damned villain,' and made use of other abusive language, which induced him (Jones) to sit up in bed. At that moment the Turnkey struck at his head with a bunch of keys, which must have proved fatal if part of the keys had not hit against the wall, which broke the dangerous effect of the blow. The Turnkey then withdrew; but returned next morning, and again opened the cell, saying, 'Come along with me, Jones, to be ironed.' 'For what,' replied Jones; 'if I had committed an offence I ought to be ironed; but I have committed none.' During this altercation the Governor came up, and beat him with a stick till he broke it to pieces; then he renewed the assault with his fists, and beat him in a cruel manner; after which, he took him to the yard and loaded him with irons, which were not taken off his limbs for several months after.[16]

Given that the prisoners' cells had been built without glazing – in line with John Howard's recommendations – Aris could legitimately excuse the cold they experienced; assuming that they received full measure of the provisions stipulated by the county's magistrates, he could also defend himself against their complaints of hunger – a defence he could be confident his employers would support since they had been actively pursuing means by which to reduce the quantity and cost of prisoners' rations, particularly those of the mutineers.[17] But surely there could be no excuse for an exhibition of such brutality towards an unarmed man – brutality, moreover, completely at odds with Howard's conviction that the primary function of a prison was to ensure 'the *safe custody* of the accused to the time of trial; and of convicts till a legal sentence be executed upon them'* and that no malefactor 'may be secretly put to death; nor murdered in a prison directly or indirectly'.[18]

Having promised the mutineers that he would make further enquiries on their behalf, Burdett asked to see next another group of prisoners: members of the London Corresponding Society, who had been found guilty of no crime, but who, in April 1798, had been imprisoned on suspicion alone under the terms of the Habeas Corpus Suspension Act.

The explosive events in France during the summer of 1789, including the storming of the prison fortress of the Bastille on 14 July 1789, had polarised opinion in Great Britain, with two men above all others crystallising the views of the opposing parties. On what would come to be called, as a direct result of the revolution, the right of the political spectrum sat the Anglo-Irish parliamentarian and philosopher Edmund Burke.** Despite his earlier support for the American colonists' resistance to taxation without representation, and his assertion that he loved 'manly, moral, regulated liberty as well as any gentleman',[19] in his influential *Reflections on the Revolution in France* of 1790 Burke would compare the revolution to 'a madman, who has escaped from the protecting restraint and wholesome darkness of his cell',[20] in the process underscoring both his objection to democratic rather than theoretically representative government and his profound ignorance of the truly horrific conditions prevalent in the majority of Georgian madhouses.

On the left stood Thomas Paine, the son of a Norfolk tenant-farmer, who had actively supported both the American and French revolutionaries and become, in the process, the *bête noire* of successive British administrations. In his *Rights of Man* – a brilliantly argued forensic demolition of Burke's defence of the propertied classes' right to rule – Paine asserted that

---

*   The italics are Howard's own.
** The terms 'left' and 'right' originated during the revolution when members of the National Assembly who supported the *Ancien Régime* sat to the president's right and those who supported the revolution to his left.

government 'is not, and from its nature cannot be, the property of any particular man or family, but of the whole community ... and a Nation has at all times an inherent indefeasible right to abolish any form of Government it finds inconvenient, and establish such as accords with its interest, disposition, and happiness'.[21]

In the febrile atmosphere generated by the successive revolutions and the public pronouncements of Burke, Paine and others, a number of societies and clubs were formed to debate and promote popular sovereignty and constitutional government. Most notable among the earliest were the Society for Constitutional Information (SCI) and the more provocatively named Revolution Society of London. Founded in 1780, the avowed purpose of the SCI was to disseminate as widely as possible 'a knowledge of the great principles of Constitutional Freedom, particularly such as respect the election and duration of the representative body ... to support a free Constitution, and to maintain and assert those common rights, which are essential to the dignity, and to the happiness of human nature'; it would also do everything in its power to encourage the people to 'contend for their rights, as men, and as citizens, with ardour and with firmness'.[22] Crucially, the society did not challenge the legitimacy of either the monarch or the House of Lords; it did, however, vehemently assert that parliamentary elections should be held annually and that there should be universal male suffrage, excepting only 'infants, insane persons, and criminals'.[23] The society's fortunes fluctuated in the decade after its establishment, in part because its need to raise funds for the printing and distribution of its literature obliged it to set its annual subscription fee at 4 guineas, thereby excluding from its membership all but the relatively well-to-do, but also because growing national prosperity during the 1780s resulted in a greater degree of complacency and acceptance of the status quo. Only when the French Revolution caused a surge in optimism regarding the potential for political reform on both sides of the Channel did the SCI experience something of a resurgence.

The event which lent its name to the second of the constitutional reform societies, the Revolution Society of London, was not, as might be supposed, the French Revolution of 1789, but the Glorious Revolution of 1688, which resulted in the overthrow of the Roman Catholic James II, the crowning of William III and Queen Mary, and the legislative safeguarding of the Protestant succession. While the celebration of this century-old event might seem an unexceptionable basis for gatherings and discussion, the society's governing committee also declared its commitment to the principles that all civil and political authority is

'Disaffected Persons': The Advocates of Radical Reform

derived from the people; that the abuse of power justifies resistance; and that the right of private judgement, liberty of conscience, trial by jury, the freedom of the press and the freedom of election, ought ever to be held 'sacred and inviolable'.

Like the SCI, the Revolution Society also emphasised the importance of ensuring that the principles underpinning the Glorious Revolution should be 'well understood, extensively propagated, and firmly maintained' and that the British people should be encouraged to 'establish Societies throughout the Kingdom upon Revolution Principles, to maintain a Correspondence with each other, and to form that grand concentrated Union of the true Friends of Public Liberty, which may be necessary to maintain its existence'.[24] If this language seemed deliberately provocative, what must the government have felt when, at its meeting on 4 November 1789, the society agreed unanimously to write to the National Assembly of France to congratulate its members on both the 'glorious success of the French Revolution' and its tendency to 'encourage other Nations to assert the unalienable rights of Mankind, and thereby to introduce a general reformation in the governments of Europe, and to make the World free and happy'?[25] The society would go on to organise Bastille Day celebrations throughout Britain, with the banquet in London attracting over 650 participants, whose joyousness led one French attendee to remark that 'the people of London are at least as enthusiastic for the French Revolution as the people of France'.[26]

The year 1792 saw the formation of a third and arguably the most important of the reform societies: the London Corresponding Society (LCS). Whereas the earlier societies had been comprised largely of members from the middle and upper echelons of society, by charging just a penny a week the LCS opened its membership to poorer working men, including artisans, labourers and shopkeepers. The vast majority of these individuals were disenfranchised, and their anger at being barred from suffrage is reflected in the radical and uncompromising tone of their very first publication:

Whereas it is notorious, that very numerous, burthensome, and unnecessary Taxes are laid on the persons and families of us and others, the Industrious Inhabitants of Great Britain, an exceedingly great Majority of whom are, notwithstanding, excluded from all Representation in Parliament:

And whereas, upon inquiry into the Cause of this Grievance, which is at once an Obstruction to our Industry and Diminution of our Property, we find that the Constitution of our Country ... has, by the Violence and Intrigue of Criminal and Designing Men, been injured and undermined in its most essential and important parts; but particularly in the House of Commons, where the whole of the supposed Representation of the People is neither more nor less than an Usurped Power, arising either from Abuses in the Mode of Election and Duration of Parliaments, or from a Corrupt Property in certain decayed Corporations, by means of which the Liberties of this Nation are basely bartered away for the private profit of Members of Parliament:

And whereas it appears to us, that until this Source of Corruption shall be cleansed by the Information, Perseverance, Firmness, and Union of the People at large, we are robbed of the inheritance so acquired for us by our Fore-fathers; and that our Taxes, instead of being lessened, will go on increasing, in as much as they will furnish more Bribes, and Places, and Pensions, to our Ministers and Members of Parliament:

Now it is resolved by us, the Members of this Society, to form ourselves into one firm and permanent Body, for the purpose of informing ourselves and others of the exact State of the Present Parliamentary Representation — for obtaining a peaceful but adequate Remedy to this intolerable Grievance.[27]

The society expanded rapidly. Forming itself into divisions of twenty members each, by November it could boast twenty-six divisions in London alone, with further divisions in fourteen cities across the country, and with every division meeting at least once a week to transact administrative business, discuss texts and debate current events.

Like its predecessors, the LCS demanded annual elections and universal suffrage; it also celebrated the French Revolution, adopted the French custom of addressing its members as 'citizens', and viewed 'with horror and detestation' Britain's war against France, declaring the conflict, which began shortly after the execution of Louis XVI on 21 January 1793, to be 'solely designed to destroy the Liberties of Britain and annihilate those of France'.[28] Unfortunately, while the revolution had attracted enthusiastic and vocal support from a wide range of individuals from all classes, the maintenance of such advocacy in a country at war with its revolutionary neighbour was deemed treasonable, and the reformers' reasonable demands for constitutional change were quickly recast by their enemies as French-influenced subversion that could only lead to such atrocities as the September Massacres of 1792 and the murder of the royal family. In this changed atmosphere the government, which had always viewed the

LCS with grave suspicion and monitored its activities closely, now took active measures to suppress it.

On 11 December 1792, 160 advocates of constitutional reform had gathered at Lawrie's Rooms in Edinburgh for what they described as a 'General Convention', to discuss the now familiar topics of wider manhood suffrage, more representative electoral districts and annually elected parliaments. According to the historian of the convention, Kenneth R. Johnston, the delegates also 'spoke intensely about a more pressing agenda: the need to forestall or outstrip government action against meetings and organisations just like theirs'.[29] They had good cause to be anxious because the government viewed the holding of a national convention as a deliberate attempt to challenge the primacy of Parliament. A number of government informers attended the first convention, but its delegates were able to conclude their four days of debate without interruption; the delegates at the second national convention, including members of the LCS, would not be so lucky when they met a year later and, crucially, after the declaration of war.

The most vocal and well-known of the Scottish delegates, Thomas Muir, was arrested on 30 July 1792, convicted of sedition at a trial in Edinburgh that has been described as 'one of the worst in Scottish, or for that matter, British legal history',[30] and sentenced to an extraordinarily punitive fourteen years' transportation by the presiding justice, Lord Braxfield – a veritable Judge Jeffreys, of whom one contemporary remarked that he was never so much in his element 'as when tauntingly repelling the last despairing claim of a wretched culprit, and sending him to Botany Bay or the gallows with an insulting jest'.[31] Arrested at the convention itself, William Skirving, the secretary of the convention, and the two LCS delegates, Maurice Margarot and Joseph Gerrald, received the same harsh punishment. Only Margarot would live to return to London at the expiration of his sentence.

Emboldened by these successes, in May 1794 the government ordered more than thirty additional arrests, beginning on the 12 May with Thomas Hardy, a poor shoemaker and autodidact who had been one of the founding members of the LCS. As well as making the arrests, the law officers seized a mass of books and papers and in the House of Commons Pitt moved for a 'Committee of Secrecy' to examine these documents. The committee, predictably made up almost exclusively of parliamentarians known for their conservative attitude towards constitutional reform, reported its findings on the 16th, stating that the objects of such societies 'must be considered as a Traitorous Conspiracy for the Subversion of the established Laws and Constitution, and the Introduction of that System of Anarchy and Confusion which has fatally prevailed in France'.[32] Pitt, himself a member of the committee, thereupon called for an Act 'to empower His Majesty to secure and detain such persons as His Majesty shall suspect are conspiring against his person and government': in other words, the suspension of the Habeas Corpus Act of 1679, which had made it mandatory for a Court to examine the legality of a prisoner's detention, and thereby prevent unlawful or arbitrary imprisonment.

The resulting Habeas Corpus Suspension Act, designed 'for the better preservation of his Majesty's sacred person, and for securing the peace and the laws and liberties of this kingdom',[33] passed through the Commons by 146 votes to twenty-eight, overwhelming a fiercely fought rearguard action on the part of Charles James Fox and his allies, and received royal assent on the 23rd. Habeas corpus would be suspended from May 1794 to July 1795, and during this period the government made full use of its ability to arrest and hold suspects merely upon suspicion of their having committed a crime, and without trial. The Act would prove particularly useful after the debacle of the 1794 treason trials during which three of the men arrested in May, Thomas Hardy, John Horne Tooke and John Thelwall, were all acquitted of treason, largely due to the brilliant advocacy of their barrister, Thomas Erskine – and much to the government's embarrassment, which in the aftermath scrapped a further 800 warrants of arrest.[34]

Pitt's most recent biographer, William Hague, has observed that 'Deterrence, not punishment, seems to have been Pitt's goal at this and later stages of popular discontent: if so, he must be judged largely successful'.[35] Certainly, for a while at least, the LCS remained on the defensive, fearful of further arrests. But anger overwhelmed fear during the summer of 1795 when a series of poor harvests caused grain prices to rise sharply, leading to bread shortages. Serious disturbances occurred in a number of cities, rioters smashed the windows of No. 10 Downing Street, and huge crowds gathered to demand peace with France, political reform and a reduction in the price of food.

Among those demonstrating were members of the LCS, who called a 'monster meeting' at Copenhagen Fields, Islington on 25 October. Well in excess of 100,000 attended to listen to speakers complaining of 'the calamities and sufferings under which the Poor at this time labour'.[36] Ministers were criticised for failing to respond to earlier calls for reform, the French government was praised and a remonstrance to the king read. This remonstrance, a reporter for the *Morning Post* observed, 'though couched in language of respect to the Chief Magistrate, as far as *title* goes, hinted at the obligations which a certain Family owe to the People for transplanting them from the obscure vale of a *Poor* Country, to rule in this land, flourishing in Commerce and Fertility'.[37]

As the king's opulent state coach rumbled from St James's Palace to Westminster for the state opening of Parliament four days later, a large crowd greeted the monarch with 'Hisses and Groans, and other marks of Disaffection', including cries of *'Down with George, No King, No Pitt, No War, Bread, Bread, Peace, Peace!'*[38] In Parliament Street the richly gilded coach was spattered with mud and detritus, and some of its windows broken; it was even suggested that 'a Ball, as is supposed from an Air-Gun ... made a round hole through one of the Glasses, intended no doubt to assassinate our *Sacred and Dread Sovereign*'.[39]

The government's response was predictable. 'The public had seen with becoming indignation,' Pitt declared in the Commons on 10 November:

> that a virtuous and beloved sovereign had been attacked in the most criminal and outrageous manner ... If, instead of stating grievances, the people were excited to rebellion; if, instead of favouring the principles of freedom, the very foundation of it was to be destroyed, and with it the happiness of the people; it was high time for the legislature to interpose with its authority.[40]

That interposition took the form of two new Bills, which would receive royal assent on 18 December: the Seditious Meetings Bill, which forbade the gathering of groups of more than fifty people without the prior consent of a magistrate, and the Treasonable and Seditious Practices Bill, which extended the definition of treason to include speaking and writing, even if such speaking and writing led to no overt act of rebellion. Under the new laws magistrates could break up any meeting – even those legally convened – if the discussions taking place were deemed seditious; speakers could be arrested; speaking disparagingly of the king or his government could be deemed treasonable; bookshops and taverns regarded as centres of radical activity could be closed; and resistance to the dispersal of a meeting became punishable by death. Just as Pitt had intended, the 'Gagging Acts', as they would come to be known, immediately succeeded in stymying political debate, particularly among those who, in Pitt's words, 'from their education, their habits of life, and their means of information, were indisputably the least capable of exercising sound judgement on such topics'.[41] The Constitutional Information Society and the London

Revolution Society had already ceased to exist, now the LCS fell into a terminal decline.

And yet, as Charles James Fox had been quick to point out, 'if you silence remonstrance and stifle complaint, you then leave no other alternative but force and violence'.[42] Denied legal means by which to agitate for reform, a number of LCS members decided to explore more extreme methods of achieving the same ends. The model they decided to follow was that of the Society of United Irishmen, which advocated not merely reform but the overthrow of the government through armed rebellion supported by a French invasion. During the winter of 1796–97 Irish revolutionaries toured mainland Britain advocating insurrection and encouraging the formation of secret societies modelled on their own. They received a particularly sympathetic hearing in the towns and cities of the north and Midlands, where a number of groups were formed under the collective name of the United Englishmen. The movement also gained some traction in London where it found willing supporters among the more radical and disillusioned members of the LCS, meeting in taverns kept by sympathetic landlords, or in the homes of those still willing to defy the government's strictures, their identities protected – in theory at least – by blood-curdling oaths and secret handshakes. Despite these safeguards, the organisation was riddled with informers and, according to one leading member of the LCS, the government was 'well informed of all their proceedings'.[43]

Disaster struck in the aftermath of the naval mutinies at Spithead and the Nore during the spring of 1797 – mutinies which, from the outset, the government had been keen to attribute to foreign influence and domestic revolutionaries. In the summer following the mutinies an Irish Catholic priest named James Coigly arrived in London. Presenting himself as an emissary of the executive of the United Irishmen and advocating ever stronger links with both Ireland and France, Coigly would serve as the catalyst for further government intervention. Described as 'a tall, stout, good-looking man of remarkably mild manners',[44] initially he succeeded in ingratiating himself with many among the higher echelons of the LCS and in January 1798 the society prepared an address to the Irish nation in which it boldly declared that if to wish 'for that happy union of mankind, when their religious opinions shall be no obstacle to the performance of their moral duties, be criminal, we also are guilty; and if to unite in the cause of reform upon the broadest basis be treason, we with you are traitors'.[45] The government pounced, arresting Coigly, John Binns of the LCS and others, in February, just as they were preparing to cross the Channel in order to meet with representatives of the French government. At the moment of his arrest, the priest apparently sat 'in a contemplative state by the fire' of the King's Head public house in Margate, but another member of the party levelled a pistol at the arresting officer and was overcome only with the assistance of a soldier fortuitously passing by.[46]

Arraigned at the Lent assizes in Kent, Coigly, who seems to have spent at least a portion of his pre-trial detention in Coldbath Fields,[47] remained calm and dignified as he heard the clerk read out the charges: that he had conspired to levy war against England, that he had plotted to assassinate the king and that he had sent intelligence to an enemy nation. His trial, presided over by Mr Justice Buller, a gouty middle-aged judge often criticised for being both hasty and prejudiced in his judgements, lasted two days, and the jury took just 30 minutes to find him guilty on all counts. In passing a sentence of death by hanging, drawing and quartering, Buller took the opportunity to remind the condemned man that he lived during the reign of a sovereign 'who was one of the best, the most just, upright, and amiable princes that ever graced a throne', and that the constitution which he had sought to overturn 'had been found to be the best calculated of any that ever existed in the world, to insure the liberty, security, and happiness of the people who lived under it'.[48] According to a Court reporter, Coigly listened to this address 'with attention, but at the same time with the greatest coolness'.[49] Given the sentence he had just received under the laws of this veritable paradise, he might also have been forgiven a derisive smile. The priest was hanged at Penenden Heath, Maidstone, on Thursday 7 June, and his head amputated by a surgeon; he was however spared disembowelment and castration, presumably on the instructions of his amiable prince.

Despite the early warmth of his reception, in reality Coigly's embassy had achieved very limited success with the LCS, with only its more extreme members being swayed by his arguments and the vast majority resisting calls to support a French invasion. But the damage was done. On 20 April, Henry Dundas, the Secretary of State for War, read to the House of Commons a message from the king in which he recommended that the House 'consider without delay of such farther measures as may enable his Majesty to defeat the wicked machinations of disaffected persons within these realms, and to guard against the designs of the enemy, either abroad or at home'.[50]

Shortly afterwards, Pitt rose once more from the front bench. 'When we know that the enemy are forming a plan to invade this country,' he declared; 'when we know that in former times ... our ancestors, without investigation, had recourse to the measure of enabling his Majesty to secure and detain those who are suspected of conspiring against his government, I say, we should be wanting to ourselves, if we hesitated in adopting the measure'.[51] There could be no doubt regarding his meaning: with the French preparing for a Channel crossing, with clear evidence of continuing activity on the part of the reform societies and with the events at Spithead and the Nore still fresh in everyone's minds – to say nothing of the abortive French landing in Bantry Bay in December 1796 – he was once again seeking to suspend habeas corpus. The suspension would not only be agreed by the House but would last until the Treaty of Amiens in March 1802 brought a temporary cessation of hostilities with France.

In fact, the government had struck pre-emptively. On the night of Thursday 19 April – the day before the king's address was read in Parliament – the Executive Committee of the LCS had met in what was described as 'a noble room on the first floor at the top of a spacious staircase'[52] in the Queen of Bohemia, a tavern on Wych Street.* The street housed an eclectic mixture of individuals and businesses in its Elizabethan buildings – rare survivors of the Great Fire – with their wooden jetties teetering towards one another across the narrow roadway. The presence of two Inns of Chancery, New Inn and Lyon's Inn, meant that lawyers in their black robes were a common sight, but the street was also home to a wide variety of tradesmen and women including booksellers, scriveners, a stationer, a truss-maker and a cabinetmaker. And yet, despite the presence of these reputable businesses, one writer tells us that it 'had borne an evil name for centuries'.[53] Certainly it is true that the squalid and unhealthy courts hidden behind the shopfronts had their less respectable denizens and up one dreary little court the notorious petty criminal and prison breaker 'Honest Jack' Sheppard had served his apprenticeship to a master carpenter in the first quarter of the century. The theatres in the area also attracted prostitution with the author and publisher John Diprose remembering nearby Newcastle Court as a particular den of iniquity where might be seen, 'in the broad glare of day, sitting at the parlour windows of nearly every house, abandoned women, young and old, decked in tawdry finery, bloated with gin and

---

* Wych Street was located where Melbourne and Australia Houses now stand on Aldwych. It ran west from the church of St Clement Danes on the Strand to the southern end of Drury Lane. In later years, Wych Street would become the site of a school owned and run by John Bickerton, one-time inmate of Coldbath Fields.

debauchery, lavishing enticing smiles, and bandying obscene expressions to entrap the unwary passer-by'.[54]

Perhaps the members of the LCS felt safe, even invisible, hidden amid this fluid and mixed community in an upstairs room of the dilapidated Queen of Bohemia. If so, they were being almost wilfully naïve given that they knew that a party of erstwhile LCS members who now proclaimed themselves United Englishmen had been arrested in Clerkenwell only the day before. In the middle of their discussions, at 11 p.m., the doors of their committee room burst open to admit a group of Bow Street Runners and king's messengers. Guided by the light of a single lamp, and led by the burly figure of the veteran officer John Townsend, these men had somehow managed to creep up the worm-eaten stairs without making a sound, and were now determined to arrest every member of the committee 'by a general warrant, or by no warrant at all',[55] and to seize every last scrap of their papers and correspondence. A reporter for *The Sun* noted that the arresting officers discovered sixteen men sitting 'in great formality, with the President in his chair. They were come upon so suddenly, that they had not time to destroy a single paper'.[56]

Ironically, at the moment of their arrest the committee were debating a resolution that even the most reactionary minister would have struggled to describe as revolutionary or treasonous. Three weeks earlier, Dundas had introduced to Parliament a Bill for 'the defence and security of the realm' which, in response to French preparations for invasion, sought to identify those civilians 'willing to engage themselves, to be armed, arrayed, trained, and exercised, for the Defence of the Kingdom'.[57] The Bill received royal assent on 5 April and the LCS had gathered not to deplore or resist its terms, but to decide whether they, as a body, could and should volunteer *en masse*. In fact, the committee had sensibly concluded that the government 'never would consent to put arms into the hands of the members of the society as a body', and they had resolved instead that each of their members should, on an individual basis, join 'some corps in his own neighbourhood'.[58]

And so, on 20 April, instead of lining up with other volunteers eager to repel an invasion that they so heartily deprecated, after a night spent confined in the home of a Bow Street Runner named Thomas Carpmeal,[59] the representatives of the LCS found themselves being grilled by the assembled Privy Council. After their initial questioning the sixteen men arrested in the Queen of Bohemia and a similar number arrested in Clerkenwell were split into groups and sent to different prisons, including Coldbath Fields. In the words of Francis Place, a leading member of the LCS who has been described as 'a ubiquitous figure in the machinery of radical London',[60] 'This stroke extinguished the Society, which never made any attempt to meet again ... the members dispersed and wholly abandoned their delegates'.[61] In another twist of fate, those men sent to Clerkenwell would now be guarded by a contingent of the Islington Volunteers – precisely the kind of corps that they had themselves decided to join only a day or so earlier.[62]

6

'The Heaviest Penalty'
Radicals in the House of Correction

In total, six of the newly arrested state prisoners would be sent to the Tothill Fields Bridewell, nine to Newgate and seventeen to the Coldbath Fields House of Correction.* In his autobiography Francis Place noted that:

> The persons seized were put together without distinction; conspirators or committee men, they were all equally harmless and no distinction was needed ... [Those] committed to the House of Correction in Coldbath Fields ... were for some days not permitted to see anybody, and when afterwards their friends were admitted, it was only on two days a week by an order from a magistrate and at the distance of two or three yards separated by gates between which a turnkey was placed. For some days they had nothing but Gaol allowance. Afterwards they were allowed to receive provision sent by their friends. They were not allowed the use of pen or ink nor to receive any letter addressed to them – all sorts of provisions sent to them were searched.[1]

A leading light of the LCS, Place himself faced imminent arrest, so he could not visit the prison in person. However, he was not only acquainted with the imprisoned members of the organisation, from his hiding place he also took charge of efforts to relieve them. We can be confident, therefore, that his testimony is closely based on the prisoners' first-hand accounts, and on those of the friends and colleagues who visited them. We can be confident,

---

* The *Morning Chronicle* of 30 April 1798 names the prisoners sent to Coldbath Fields as Thomas Evans, Robert Keir, Edward Despard, John Bone, [George?] Ebsworth, Purnell, John Webb, Edwards, Thomas Goodluck, John Roberts, Neagle, Charles Clay, Crank, Campbell, Fushard, George Cowle and Humphreys.

too, in the accuracy of his description of the very different experiences of the group who had been sent to the 'State side' of Newgate Prison. In spite of that prison's notoriously forbidding appearance, these men found themselves 'tolerably well-lodged, well-fed, and respectably treated by the Gaoler'. In contrast with the inmates of Coldbath Fields, they were also allowed 'whom they pleased to visit them all day long'.[2]

Of course, by no stretch of the imagination could Newgate be described as a model prison and even after its complete rebuilding in the early 1780s overcrowding remained a chronic problem. In his *Letter to the Livery of London*, the radical publisher, reformer and Sheriff of London, Sir Richard Phillips, asserted that in describing the prison's conditions, 'the most apt comparison' would be with an engraving of the slave decks of the '*Brookes*', which had been distributed to great effect by abolitionists during the 1780s:

> When the prisoners lie down on their floors by night, there must necessarily, at least in the women's wards, be the same bodily contact, and the same economical disposition of heads and legs, as were represented in that drawing ... The horrors of such a situation, during the night, when the prisoners are all locked up in their respective wards, especially during the heat of the summer, may be better conceived than described.[3]

And, inevitably, overcrowding and poor sanitation led to the spread of disease – particularly the ever-present typhus, which killed five or six prisoners every day during an outbreak in 1789. The state prisoners did not experience the worst of these conditions, but even John Thelwall, who had been an inmate prior to his treason trial in 1794, described the prison's 'noxious gloom', 'damp foul floor', 'ragged wall' and 'shattered window, grated high', in his dreadful *Poems Written in Close Confinement in the Tower and Newgate*.[4]

Located within the City of London, Newgate was controlled by the mayor, sheriffs and aldermen, from whom the City's magistrates were chosen. Coldbath Fields, on the other hand, lay outside the City and therefore fell under the jurisdiction of the Middlesex magistrates, who were themselves appointed by the Lord Lieutenant of the county. Though the men arrested on 18 and 19 April had been detained on the instructions of the government, there is no evidence to suggest that Pitt and his ministers directly influenced the conditions in which they were held, instead leaving routine matters of security and discipline in the hands of the gaolers and their employers. While the City authorities seem to have been fairly relaxed about such matters, after the escape of the mutineers in April the

'The Heaviest Penalty': Radicals in the House of Correction

Middlesex magistrates most certainly were not. In the aftermath they had complained to the Duke of Portland that they had 'found by painful Experience that the Discipline as well as Security of the Prison is much interrupted and endangered by the Reception of State Prisoners', and asked him to deliver them 'from the burthen of such Additional responsibility'.[5]

Predictably, the Secretary of State had ignored their plea and they had felt it necessary to adopt a stricter approach to state prisoners, placing tighter restrictions on visitors' communications with inmates, and enforcing the requirement for them to obtain a signed pass before entry. But surely these differences did not, in themselves, cause Place to describe one group as being made 'as comfortable as persons in prison could well be made', while the other suffered 'the heaviest penalty which could be inflicted on the most incorrigible felons'.[6] It seems more likely that the disparity was caused by the very different characters of the men into whose hands the two groups fell.

From November 1792, the governor of Newgate had been John Kirby.[7] Born in the North Yorkshire village of Scruton in 1727, at one time Kirby had run his own grocery business in Hull, but in 1754 he had been arrested for a debt of £60 and imprisoned in the Wood Street Compter in the City of London, where the notorious Jonathan Wild and the Gunpowder Plot conspirator Robert Catesby had once been held. Kirby would spend seven years there, being released only with the passing of the Insolvency Act of 1761, which forced his creditors to accept the residue of his estate in lieu of the value of their demands. Apparently recognising that his old life was over, instead of returning to Yorkshire or to his business as a grocer, Kirby decided to turn his recent experiences to his advantage by accepting the post of deputy keeper of the prison where he had spent so many years. His biographer has suggested that 'It was probably his familiarity with the gaol and his business background that led to Kirby's hiring, appearing a more trustworthy deputy than the traditionally working-class turnkeys',[8] and certainly his first-hand knowledge far exceeded that of appointees like Aris, who had only ever observed prison from without.

This awareness and his own character also enabled Kirby to empathise with his prisoners and, from 1766, when he was promoted to become keeper of the compter, he began to introduce changes that would substantially improve the lot of the debtors in his care. Not only did he take personal control of the distribution of charitable donations intended for the prisoners' benefit, thereby curtailing the tendency to squander that had left so many in dire straits, he also paid for apothecaries and other medical professionals to attend the inmates, successfully campaigned for the appointment of a permanent physician to the staff, and even used his own private funds to pay for the release of those debtors who owed the most derisory sums. As governor of Newgate, Kirby continued his philanthropy by ending the age-old custom of charging rent for the debtors' rooms: a decision which certainly reduced his own income but which the prison reformer James Neild considered entirely 'consistent with his wonted humanity'.[9]

Nor, despite his charitable proclivities and his rotund, even Pickwickian appearance, could even his worst enemy call Kirby a milksop. When a group of twenty prisoners armed with knives seized a turnkey and tried to make their escape using the unfortunate man as a human shield it was the newly appointed Kirby who led his men in a counter-attack and foiled the attempt, 'at the hazard of their lives'.[10] Only one man, a thief nicknamed 'Irish Jack' who was awaiting trial for stealing a large quantity of gold coins out of a ship on the Thames, evaded him, 'having previously sawed his irons off, he jumped over the hatch before any assistance could be got to prevent him'. On another occasion a knife-wielding and seemingly deranged prisoner attempted to stab his own solicitor, and once again it was the vigilant and active septuagenarian governor who intervened and disarmed the assailant.[11] All in all, then, it would be difficult to find two men more dissimilar than John Kirby and Thomas Aris.

According to Aris's accounts of the interviews conducted by Burdett during December 1798, the dominant feeling among the political detainees in Coldbath Fields was one of bewilderment: when the baronet enquired of a man named Thomas Evans, a brace maker in Newcastle Street, why he had been arrested, 'Evans said he did not know; he had been taken up and examined before the Lord Chancellor'.[12] In fact, this claim of ignorance seems barely credible. Described by Place as 'a strange creature, with very contemptible reasoning powers, a sort of absurd fanatic, continually operated upon by impulses and capable of undertaking any folly of which he could make himself one of the leaders',[13] Evans had been a prime mover in the establishment of the United Englishmen and when arrested he had been carrying a copy of the oath to be sworn by its members, committing them to 'Truly and sincerely engage to defend my Country ... for which Purpose [I] am willing to join the Society of True Britons, to learn the Use of Arms, in order that equal Rights and Laws should be established and defended'.[14] He must have known that if caught in possession of such inflammatory material his arrest was guaranteed.

Asked the same question, John Webb, a musician, composer and 'very precise careful young man'[15] who had loaned Place books in French to facilitate his language studies, replied that 'he could not tell; but only that he belonged to the Corresponding Society'. Aris observed that Burdett smiled at this response 'and the person who accompanied him said, "Is that all?" Either Sir Francis or the said person then said, "Why, I belong to it."' The next prisoner proved to be the bookseller John Bone, who, along with two unfortunate customers who happened to be in his shop at the time, had been arrested in Holborn on 20 April.[16] Described as 'a good honest man ... a saint, and a busy man privately in his endeavours to make converts',[17] Bone had written exasperatedly of the government's desire to turn 'those laws which were made for the punishment of criminals into a scourge for every honest man who would oppose their arbitrary measures'.[18] Despite his strong support for the LCS's manifesto — so strong, indeed, that the society's Committee of Correspondence had felt obliged to tone down his declarations prior to their publication[19] — in speaking with Burdett Bone focused not on the injustice of his and his colleagues' detention, but on the fate of another inmate: a 50-year-old vagrant who gloried in the name of Obaker Higgles.

The date of Higgles's arrest is uncertain, but we do know that he was committed to Coldbath Fields on 7 December for a term of seven days, that he died on the sixth day of his detention, and that he was buried in an unmarked grave in St James's churchyard, Clerkenwell, on the 15th.[20] Now Bone asserted that Higgles 'had come by his death in a very unfair way',[21] and that he and his companions were very dissatisfied with the coroner's verdict of death 'by the Visitation of God', a whitewashing phrase which has been described as being 'as nonspecific as it was unassailable',[22] and which was intended to indicate a death by natural causes. The bookseller added that two other men had died 'much in the same way'.

At this point, Aris interrupted to demand 'what he meant by that expression, and whether he meant to insinuate that they had been murdered?' When Bone replied, 'literally so', Aris exploded, denouncing his accuser as a purveyor of falsehoods and stating that he would ask a committee of magistrates to look into the story. Faced with this claim and counter-claim, for the time being Burdett could do little but praise Bone for having brought the circumstances of the vagrant's death to his attention. But that would not be the end of the matter: very soon Higgles, a man who had stood on the very lowest rung of the social ladder in Georgian England, would become the subject of passionate debate in the House of Commons.

In a paper later found in a cell and confiscated by Thomas Nicholson, the prison's clerk, Evans, Bone and other prisoners recorded more details of the treatment they had received in the house of correction. The cells they occupied measured 9ft by 6ft, with half the width taken up by the bed, which was 'laid across on hanks' and consisted of 'a bag of straw, one blanket, and a very thin rug of the quality of a horse cloth'.[23] The only other facilities were 'a tin can and chamber pot', the can presumably intended for carrying drinking water from the pumps in the yards. Evans claimed that on first being admitted he had been told that he could have better accommodation if he paid a guinea a week: 'This he declined ... and was conducted to a common cell and left the remainder of the day without bed clothes or even a Urinal'.

From their arrest in April until the end of June, the men spent 23 hours a day locked in their cells, after which they were allowed out for 6 hours in the 24. During the former period, Keir, Goodluck and Neagle had been confined for six weeks at a time in what they described as 'dark cells', with Neagle's situation being particularly pitiable:

> for near his cell door was placed a tub, which served the purpose of a Privy to a Gallery of Thieves, the stench of which added to the Closeness of his Confinement and want of Air reduced him to so low a state of health that he was barely able to get up and down stairs after his removal.[24]

For his part, initially at least, Keir remained defiant, drawing a guillotine and a beheaded figure on his cell wall and scrawling the captions 'This is the base Pitt' and 'This is a cure for the King's Evil',[25] a provocation that resulted in his being confined in a dark cell until August. In November, 'in the midst of Frost and Snow', they remained locked in their unheated cells for 16 hours each day, the cells being rendered both dark and damp when the plummeting temperatures forced them to close the wooden shutters on the unglazed windows.

During the earlier part of their imprisonment the men were 'continually threatened with Fetters, Dark Cells and to be knocked down for talking, singing, or looking out of the Grating', and if any dared mention their treatment to their visitors they would be placed in solitary confinement and denied visitors altogether. In order to save money, the prison authorities believed that the families of state prisoners should provide their food, but with the families' breadwinners in gaol this became increasingly difficult and in June they submitted a petition to the Duke of Portland, 'setting forth the distresses of their families, and the inability of the latter to assist them'.[26] The duke agreed that the prisoners in the house of correction should be put on the same rations as those in Newgate, but even then Bone and his companions believed that the quantity and quality of their food was decided upon by the governor, and consisted of two slices of bread and butter and a pint of 'very bad tea' for breakfast, a plate of meat and one pint of porter at 1, 2 or 3 p.m., the meat 'sometimes stinking and often very bad in quality', with the prisoners allowed no knife, fork or other utensil with which to eat. Their last meal of the day would be made up of another pint of tea and another slice of bread and butter. And, of course, any complaint regarding treatment or provisions would be rewarded with more time in the cells.

Naturally, Burdett became increasingly appalled as these details gradually came to light – but it was the fate of another imprisoned member of the LCS that he would use to drag the abuses of the Coldbath Fields House of Correction into the cold light of day. That man was in no way typical of the disenfranchised, working class membership of the organisation and could not be dismissed as a mere penny pamphleteer or rabble-rouser; instead, Colonel Edward Marcus Despard was not only a member of the landed gentry who had spent his entire adult life in the service of his king and country, he had actually been lionised as a British hero and assured of the king's 'royal approbation'.[27]

The scion of a Protestant Anglo-Irish family of French Huguenot descent, Despard was born on 6 March 1751 in Coolrain, Queen's County, roughly halfway between Limerick and Dublin. In line with his family's long tradition of military service, he had joined the 50th Regiment of Foot as an ensign in 1766, and, with the exception of six years on home service, had spent his entire military career in the Caribbean and Central America, initially in Jamaica, where he worked on shoring up the island's defences in readiness for a predicted attack to be launched by the combined forces of France and Spain in support of their allies, the American revolutionaries. The attack did not materialise, but Despard gained useful experience in military engineering and his work brought him the praise of both his superiors and the island's authorities.

One highly critical biographer suggests that Despard's employment on tasks that separated him from the usual discipline of regimental life and encouraged him to operate with a high degree of autonomy may have resulted in his loss of 'any idea of obedience that he may have imbibed during his years of service as a very young ensign'.[28] If so, there was no sign of this weakness in either his performance or willingness to comply with orders during his next posting early in 1780; indeed, the character and abilities that he was about to display won for him the lifelong friendship and admiration of one of Britain's greatest military heroes: Horatio Nelson.

As captain of the twenty-eight-gun frigate HMS *Hinchinbrook*, Nelson had been placed in command of the naval contingent for a daring – or, as it would prove, foolhardy – attack on the Spanish province of Nicaragua.[29] Later characterised as 'one of those nightmare expeditions to which British statesmen ... frequently condemned a handful of British soldiers',[30] the plan was the brainchild of General John Dalling, the ambitious governor of Jamaica, and involved a rag-tag force of perhaps 3,000 men, made up of regulars, irregulars, native troops and a contingent of Miskito Indians under the command of Major John Polson, landing on the Caribbean coast of the province and then forcing their way up the San Juan River to take the strategically vital towns of Granada and León to the north-west of Lake Nicaragua. If the invading force could fight its way to the Pacific coast, and if a Royal Navy squadron could meet it there, then Spanish possessions would be cut in two and Britain would have taken a huge leap towards dominating both the Atlantic and Pacific oceans, enabling it to blockade Spanish-American ports and thereby strangle the supply of gold to Spain, crucial for the Spanish Empire's continued military support for the rebelling American colonists.

With such a goal in view, optimism among the British ran ludicrously high: 'Happy was every man who had hopes of bearing any part in the enterprise', wrote one contemporary commentator closely associated with the expedition. 'Enthusiasm never was carried to greater height, than by those who had promised to themselves the glory of shaking Spain to her foundation'.[31] Despard's role in this grandiose scheme would be to use his newly acquired engineering skills to construct a gunboat for use on Lake Nicaragua, to scout for campsites ahead of the main force, to survey and chart the waterway, to site the artillery batteries for the assault on the Castle of San Juan, which guarded the entrance to the lake, to build fortifications and to prepare siege equipment.

As is so often the case, the origins of the expedition's ultimate failure are to be found in its timing, or mistiming. The first troops, escorted by the

Hinchinbrook, did not land on the Nicaraguan coast until 14 February 1780 and, after delays in co-ordinating the various contingents, it was not until 24 March that they reached the mouth of the San Juan River. After further delays, a party of some 200 regular troops began their 100-mile journey up the river in canoes skilfully piloted by the local Miskito people. But so close to the end of the dry season, low water levels meant that progress was constantly interrupted by the need to navigate shoals, often requiring the sweating, broadcloth-clad troops to disembark and fight their way through the jungle on shore. On 11 April, having already taken a number of small Spanish outposts, they finally reached the fortress of San Juan, some 69 miles inland, and began its siege some 48 hours later. After eleven days, when its freshwater supply was cut, the castle's governor surrendered, with the loss of just a handful of besiegers killed and wounded. But, despite this success, the expedition was already doomed.

With the onset of the rainy season, and with the river quickly swelling so as to become all but unnavigable, the victors found themselves imprisoned in the castle they had just captured. Dr Benjamin Moseley, a Jamaican physician and the earliest historian of the expedition, wrote of the 'foul vapours, which clog the atmosphere' in the dark, dank jungle of Nicaragua, and noted how the 'troops and the Indians were attacked with fluxes and intermittents, and in want of almost every necessary ... languished in the extremest misery, and gradually mouldered away, until there was not sufficient strength alive to attend the sick, nor to bury the dead'.[32] On the disease-ridden coast to the east the sailors fared no better than the soldiers, and of the 3,000 men who took part in the expedition more than 2,500 would die, mostly of yellow fever, malaria and dysentery, which tore through camps, barracks and ships with equal fury.* Further attempts were made to push on to Lake Nicaragua, but in the face of stiffening Spanish resistance and sinking morale all failed and by 30 November the campaign was over. Thus, in Moseley's words, 'the best concerted and most important enterprise that had been conceived during the war, was totally defeated, and a considerable national expense and mortality incurred'.[33]

---

*   *The World* for 22 July 1791 would report that, as of that date, of the officers who had taken part in the expedition up the San Juan River only two were still living: Despard and 'another Gentleman, a subaltern in the West-Indies'. It must be assumed that Royal Navy officers were not included in the statistics, as Nelson would live for another fourteen years.

Miraculously, despite serious illness, Despard survived the expedition and remained with it until the very end – his resilience perhaps explained by a combination of an iron constitution and a high degree of immunity gained during eight years of service in Jamaica. Nelson was not so lucky, falling so desperately ill before the walls of the Castle of San Juan that he was eventually evacuated to Britain, and survived by only the narrowest of margins. But Despard had not only survived, he had become a hero, having been so constantly at the forefront of the action that Polson later reported that, during the siege, 'There was scarcely a gun fired but was pointed by [Nelson] or Lieut. Despard, chief engineer, who has exerted himself on every occasion'.[34]

Fully recovered from the rigours of jungle warfare, Despard next saw action on the coast of Honduras. In March 1782 a Spanish force captured the town of Black River, the de facto capital of the British territories in the region, and the newly promoted Lieutenant Colonel Despard was tasked with recovering it. With a total force of around 1,400 men at his command, on 17 August he despatched 400 under the command of Captain John Campbell to retake the smaller of the two forts at Black River – a task which Campbell completed on the 21st, but with considerable loss of life among the Spaniards, with over half of the defenders being massacred. Despard, meanwhile, turned his attention to the larger fort, and its garrison of 750 officers and men. Knowing themselves to be outnumbered, and no doubt aware of the fate that had befallen so many of their comrades, the Spaniards' only hope lay in the arrival of reinforcements – a hope destroyed when Despard captured an incoming troop carrier with all the troops on board. On his arrival at the fort on 28 August he demanded that its governor surrender without resistance, which he did almost immediately, preferring to avoid any further loss of life.

For the British it had been a morale-boosting and bloodless victory, particularly welcome after the San Juan debacle, and the newly appointed governor of Jamaica, Archibald Campbell, reported delightedly to Whitehall that the British settlers along the Mosquito Coast now anticipated 'a fair Prospect of enjoying their Plantations in Tranquillity; while the Spaniards, who have been at an immense Expence and Fatigue, have lost the Fruits of their costly and laborious Exertions'.[35] Two months later the Home Secretary, Thomas Townshend, replied on behalf of the king, signifying His Majesty's 'highest satisfaction at … the judicious conduct and gallant services of Lieutenant-Colonel Despard'.[36] Less than a year later, with the end of the American War of

Independence in September 1783, hostilities between Britain and Spain came to an end.

One of the conditions of the Treaty of Paris, signed on 3 September 1783, was that the whole of the Mosquito Coast should be surrendered to the Spanish and its 2,000 or so British settlers and their slaves relocated to the Bay of Honduras Settlement at Belize. However, this agreement had been reached without any consultation with the settlers themselves and, furious at what they saw as a betrayal by the British government, they refused to move. Facing the risk of the growing tension flaring into outright war, the British and Spanish returned to the negotiating table and eventually hammered out a revised agreement, the Convention of London of 1786, which included sufficient additional Spanish concessions – in particular the granting of more land to the settlers and the right to fell valuable mahogany trees – for them to agree, albeit reluctantly, to their being evacuated to Belize. At the earnest request of the Mosquito Coast settlers, the man appointed to be the new superintendent of the British logwood concessions was no less a person than the victor of the Black River campaign, Colonel Despard. His appointment would prove to be a poisoned chalice, and its contents would set him on an irreversible course from national hero to reviled and imprisoned rebel.

After 1786, the inhabitants of the Bay of Honduras Settlement could be divided into two groups: on the one hand the 'Baymen', the 700 members of the small log-cutting and trading community who had made the settlement their home for well over a century; on the other, the 'Shoremen', the 2,000 incomers expelled from the Mosquito Coast. Conflict between the two began almost immediately and for the entire duration of his command, from April 1786 to May 1790, Despard found himself 'in one constant round of disputes and protests'.[37] The primary cause of complaint was the distribution of the additional land granted to the settlers under the terms of the Convention of London. According to the instructions issued to Despard by Thomas Townshend, now raised to the peerage as the first Viscount Sydney:

> His Majesty conceives that the Mosquito Settlers who have been obliged to relinquish their possessions ought first to be attended to, especially in the disposal of those lands which may in some degree be looked upon as a consideration for their Settlements upon the Mosquito Shore. Upon this ground His Majesty has commanded me to instruct you that the late inhabitants of the Mosquito Shore who may arrive at the

Honduras Settlement are to be accommodated in preference to all other persons whatsoever.[38]

Reasonable though this instruction might appear, it did not take into account the fact that practically every square inch of the additional land granted by the Spaniards had already been claimed – albeit illegally – by the Baymen, who now faced expulsion. Worse still, in the eyes of both the Baymen and the wealthier Shoremen, Despard sought to redistribute the land 'without any distinction of Age, Sex, Character, Respectability, Property, or *Colour*'.[39] In essence, this meant that under his system of land allocation the poorest free black had just as good a chance of acquiring a plot of land as the richest white settler. Confident in his unambiguous instructions from the Crown, Despard refused to give way and relations between the superintendent and the settler elite continued to deteriorate, with both ultimately seeking the intervention of Lord Sydney.

Back in London, in the face of the conflicting accounts, Sydney dithered. While supporting Despard and deploring the settlers' audacity in defying the authority of the king's representative, he also wished that the superintendent had made:

> some Distinction in the Extent of Lots so as to be disposed of, between affluent Settlers and Persons of a different description, particularly people of Colour, or Free Negroes, who, from the natural Prejudices of the Inhabitants of the Colonies, are not ... considered upon an equal footing with People of a different Complexion.[40]

Put another way, Despard should have second-guessed the king and assumed that when told to accommodate 'the late inhabitants of the Mosquito Shore ... in preference to all other persons whatsoever', the late inhabitants alluded to were the white European settlers. As well as being an unreasonable (and entirely retrospective) expectation on Sydney's part, it was a distinction with which Despard is very unlikely to have felt the slightest sympathy as just two years later he would marry Catherine Gordon, the daughter of a free woman of colour from Jamaica.[41]

The impasse could have lasted indefinitely, had it not been for an important change in the Home Office. On 5 June 1789, William Pitt dismissed Sydney as home secretary, and replaced him with his own cousin, William Grenville. According to James Bannantine, Despard's secretary and admirer, the settlers immediately realised that Grenville, unlike his predecessor, would not be familiar with the history of the dispute, and they seized their opportunity, presenting 'several memorials to him, filled with the most audacious lies, and charging Colonel Despard with the grossest injustice, tyranny, and oppression'.[42] Unable at such a distance to separate fact from fiction, Grenville decided that he had no option but to suspend the superintendent while the case was investigated. Given the choice of remaining in the settlement while Grenville's representative undertook his unenviable task or sailing home, Despard chose the latter course, embarking for England on 3 June 1790, wearied by the conflict but no doubt relishing the prospect of presenting his case in person.

The relish would quickly evaporate. Expecting that his years of dutiful service would result in an early hearing, Despard instead found himself pushed from pillar to post, his path to Grenville, and to his replacement Henry Dundas, barred by polite but intractable functionaries. Days stretched into weeks, weeks into months, and months into years without any indication that he would be regarded as anything but another inconvenient suppliant haunting the corridors of power, his case receiving nothing but the most cursory consideration. A sorrowful Bannantine wrote that 'all his efforts were in vain', and that 'after two years constant attendance upon all the departments of Government' the most he ever received was a mealy-mouthed acknowledgement 'that there was no charge against him worthy of investigation'.[43]

Despard had been deemed guiltless, but the 900 pages of evidence and affidavits that he had gathered (at Grenville's request) had been ignored; he had not been reinstated, or offered any alternative post commensurate with his rank and experience; and the considerable personal expense that he had incurred while acting as superintendent would not be reimbursed, leaving him substantially out of pocket. Worse still, in order to protect the trade of the Honduras Settlement, Despard had found it necessary to seize ten American vessels; now – and despite his actions having received official approval at the time – he found himself abandoned by the government when the owners of those vessels pursued him for damages, involving him in a vexatious lawsuit and yet further costs, which the administration refused to reimburse and which resulted in his spending over two years in the King's Bench Prison as a debtor.

Despard had every reason to feel let down, even betrayed, by the existing system: he had served it honourably and well for decades, only to find himself ignored, imprisoned, unemployed and broke. The point at which his resentment turned into active resistance to the government is uncertain, but by 1794 he had joined the LCS. As his most recent biographer has asserted, 'Despard's conversion to politics was a dramatic change of career, but not an entirely puzzling one'.[44] Throughout his years of service he had demonstrated broadly liberal attitudes: not only had he gained the admiration and trust of the indigenous Miskito people in his dealings with them, he had shown an unyielding commitment to the equal rights of the Shoremen during their resettlement in Honduras – no matter how lowly their status and no matter what their race or colour – and he had sought to run the colony on democratic principles, with the votes of rich and poor possessing equal value. Of course, he believed that his policy of land allocation accorded with the instructions he had received from his masters in London, but it seems likely that many appointees would have employed far greater latitude in interpreting those instructions for the benefit of white settlers – just as the home secretary had apparently expected him to do. Finally, while mixed-race marriages were not extraordinary they remained unusual, and Despard's union with Catherine Gordon therefore suggests a degree of open-mindedness shared by few contemporaries of his rank. Given these attitudes, it does not seem surprising or in any way out of character for him to sympathise with the goals of the LCS, particularly their quest for equal representation.

By 1794, the gentlemanly confederacy of campaign groups like the Society for Constitutional Information had withered on the vine, strangled by the bloody events of the Terror in France, by the declaration of war and by the hardening of the British government's attitude to dissent. Those who continued to call for constitutional change found themselves effectively gagged and at imminent risk of being arrested and imprisoned. It has been suggested that Despard may have been a member of the United Irishmen ever since 'its genteel days under Wolfe Tone',[45] and in the prevailing atmosphere of repression there can be no doubt that, over time, he came to agree with the arguments of James Coigly and others that the likelihood of the reformists achieving their aims through passive resistance was diminishingly small. It is also true that he alone among the prominent members of the LCS had the necessary military training and experience to lead an armed insurrection. But sympathy with the aims of the group that now called itself the United Englishmen and the possession of the skills and knowledge that would offer them the best chance of success did not automatically translate into a desire for immediate action, and Francis Place, who knew Despard very well, believed that in the spring of 1798 the colonel shared his own view that the plans of the United Englishmen for an armed uprising were 'equally absurd and mischievous'.[46]

But the government was well aware of Despard's sympathies – partly through the work of its network of spies and partly because of his openness in avowing his beliefs – and on 12 March, in the aftermath of the capture of James Coigly, four king's messengers and several Bow Street officers burst into his bedchamber in Meard's Court, Soho, tore him from the arms of 'a black woman' (his wife) and arrested him.[47] However, any glow of satisfaction the intelligence services may have felt as a result of their foiling of Coigly's plans quickly paled when they realised that they had thrown their net too wide and caught in its meshes not only Edward Despard, but also his brother, General John Despard – a man of unquestionable loyalty who had become estranged from his younger sibling and had dismissed his recent conduct as 'extremely foolish'.[48] Embarrassed, the home secretary ordered the release of both men – only to arrest Despard again on 22 April, two days after the suspension of habeas corpus. This time, though, the arrest was made rather more discreetly by just two Bow Street Runners, Edward Fugion and John Rivett, who had arrested Coigly in Margate. After a brief interview by the Privy Council, Despard was despatched to Coldbath Fields where, eight months later, he would meet Sir Francis Burdett, Billy Bosville and John Courtenay.

7

'Everybody Knows the Bastille'
BURDETT'S CAMPAIGN

The first public statement made regarding Despard's treatment after his arrest was delivered by Courtenay on 21 December 1798 during his parliamentary speech in opposition to the extension of the suspension of habeas corpus. One of the prison's inmates, he told the House, 'was a Gentleman whom he had known in His Majesty's service more than 30 years ago', who now lived 'secluded from every one of his friends', and not allowed to speak even to his wife except 'through the bars of an iron gate'.[1]

Of course, what made Despard's case conspicuous were his aristocratic background and his distinguished career in the service of the king. In all other respects, the conditions he endured were precisely the same as those experienced by the other state prisoners, and which Courtenay believed to be 'unexampled in severity and rigour':

> denied every kind of society – exposed to the cold and rain, which in that inclement season ... entered by the iron bars of their cells – only allowed to breathe the air out of their cells for about an hour – denied every comfort, every innocent amusement – excluded from all intercourse with each other, and each night locked up from all the rest of the world.[2]

He went on to state that having visited the prison he had asked several gentlemen, all 'eminent in the profession of the law', whether there existed a precedent for such treatment. 'They uniformly answered, that they never had heard of such severity ... and that they could not imagine that any men were used in such a manner in this country'.³

But the ignorance of these eminent lawyers was not shared by the people from whose ranks most of the prison's inmates came. Naturally, the prostitutes, petty thieves, vagrants and other misdemeanants who had been released after the expiry of their short terms of imprisonment soon told their families, friends, neighbours, and drinking and gaming partners what they had seen and experienced while interned, and some wit among them had made the inevitable comparison with the infamous French fortress that had come to embody the oppression of the *Ancien Régime*, and the destruction of which had heralded the eventual fall of the Bourbons: the Bastille.* The prison's new nickname quickly gained currency, and Courtenay told the House that in taking a coach to Clerkenwell from Oxford Street in order to rendezvous with Burdett and Bosville, he had given the coachman the simple two-word instruction, 'The Bastille'. Surprised that the driver seemed to know exactly where he wished to go, he asked him if he really knew the place, and received the reply, 'O yes, I know it – why everybody knows the Bastille in Coldbath Fields'.⁴

The Secretary of State for War, Henry Dundas, had little time for such tales. A Scottish lawyer renowned for his powerful and articulate argumentation in Court, he dismissed them as having 'no relation whatever to the question before the House' and reminded Courtenay that 'every gaol was under the direction of some Magistrate, to whom application ought to be made for redress of any grievance that might take place within it'.⁵ Such matters should be brought to the attention of Parliament only in those cases where the magistrates failed to act. Furthermore, he suggested, had Courtenay made such an application in a timely fashion instead of attempting to use the supposed abuses at the prison as political capital, they might long since have been remedied.

Besides, Dundas went on, did some of the so-called abuses really stand up to scrutiny? Courtenay complained that the state prisoners were excluded from society. What did he, or they, expect? After all, isolation 'was a circumstance which naturally arose out of the situation of all prisoners, and would always occur whenever there was a necessity for keeping

---

* The first published use of the term 'Bastille' to describe the house of correction seems to have occurred in a letter from the Reverend Christopher Munnings of Bilney Hall in Norfolk to Lord Kenyon, published in the *Telegraph* on 15 February 1797.

men, of whatever description they might be, in a state of confinement'. As to the prison being nicknamed the Bastille, of course a name would enter common parlance if gentlemen insisted on using it, and the 'same shilling that paid for driving them would teach the coachman to know it by that name, and in this manner the appellation of Bastille might be given to any edifice in London'. A name so taught, he contended, meant nothing.

Next to speak was George Tierney, an Irish Whig who could claim the unusual distinction of having fought a duel with the sitting Prime Minister after Pitt accused him of deliberately compromising the defence of the country by opposing an Emergency Bill to increase manpower for the Royal Navy.* Opposed to the continued suspension of habeas corpus, Tierney opined that Courtenay had been quite correct in drawing attention to the way the state prisoners had been treated because his remarks revealed that individuals arrested under the terms of the Act were not treated as people under suspicion, but 'as if they had been convicted of some great felony'. As for the solitary confinement in which they had been kept, while magistrates continued to argue over its utility, 'he never yet heard its warmest supporters say that an Englishman, who had been convicted of no crime, should be confined in one of those cells'.[6] In other words, Courtenay's investigations had brought to light a shocking abuse of power which the House should feel compelled to remedy now and prevent in future.

This game of parliamentary tit for tat continued when Sir John Scott, the Attorney General who had been humiliated by the failure of his prosecutions during the 1794 treason trials, rose from the government benches. Calling prisons like Coldbath Fields 'Bastilles' was, he stated, 'perfectly childish – they were fit places of confinement for those who endeavoured to overthrow all law, all government, all morality, and all order'.[7] With respect to the hardships some prisoners claimed to suffer, while he agreed with Dundas that ample means existed to redress any such wrongs, in reality it seemed highly improbable that cruelty would be practised by gaolers who, as a body, were so desirous 'of standing well in the opinion of the public, that they were often induced to go beyond the bounds [of leniency] which their sober reflection would approve'.

---

* Pitt and Tierney fought with pistols on Putney Heath on 27 May 1798; neither man sustained injury and the duel came to an end when their seconds declared that honour had been satisfied.

William Wilberforce, the abolitionist and evangelical Christian, whose arch-conservativism and resistance to all forms of reform at home had led to accusations of gross hypocrisy from Fox and other Whigs, continued in a similar vein. He stated that a letter he had received from a friend 'well acquainted with the subject' completely exonerated the Middlesex magistrates of any charge of neglect, while one of the magistrates (probably Samuel Glasse, whom Wilberforce accepted as an unbiased witness) had assured him that 'many persons had returned to society after their confinement much improved in their morals'[8] – an achievement particularly satisfactory to a politician and campaigner who, eleven years earlier, had played a leading role in persuading the king to issue his largely ineffective Proclamation for the Discouragement of Vice. If an improvement in the ex-prisoners' morals could be discerned then the prison must surely be considered a 'valuable institution'. He concluded by reading from a letter written by yet another magistrate who asserted, incredibly, that 'the prisoners enjoyed good health, and were allowed as good food as ever he had at his own table' and that 'the place deserves rather the name of an hospital than a prison'.[9]

Only two defenders of the prison had actually visited it. For his part, Rowland Burdon, the MP for County Durham, accepted the magistrates' assertion that the prison had not been designed for state prisoners,[10] but he had seen nothing objectionable during his tour and, with respect to regulations and economy, 'everything seemed to be conducted in the best manner of which such an establishment was capable ... and everywhere the greatest neatness, regularity, and propriety prevailed'.[11] William Mainwaring, meanwhile, defended Thomas Aris as a man 'remarkable for humanity', who used no severity and treated the prisoners with 'every indulgence that could be shewn them'.[12] And Mainwaring, despite being dismissed by the king as 'the son of some tradesman' and a cuckold,[13] could speak with authority, being not only an MP for Middlesex but also a senior magistrate for the county and chairman of the Middlesex and Westminster Quarter Sessions. He therefore knew the prison and its governor better than anyone else taking part in the debate. Of course, it could also be argued that in terms of reputation he had far more to lose should the accusations of mismanagement and cruelty be proved.

Burdett, speaking publicly about Coldbath Fields for the first time, observed that while it was important to avoid exaggeration he believed that 'great severity had in some instances been used',[14] citing as an example the case of a number of Manchester radicals arrested under the Act and then driven 200 miles south to Clerkenwell:

> They were loaded with irons ... From the effects of travelling in this state, their legs were very much swelled, and when lodged in the prison, the Bow-street Officers ordered the irons to be knocked off, which was then a very painful operation. They were then thrown into places quite unprepared for their reception, and next day taken before the Privy Council. They were exposed to great inconvenience, as, though several of them were manufacturers, they had no opportunity of giving directions about their affairs, nor of obtaining redress, as nobody was permitted to see them.[15]

As for Burdon's statement that he had seen nothing objectionable in the cells, Burdett asked whether he had considered the probable condition of such a chamber 'after a person had been in it for some hours, or when persons were confined for many weeks without being permitted to go out but for a few minutes to wash themselves?' It was also self-evident that unheated cells with bare brick walls must become damp in cold or wet weather.

Despite the efforts of Dundas, Scott and their supporters to dismiss the complaints regarding conditions at Coldbath Fields, inevitably the topic resurfaced when the debate on the extension of the suspension of habeas corpus resumed on 26 December. On this occasion, Courtenay took the opportunity to quote from a letter written by Catherine Despard after she had read accounts of the earlier debate. Her husband, Catherine wrote, had been confined for nearly seven months in a damp cell, 'not seven feet square, without either fire or candle, chair, table, knife, fork, a glazed window, or even a book to read'.[16] For corroboration of her account, she referred any doubters to Valentine Lawless and John Reeves, who had also visited Despard during the first few months of his imprisonment.

Unfortunately, in Lawless, Catherine had chosen a witness whose testimony the authorities would happily disregard. A member of the Anglo-Irish Protestant Ascendancy, he was nonetheless an enthusiastic advocate of Catholic emancipation and an early recruit of the United Irishmen; moreover, his views were so well known that by the time Courtenay read Catherine's letter in the Commons, Lawless, too, had been arrested and imprisoned in the Tower of London, where he would remain, without trial, until March 1801. As a result, his support for

Despard would count for very little with the government and could easily be ignored.

The same could not be said of the testimony of John Reeves. An ardent royalist – so ardent, indeed, that his enemies accused him of being a Jacobite and a believer in the divine right of kings – in the aftermath of the French Revolution Reeves had described Englishmen who sought constitutional reform as being 'influenced by a defect of mind ... so that by the strength of the will, or the weakness of the wit ... [they] go on from error to error, and are almost always in a heat from the pursuit, and from the disappointment attending it'.[17] Disturbed that so many challenged his Panglossian view of the British constitution, in 1792 Reeves had founded the Association for Preserving Liberty and Property against Republicans and Levellers which successfully disrupted radical meetings and actively pursued the prosecution of the publishers of Paine's *Rights of Man* and other 'seditious' writings. Despite Reeves's maggoty-headed obsession with eradicating the pernicious influence of French Jacobins, Lawless believed that his friend's 'toryism never interfered with the promptings of his kindly and benevolent heart'[18] and the two men were equally shocked by the conditions in which Despard was kept – Lawless noting that, by the time of their visit, the 47-year-old 'appeared to be about sixty'. Crucially, as well as being an active and high profile campaigner very much in tune with the government's agenda, Reeves served as a Middlesex magistrate and his representations to those in power had resulted in the colonel being moved to an upper room with a fireplace, provided with fuel and chairs, and permitted longer and more frequent visits from his wife, although Catherine noted that this amelioration did not occur until 'his feet were ulcerated by frost'.[19]

Having listened to the contents of Catherine's letter, the attorney general observed that her words had been published in a newspaper* and that if the House was to discuss accusations of cruelty made against respectable public officers, then he believed that 'there was no cruelty more harsh than that of a Member of Parliament stating in his speech as an authentic account, something that he had seen in a newspaper'.[20] He admitted that the Duke of Portland had received a letter of complaint from Catherine in June; however, the complaint had been investigated and the duke had given instructions that the prisoner should be shown 'every indulgence which the nature of the Warrant under which he was committed, and safe custody, would admit'. He did not deny the conditions in which Despard

---

* *The Morning Post*, 24 December 1798. Catherine's letter was dated 23 December.

had originally been kept, nor did he choose to call upon John Reeves for any corroboration of Catherine's account. Given the improvement in the colonel's circumstances, he believed that Courtenay was raking over old ground for purely political purposes. Besides – and here Scott played his trump card – when he heard that his wife had complained of his harsh treatment, Despard had apparently expressed surprise 'and added, that if necessary, he would contradict it himself'. Finally, Scott asked with staggering condescension, had Catherine really written the published letter? 'It was,' he acknowledged, 'a well written Letter, and for a certain purpose well adapted', but he felt sure that 'the Female Sex would pardon him, if he said it was a little ... beyond their style in general'. Perhaps the letter bearing her name had been penned, in part at least, by 'artful men' who had taken advantage of her.

Burdon chipped in to provide more details regarding Despard's denial of harsh treatment, informing the House that having read Catherine Despard's letter in the newspapers he had visited the prison and spoken with the colonel. Despard had 'told him that he had nothing to allege against the conduct of the Governor ... and that he had been treated as well as the nature of the prison would admit'. As to his ulcerated feet, he had suffered nothing worse than chilblains in his heels, 'which he thought so lightly of, that he would not suffer the Surgeon to apply any remedy to them ... that he was an old soldier who had borne much greater hardships; and that he could cure himself'. He again denied that he knew of his wife's letter, and said that 'if he had, he must have disapproved of it'.[21]

Completely wrong-footed by Despard's reported denials of mistreatment, a deflated Courtenay had little choice but to say that he 'would examine every matter again, if he was permitted to visit the place, and if he found he had been in an error in anything he should be perfectly ready to acknowledge it'.[22] Angry and embarrassed, he was then obliged to listen as Wilberforce dismissed accusations of neglect and cruelty as 'much exaggerated' and the product of Courtenay's own prejudice. Picking up on Scott's questioning of Courtenay's motives, Wilberforce then suggested that his visits to the prison had been prompted not by humanity but by a desire to score political points for the benefit of the radicals. 'The persons whose cause is now so pathetically pleaded,' he sneered:

> might heretofore have been objects of humane compassion. But where was the Honourable Gentleman's humanity and friendship for them before they were accused of High Treason? Where was the Honourable Gentleman's curious anxiety to visit the prisons and pry into their

regulations before the State Prisoners were confined in them? – Has he examined into the treatment of vagrants with equal solicitude?

Perhaps recognising a degree of justice in Wilberforce's question, the usually voluble Courtenay made no reply. Burdett, however, felt no reluctance. Having read to the House a series of letters from the Manchester radicals whose plight he had described on 21 December, he told his fellow MPs that if a proper investigation of the conditions at Coldbath Fields proved his claims to be false he would not only 'make an *amende honorable*', he 'should also enjoy the happiness of having his feelings relieved from the idea that such foul atrocities had been practised in a country he was taught to look upon as free and humane'. With mock seriousness, he then returned to the words of Wilberforce's pet magistrate, arguing that if, as had been asserted, the prison more closely resembled a hospital than a place of confinement, an investigation was no less necessary because, if true, then the prisoners were enjoying 'a luxury that ill-suited a place of correction, where legal chastisement should be inflicted'. Either way, an investigation must be instigated, and the resulting evidence brought to the bar of the House.

By requesting an inquiry, Burdett had successfully turned the tables, because it quickly became apparent that an inquiry was the very last thing the government wanted. The first to respond to his suggestion was Burdon, who argued that such an inquiry could serve only to 'traduce the fair character of respectable men, and particularly of the Magistrates whose conduct should not be lightly arraigned'. Bizarrely, he went on to argue that it would also 'injure the credit and character of that eminently humane man [John Howard] who laboured so strong and so strenuously in meliorating the state of prisons throughout the country', in the process ignoring the obvious fact that Howard, who had died in January 1790, would have been the first to publicise abuses, even in a prison built upon the principles that he had laid down two decades earlier.

The last word in the debate went to George Canning, the rising young Tory orator, who, recognising that Burdon's resistance to an inquiry sounded too much like bluster, opposed it on stronger grounds, arguing that every suggestion regarding the existence of abuses in the prison had been contradicted, and no new evidence brought forward. More importantly, so far as Catherine Despard's letter was concerned, 'Here was an illiterate woman, whose former letters could scarcely be understood, who came forward with a well-written letter ... and all the statements of this letter were disproved by the acknowledgement of the party to whom it alluded'.²³ An inquiry could not, and must not, be commissioned on the basis of lies and half-truths.

For all his brilliance, Canning made a serious tactical error in his dismissal of Burdett's allegations. 'He did not mean to charge the Hon. Gentleman opposite to him as the author of this letter;' he quipped, 'for he was capable of writing better things. But he hoped that the Hon. Gentleman would learn from this circumstance, not to state facts again without a sufficient enquiry'.²⁴ Rather than conclusively scotching the idea of further investigations, in effect Canning had invited the baronet to undertake them personally – something Burdett had already proved very willing to do. No doubt spurred on by Canning's suggestion that he keep 'his facts for Newgate; and his jests for the hackney coachmen who should drive him', he again visited the house of correction on 29 December and, having marshalled his evidence, on New Year's Eve he gave notice in the House of Commons that 'immediately after the holidays he should make a motion relative to the treatment of the persons confined in Coldbath Fields Prison, and respecting the management, &c. of that Prison in general'.²⁵

There can be no question that, by this time, one of the MPs paying closest attention to Burdett's activities was the Prime Minister himself. Fully aware of their radical sympathies, Pitt knew that Burdett and his supporters would use any fresh evidence of the misuse of state prisoners to launch a much more wide-ranging assault on the government's repressive policies. And, by now, he must have been all too well aware that the conditions in the prison would not bear close scrutiny. Clearly believing that attack would be the best form of defence, he immediately took measures to undermine Burdett's case and, following the celebrations to mark the beginning of the New Year, he rose from the government benches to announce that various papers existed 'very material to have laid before the House',²⁶ and that these papers should be examined prior to there being any discussion regarding his honourable friend's motion; predictably, his request was duly granted by the Speaker of the House, Henry Addington, a childhood friend and long-time supporter. The documents in question consisted of an affidavit made on 31 December by the prison's governor before Sir Richard Ford, the Middlesex magistrate, and a letter on the subject written by the Home Secretary, the Duke of Portland. Both papers were laid before the House on Friday 4 January 1799.

As we have already seen, in his affidavit Aris described Burdett's visits on 28 November and 29 December, but also – embarrassingly for Scott and Burdon – he noted that in his conversation with the baronet Despard had denied outright Burdon's assertion that he had disassociated himself from his wife's complaints regarding his treatment. As for Portland's letter, this was addressed to his son, the Marquess of Titchfield, who also happened to be Lord Lieutenant of the County of Middlesex, and therefore the man who appointed the magistrates in control of the prison. Writing from Whitehall on 2 January, Portland accused Burdett of having conducted himself during his visits 'in a manner that tended to affect the discipline and good government of the Prison, and to give countenance and encouragement to prisoners confined there under the sentence of the Law for the most heinous offences'.[27] As a consequence, he had instructed Aris, and the keepers of Newgate and Tothill Fields Bridewell, where the other state prisoners were held, to 'on no account permit Sir Francis Burdett to visit'. As well as refusing an official inquiry into Coldbath Fields, the government had now prevented any private investigation from taking place.

But, via Portland, the king had instructed the Middlesex magistrates 'at their ensuing Quarter Sessions, to make due enquiry into all the circumstances of this case',[28] and they had no choice but to obey. Their report, which was read in the House of Commons at the beginning of March, proved to be a whitewash, the inspectors expressing their 'perfect satisfaction of the cleanliness of the prison, the wholesomeness of the provision, the treatment of the prisoners, &c.', all of which, they thought, did nothing but 'honour to the Magistrates, and others, who have the direction and management of the same'.[29] The supporting papers repeated all of the well-known accounts of Despard's imprisonment, of his satisfaction with his improved conditions and of his disapproval of his wife's published letter. Witnesses including Aris, Thomas Nicholson, the clerk and Thomas Webbe, the prison's apothecary and surgeon, described the visits made by Burdett, Courtenay and Bosville, and their conversations with various prisoners, some of whom complained, while others expressed themselves entirely satisfied with their lot.

In his evidence, Webbe opined that 'there can't be a wholesomer place than the prison is',[30] and told the investigating magistrates that he had conducted a number of experiments with thermometers and seaweed in order to monitor the temperatures and dampness of the cells – tests which, needless to say, had demonstrated beyond all reasonable doubt the salubrious conditions prevailing in the prison. He also described a number of instances where the sick and the lame had been cured during their incarceration, including one man whose leg was to have been amputated prior to his admission, but who, on the completion of his sentence, 'left the prison in a perfect state of health'.[31] He might almost have quoted from the *Acts of the Apostles*: 'many taken with palsies, and that were lame, were healed'.[32] As an expert witness, he defended the verdict of the coroner's inquest into the death of Obaker Higgles, who, he said, had entered the prison extremely ill and had received every care possible prior to his demise due to the 'Visitation of God', and he concluded his remarks by paying tribute to Aris, noting that 'I have not only been an eyewitness to his attention and humanity, but have frequently heard the prisoners express their gratitude for his kindness to them'.[33]

And yet, the governor told the magistrates, despite the benign conditions they enjoyed, some of the ungrateful mutineers had hatched a plan to murder both the surgeon and one of his own sons who worked as a turnkey. One of these prisoners 'was to pretend to hang himself, and upon the alarm being given by the others, in case the Doctor or my Son came, they were immediately to be destroyed'.[34] The plot had been foiled only because one of the mutineers had betrayed his companions. Aris believed that such behaviour resulted directly from the visits of Burdett, who had encouraged the mutineers to hope, and in so doing 'excited so turbulent a spirit ... that great danger is to be apprehended'.[35] The implication was clear to all: given such instances of unrest, the moratorium on Burdett's visits should remain in place.

With the magistrates' glowing report on the table of the House of Commons, the government now felt confident in acceding to the continued calls for a further investigation to be conducted by members of the House itself. On 1 March – the very day of the report's submission – Rowland Burdon gave notice that it would be referred for further scrutiny by a Select Committee on Tuesday 5 March. Given that the Committee resolved not to examine any of the prisoners,[36] and that its ranks were dominated by Pittites including Wilberforce, Richard Ellison, Viscount Belgrave, Sir John Mordaunt and William Dundas (the dutiful nephew of the secretary of state for war), its findings were a foregone conclusion.

Reporting to the Commons on 19 April, Dundas told the assembled MPs that the prison stood in a high, airy and dry situation; that the Committee had found it to be clean; that the health of the prisoners was good and their provisions wholesome; that the treatment of Colonel Despard had been at all times reasonable; and that no complaints had ever been made to the inspecting magistrates.[37] In an attempt to demonstrate balance, he also acknowledged that the prison's printed regulations had not been displayed as they should, and that its journal had not been properly maintained. But these were trifling shortcomings and in all other respects he and his colleagues thought the prison 'unexceptionable; and from the attention of the visiting Magistrates they were convinced that no abuse on the part of the gaoler would have escaped their vigilance'. They went further still, expressing the hope that their work 'would serve as a sufficient answer to the absurd and wicked reports which had been circulated respecting the prison, which in every way seemed to fulfil the purposes for which it was intended'.[38]

Unfortunately, the following day, Dundas was forced to admit that in examining Nicholson's private journal an entry had been found in which the clerk described how, on 21 March, Despard had called Rowland Burdon 'a villain! a scoundrel! a perjured man! – that he would have his revenge as soon as he got out! – that he would spit in his face! ... that to tell a falsehood in the House of Commons, though not upon oath, was as atrocious as perjury!'[39] There could be little doubt that the cause of Despard's outburst was the MP's continued assertion that the colonel had repeatedly denied that he had been poorly treated and that he disowned his wife's account of his circumstances. However, rather than admit that this evidence shed new light on the inquiry, Pitt preferred to look upon Despard's utterances as a 'matter which materially concerned the dignity of the House and the public peace'. His anxiety, therefore, was not that Burdon might have misrepresented the facts, but that a sitting MP had been insulted by a prisoner accused of High Treason.

On 21 May, the Commons debated the three resolutions contained within the Select Committee's report: that the prison was well situated and suitable for its purpose; that it was clean and healthy, and its provisions good; and that the work of the visiting magistrates should be described as exemplary and meritorious. Pitt had always expected that Burdett would use the abuses at Coldbath Fields as a vehicle for a broader critique of government policy, and he would not be disappointed. As the baronet stood before his peers to attack the report and to demand a full and proper inquiry into conditions at the prison, it quickly became apparent that he could barely contain his furious indignation. Beginning with a rhetorical flourish, he observed that, in the current climate, he could not hope to meet with success; but at one time things would have been very different, because then:

> before the Minister had seized upon the Bank, the produce of the East and West Indies had been converted into engines of ministerial corruption

and power, the National Debt increased to 400 millions, and the Habeas Corpus destroyed – before Secret Committees had forestalled the privileges of Grand Juries, and the conduct of Englishmen had been subjected to the scrutiny of salaried Police Officers and pensioned Informers, no House of Commons would have suffered such treatment as existed within the walls of that prison, much less would it have patiently borne with those insults to one of its own members which he had received.[40]

But that time had passed, and it was too late to complain of such treatment because 'a new-fangled system had gained ground, by which the Crown was everything, and the people nothing'. In pursuing his own investigations into the Coldbath Fields House of Correction he had been doing nothing but his duty, but at every stage the government and its supporters had sought to place obstacles in his way, appointing secret committees and traducing his reputation and conduct. The reason for their behaviour was, he told the House, obvious: they knew that they must do everything possible to disguise the cruelties their own actions had given rise to: 'They acted with becoming caution, for a fouler system of torture had never been practised in any nation' and, if allowed the opportunity, he would 'adduce proofs capable of covering with confusion the faces of men not much accustomed to blush'.

Burdett swiftly moved on to cite disturbing admissions made during the examinations of the prison's staff. The governor, he pointed out, 'acknowledged upon oath, that he struck the prisoners both with his stick and his fist', prisoners whose persons, he contended, 'ought to be as inviolable as that of a King'. But Aris defended his actions on the basis that he feared for his life; the surgeon, too, claimed to be fearful of the prisoners and both men suggested that their lives had been plotted against. Was it not strange, Burdett asked, 'that prisoners should entertain a design of butchering their humane keeper and their health-bearing Surgeon'? As for the death of the vagrant, Obaker Higgles, on 13 December 1798, he observed that, in his inquest report, Edward Walter,* the coroner, recorded that on the day prior to his death Higgles had eaten some broth, 'and it also appeared that

---

* Of the 531 deaths for which Edward Walter conducted inquests between 23 October 1800 and 18 April 1802, and during 1803, a total of 93 (17.5 per cent) aroused the suspicions of Mary Beth Emerichs, who cites the low levels of investigation by the police and coroners as a primary reason for the high incidence of verdicts such as 'Died by the Visitation of God' and 'Found Dead'. See Mary Beth Emerichs, 'Getting Away with Murder? Homicide and the Coroners in Nineteenth-Century London', *Social Science History*, 25, 1 (2001), pp. 93–100.

he was amply provided with bed clothes as there were three beds in the room, two of which were unoccupied, [and] he had taken the whole of the clothes, all of which were found upon him in the morning'.[41] Thus, cried the baronet, 'It had been proved that the poor wretch swallowed two quarts of broth a few hours before his death. I would ask you, Mr Speaker, whether he was hungry? He was covered with the clothes of three beds; I would ask you, whether he was cold?'[42]

Burdett went on to refer to another two prisoners who had died of consumption, their disease being brought on, he felt convinced, by the ill-treatment they had suffered during a confinement of eighteen months. And what of the extortion routinely practised by Aris, who, he claimed, had made more than £1,000 by charging fees for every article of food, and even demanded a fee for admission to the hospital? Gaolers, Burdett concluded:

> had seldom been humane, but it was the interest of this steeled Gaoler to be cruel. The question, however, was not now respecting what he might be supposed capable of doing, but respecting what he had actually done. He and his servants had the power of depriving the objects of their resentment of pen, ink, and paper, and consigning them cold, hungry, motionless, and heavy-ironed, to dark cells, where they could, unobserved, inflict upon them blows, torture, and death. His charge was that this power had been used. His complaint was that some of his ill-fated victims had died, and that others were now dying under such punishments.[43]

Rather than approve the resolutions of the Select Committee's report regarding the prison's good management, he would prefer to be locked in one of its loathsome cells – a fate to which, he wryly noted, 'he was perhaps already destined by the Minister'. The Committee's report should be laid aside, and a new inquiry immediately initiated.

Burdett had begun his oration by expressing his conviction that his motion to have the Select Committee's report rejected would be defeated; unsurprisingly, his prediction came true. Despite the well-argued and witty support of Richard Brinsley Sheridan and William Wilberforce Bird – a cousin of the abolitionist and one of the few members of the Committee who deplored his colleagues' refusal to take the evidence of prisoners – the report received the overwhelming approval of the House. With just five MPs voting with Burdett, his defeat would have been assured even had the seceding Foxites returned to the Commons to support him. His one minor success was the acknowledgement of Sir William Young, a member of the Committee and author of the anti-democratic tract *The Rights of Englishmen*, that Aris should have been disciplined for borrowing money from prisoners, and that 'he ought not to have been suffered to remain a moment longer in his situation'.[44] If, however, this overwhelming victory convinced the government that it had finally laid the issue to rest, it would soon find itself very much mistaken.

John Howard (1726–90) drawn and engraved by Thomas Holloway, 1791. It was Howard's impassioned criticisms of Britain's crumbling prisons that led to the construction of the new house of correction at Coldbath Fields. (Wellcome Collection)

A view of the prison from Gray's Inn Lane. Wood engraving by James Peller Malcolm for *The Gentleman's Magazine* (1796), and one of the first published images of the new prison.

'House of Correction, Coldbath Fields', drawn by Thomas H. Shepherd and engraved by W. Watkins for *London and its Environs in the Nineteenth Century* (1829).

James Gillray's 'Citizens Visiting the Bastille' (1799) depicts the arrival of the campaigning Sir Francis Burdett at the gates of Coldbath Fields House of Correction. The troll-like gaoler is presumably the prison's governor, Thomas Aris (1743–1840). (Staatliche Museen zu Berlin, Kunstbibliothek/Dietmar Katz)

Sir Francis Burdett (1770–1844) lithograph by Antoine Maurin after a portrait by Sir Thomas Lawrence. Despite having been encouraged to enter the House of Commons as a means of distracting him from womanising, Burdett would prove to be a passionate conviction politician and the prison's chief critic. (Via www.lacma.org)

John Courtenay (1738–1816) by James Sayers. Soldier, poet, literary critic and MP, Courtenay would prove an able lieutenant to Burdett during his campaign against the prison and the government that maintained it. (Courtesy of Princeton University Library)

William 'Billy' Bosville (1745–1813), detail from a cartoon by James Gillray (1806). An ardent Whig and champion of political reform, Bosville accompanied Burdett and Courtenay on their very first visit to the prison in November 1798. (Via Art Institute of Chicago)

Richard Brinsley Sheridan (1751–1816) by Thomas Williamson, after Sir Joshua Reynolds. The Anglo-Irish playwright would become the prison's most eloquent critic in the House of Commons. (Library of Congress)

George Tierney (1761–1830) by George Hayter. Another vocal supporter of Burdett in the House of Commons, Tierney enjoyed the unusual distinction of having fought a duel with the sitting Prime Minister, William Pitt the Younger. (National Gallery of Ireland, Wikimedia Commons, CC A 4.0)

A later illustration depicting seamen complaining about their rations prior to the Mutiny at the Nore. (*Cassell's Illustrated History of England*, 1865)

Colonel Edward Despard (1751–1803) by an unknown artist after Thomas Lawrence, *c.* 1790. A war hero and progressive colonial administrator, Despard was arrested on 22 April 1798 under the terms of the Habeas Corpus Suspension Act, and would become Coldbath Fields' most high-profile inmate.

William Mainwaring (1735–1821), shown (right foreground) in James Gillray's 'A Hackney Meeting' (1796). As chairman of the Middlesex Sessions and an ardent defender of Thomas Aris, Mainwaring was the magistrate who became most closely associated with the abuses practised at Coldbath Fields. He would also stand against Burdett in the Middlesex parliamentary election of 1802. The other foreground figures are (centre) George Byng (1764–1847), MP for Middlesex, and (left) Charles James Fox (1749–1806). (Yale Centre for British Art/Yale University Library)

Gillray's depiction of the 1804 Middlesex election shows Burdett's supporters dragging his coach in time-honoured fashion. One banner proclaims, 'No Bastille', while another portrays William Pitt whipping Britannia. The headgear of the figures in the right foreground suggest that Burdett's supporters were Jacobins. (Via Art Institute of Chicago)

An early illustration of William Cubitt's 'Discipline Mill', or treadmill as it would more commonly be known. First installed at Bury St Edmunds in 1819, by early July 1822 eight had been installed in the yards at Coldbath Fields.

Prisoners picking oakum under the 'Silent System', c. 1860. The system was introduced at Coldbath Fields on 29 December 1834, in preference to the alternative 'Separate System'. Both were imported from the United States.

8

'Disgraceful to Humanity'
Debates and Inquiries

During his campaign for a properly constituted inquiry into the mismanagement of Coldbath Fields, Burdett had been criticised for using the suffering of state prisoners for party political purposes, and for not having investigated sooner the conditions of the misdemeanants who made up the bulk of the prison's population. Of course, he and a number of supportive Whig MPs had used the treatment of state prisoners to highlight the abuses to which the suspension of habeas corpus lent itself, and it was neither surprising nor reprehensible that his researches had broadened only with the passage of time. As radicals and Whigs alike had repeatedly asserted, imprisonment without charge or trial would inevitably attract widespread condemnation, and Burdett had naturally begun his investigations with those cases that had seemed most egregious under the terms of the British constitution. Nonetheless, in the face of the continuing jibes, he must have felt a degree of satisfaction when, in May 1800, he received another shocking report, the publication of which even his most determined opponents would struggle to dismiss as being politically motivated, the victim in the case being neither a radical nor detained under the terms of the Act.

Burdett's informant was William Dickie, a stationer on the Strand who, as well as having the unusual distinction of being J.M.W. Turner's preferred supplier of sketchbooks,[1] had served as foreman of the Traverse Jury for the County of Middlesex during May. According to the information provided by Dickie, a 13-year-old girl named Mary Rich* had been

---

* Possibly Mary Rick [sic], the daughter of Sarah Rick, who was born in Gray's Inn Workhouse on Mount Pleasant, Clerkenwell – just yards from where the prison would be built – and baptised on 1 November 1786 at St Andrew's, Holborn.

brought to testify before the county's Grand Jury during its examination of William Dell, whom she accused of rape. However, on the day of her appearance at the grandiose Sessions House towards the end of May the filthy, rag-clad Rich had been so weak that she could barely sit upright, and the jury deemed her too ill to give evidence. In a stark example of the topsy-turvy practices of the day, as a material witness who also had the misfortune to be indigent, Mary had been committed to prison while her alleged assailant roamed free. When asked by the jurors how she had become so debilitated, she explained that during the month or more she had spent in the house of correction, she had been given nothing but bread and water to eat and drink, and her only defence against the cold of her cell had been a threadbare blanket – and even this had been taken from her when another prisoner gave birth: a facility equipped for the detention of hundreds of prisoners supposedly having no other wrapping suitable for the newborn baby.

Having listened to Rich's story, the jury immediately requested the attendance of the responsible members of the Middlesex magistracy in the jury room. When questioned, the magistrates, in turn, expressed themselves dismayed by the child's condition and ordered the governor and the surgeon to appear before the jury, bringing with them the order for Rich's commitment. We have no way of knowing whether the jurymen knew of the glowing report on the prison issued by these magistrates the previous year, but given the wide publicity it received at the time, and the equally well-publicised derision that it and the prison's management more broadly had provoked in some quarters it seems highly probable that they had. In recent weeks the heated exchanges in Parliament had been widely reported in the newspapers, and commentators as disparate in style and attitude as Samuel Taylor Coleridge and James Gillray had joined the fray, the former suggesting that the Devil would happily take Coldbath Fields as a model 'for improving his prisons in hell',[2] while the latter, in his 'Citizens Visiting the Bastille' (January 1799), had portrayed Burdett as a Jacobin rake and Aris as a corpulent troll. Either way, determined to get to the bottom of the matter, and fearing that 'some misinformation' might be given by Aris and the surgeon when interviewed, the eighteen members of the jury decided to visit the prison themselves.

They issued their report, or presentment, to the General Session of the Peace on 27 May. It was not as damning as some might have anticipated; indeed, 'from the cleanliness and good order preserved there', the jury considered the house of correction to be the 'best conducted prison we ever saw, for prisoners after conviction, the article of bedding alone excepted, which certainly appears to us by no means sufficient, even for the summer season'.[3] For those held without conviction, on the other hand, they thought 'directly the contrary, inasmuch as no provision is made for them, but bread and water, and the difficulty, if not the impossibility, of obtaining admission for their friends to see them, renders it a melancholy and dangerous situation'.[4]

They also opined, very much in the spirit of Burdett, Courtenay, Tierney and others, that keeping men, women and children in such conditions 'appears to us contrary to the principle of our happy Constitution, which has wisely provided that no punishment ought to take place till after conviction'.[5] As for Mary Rich, they believed that she should be immediately removed and given 'every comfort and convenience the nature of her case requires'. The appearance of the infirmary they considered very good, but noted that they had discovered two prisoners 'in separate cells (one locked up), both very ill' who had not received medical aid or been transferred to the infirmary, despite its being practically empty of patients. They ended their report with a recommendation that the magistrates themselves undertake a 'serious and attentive enquiry' into these issues, 'trusting, at the same time, that the same sentiments that induced us to obtain this information will also influence you to render the situation of the unhappy persons confined there as free from complaints of this kind as the nature of their cases will admit'.[6]

This would not be the end of the matter. In English law, the role of a Grand Jury was to examine the conduct of any person accused of a crime and, if the evidence warranted it, to make formal charges on which the suspect would later be tried. In this respect, its functions might be compared to those of the modern Crown Prosecution Service, but with its duties undertaken at a local rather than a national level. A Grand Jury would not determine guilt or innocence; nor would its dealings with a witness usually go beyond testing their evidence. In contrast, the role of a Traverse, or Petit, Jury was to try the accused under the supervision of a trial judge. For either jury, let alone both, to investigate the conditions in which a witness, or even an accused person, had been held was highly unorthodox – and yet this is what now happened. Apparently inspired by the work of the Grand Jury, the members of the Traverse Jury for Clerkenwell decided to conduct their own inquiry, even though the trial of William Dell had not even commenced.

Led by William Dickie, the jurors visited the prison twice, on 30 May and 4 June. They spoke first with the Nore mutineers, but not before asking the turnkeys to withdraw so that the prisoners 'might with the greater freedom communicate to us the treatment they received; because when we first questioned them they hesitated, being fearful of answering, dreading the severity of the Governor in case he should know they made any complaint'.[7] So far as provisions were concerned, the mutineers acknowledged that their allowance had increased somewhat as a result of the previous inquiries, but they remained constantly hungry nonetheless. There had been no improvement whatsoever with regard to the extreme cold that they suffered, with each prisoner's bedding limited to a thin mattress filled with chaff, a small horse-rug, and a coarse blanket, 'all of the worst quality, and which we consider by no means proper or sufficient bed or covering for any human being'. Many prisoners also complained that 'they had scarcely a bit of shoe to their feet' and that the rapacity of the governor and his staff continued unchecked, with money being both stolen and extorted from them.

After interviewing James Jones, the mutineer who had been so severely beaten by Aris that he still remained confined to his bed, the jurors moved on to the kitchen. Here they found the cooks preparing a meat broth which, on tasting, they thought 'rich and very good' – until they learned that, prior to being distributed, it would be mixed with at least three times as much water, 'with oatmeal, rice, and sometimes potatoes'. Such a mixture, they agreed, must make a 'very poor broth'. At this juncture, did they recall that one magistrate had told William Wilberforce that the prisoners enjoyed 'as good food as ever he had at his own table'?

Like the Grand Jury before them, the Traverse jurors found the infirmary unobjectionable but suspiciously empty, and in one of the yards they met several men and boys who seemed very ill and desperately hungry, but who were denied both medical assistance and admission to the medical ward, including one inmate who 'said he had been greatly afflicted with the flux for two years past, which his weak appearance denoted'.[8] Having seen this much, they stopped to consult and concluded that, while they had met several prisoners who had good cause to complain at their treatment, every part of the prison that they had so far seen appeared to be very clean. Here they might have been expected to bring their investigation to an end – but they remained suspicious 'in consequence of some information we obtained, that we had not seen all the prisoners, or been taken to the worst part of the gaol'.[9] It was these suspicions that led them to return on Wednesday 4 June.

On their second visit, the jury made their way into a gallery they had not previously inspected, where they found many more prisoners who complained of illness and malnourishment, attributing their ailments 'to bad treatment and want of sufficient food'. They claimed that the medicine they received provided no alleviation of their symptoms 'as they believe it is nothing but vinegar and water (we have since been informed that it is vitriol and water),* and the same sort of medicine is administered for every different disease'.[10] These inmates also repeated the accusations of neglect by Thomas Webbe, with one man 'who seemed to be in a high fever, and unable to sit up' claiming that the surgeon had not only refused to visit him more than twice during an illness lasting many months, but also told him that, if he could not digest the standard prison food, 'he might go without any'. The surgeon's only concession had been to allow him one pint of milk each day.

If the conditions in which these men lived seemed deplorable to the jurors, they could hardly find words to describe those endured by the prison's population of debtors, paupers and vagrants, whose wards 'exhibited a *true picture of wretchedness, disgraceful to humanity*'.** In a corner of the first of these rooms, they met a man named Davis who had 'scarcely a rag to cover him'. Dickie, 'anxious to ascertain the real situation of the prisoners' approached him, 'but was so overcome by the disagreeable stench of the place that he could hardly retire without fainting'.[11] Next, they proceeded to an upper room occupied by those detained under the Vagrancy Act of 1792, meaning a constantly changing population made up from what George Rudé has described as 'the floating population of vagrants and beggars, the "miserable", the destitute, the unemployed and unemployable, the indigent, the aged, the part-time domestic workers, the casual workers, the poorest of the immigrant Irish and Jews'.[12] Here the jurors witnessed yet more scenes of abject misery: prisoners, emaciated, filthy and semi-naked, 'tortured with vermin, which they caught from the filth of the place', living on just 1lb of bread and water per day, and with eight men sharing just three threadbare mattresses. And poverty, declared the outraged jurors, 'is the offence which subjects our fellow-creatures to such cruel treatment!'

Burdett read both reports in their entirety to the House of Commons on 11 July. Having done so, he forbore to comment any further on their contents, merely stating his wish that they should be laid on the table of

---

*   Possibly cupric sulphate, or blue vitriol, which was used as an emetic.
** The italics are the jurors' own.

the House, that the assembled MPs should form a committee to consider the facts placed before them, and that the jurors and the Middlesex magistrates should be called to the bar to be examined.

In seconding his friend's motion, Sheridan was altogether less circumspect. If the House refused an inquiry in the face of such 'shameful and incontestable facts', he argued, 'it would be lost to every sense of what was due to its own dignity, its justice, and its humanity':

> When he supported the worthy Baronet on the subject last year, he was fully impressed with the real injuries to which the poor unfortunate persons confined in Coldbath-Fields were exposed; but from the papers which the House had just heard read it appeared that the mischief was not then distinctly and wholly felt; the situation of the prison was imperfectly known. The Magistrates were then imposed upon by the artifices of the Governor, so as to give a favourable account of the state of things; the Judges who approved of the conduct of the Magistrates from their benches had been imposed on; and in consequence of that the House was also imposed on. The House, therefore, was unintentionally made a party in all that exaction, oppression and cruelty, which had since taken place within those walls.[13]

As might be expected of the author of *The Rivals* and *School for Scandal*, Sheridan had turned his phrases very carefully. While accusing the magistrates of a dereliction of duty in not properly supervising the management of the prison, he placed the blame for the cruelty and corruption not at their feet, but at those of Thomas Aris, who showed them only 'those places which would best bear inspection, and everything which would tend to criminate him in the least, was studiously kept out of sight'. In effect, Sheridan was offering William Mainwaring and his fellow magistrates an opportunity to avoid much of the blame if they would support a full inquiry, and thereby demonstrate their own desire to get to the truth.

Mainwaring, however, was in no mood to accept the implicit offer, preferring instead to challenge the legitimacy of the Traverse Jury's report. With 'some warmth' he called it 'unauthentic, inflammatory and false', and declared that while he and his fellow magistrates had received the presentment of the Grand Jury, all the Traverse Jury had ever submitted to them was a copy of their rough notes or memoranda. On receipt of these documents, the magistrates' Prison Committee had amended the prison's regulations to address the issues that had been brought to their attention and, to support his assertions, he read a list of all the fixtures and fittings that the Committee had found to be serviceable in the prison, though he chose not to mention that the list had been compiled by Aris, rather than by the Committee members themselves.[14]

The magistrate then turned his attention to the case of Mary Rich. This girl, he told the Commons, lived in extreme poverty, being one of six children whose mother undertook piecework, making soldiers' buttons at a penny a dozen, while her father earned about 12s a week. All they could afford was 4 or 5lb of meat each week to feed a family of eight. In the opinion of the magistrates' Prison Committee, these facts suggested that Mary 'was treated better, and lived more comfortably in the gaol than ever she had done with her parents'. Mainwaring concluded by observing that if Burdett's motion for documents to be laid on the table of the House was restricted to the Grand Jury's presentment and the report of the committee of magistrates, he would not object.

With Burdett, Sheridan and Tierney ranged on one side, and Mainwaring, Sir John Mitford (Scott's replacement as Attorney General) and William Windham, the Secretary at War, on the other,* the toing and froing continued, the radicals demanding that the reports of both juries should form the basis of any inquiry, while the magistrate and ministers objected to that of the Traverse Jury being included, on the basis of its not being 'perfectly official'. In the process, Tierney took umbrage when Mitford seemed to doubt that his motives were altruistic rather than political, but the attorney general, no doubt remembering the Irishman's reputation as a fire-eater and duellist, swiftly apologised. Sheridan, meanwhile, mocked the Prison Committee's implied suggestion that, because Mary Rich's 'parents were poor, the wretched meagre diet of the gaol was excellent food', and asked what had happened to William Dell, the alleged rapist? He, it seemed, remained at large, while his victim was imprisoned, perhaps at the behest of Dell himself who, given the reputation of Aris and his myrmidons, might even have bribed them to keep and starve the poor child. 'Where, in the law of England,' he demanded, 'do the Magistrates read that a person complaining of an injury, a prosecutor, is to be detained in his own cause; and kept on bread and water?'[15]

The debate ended in a truce, its terms allowing for the presentment of the Grand Jury, the report prepared by the magistrates' Prison Committee

---

* The Secretary at War was responsible for running the War Office, the post being distinct from, and subordinate to, the Secretary of State for War.

and the notes of the Traverse Jury to be laid before the House. However, the questions regarding the formation of a Committee of Inquiry and the inclusion of the Traverse Jury's full, if unofficial, report remained unresolved. These issues would be decided at a later date once the first tranche of documents had been examined.

The second debate took place on 22 July. As previously agreed, the Prison Committee's report of 10 July had been submitted for the inspection of the House, but its contents did nothing to allay the concerns of the radical members – quite the opposite. After quizzing Mary Rich about her parents and diet when living at home, the committee had noted that she had not complained regarding her treatment to either the turnkeys or to Webbe, the surgeon. Moreover, when they questioned the prison's nurse (herself an inmate) regarding the child, she had stated:

> that from the conversation she had had with Mary Rich she was sure she was a bad little girl; that she had told her that she had been with several boys on the stairs in a way not proper to mention, and had received half pence from them; and that if the gentleman who she had indicted for assault upon her had given her what he promised her, she would never have made any complaint against him, or made any alarm.[16]

This evidence, the committee declared, had convinced them that Rich had been 'properly treated during her confinement and that every necessary care and attention had been paid to her'; in fact, they believed that 'she had lived better since she had been in the Prison than in her usual mode of living with her Father and Mother'.

So far as the disgusting conditions in the vagrant, pauper and debtors' wards were concerned, Aris had explained to the committee that 'it is impossible to keep [them] so clean as he ought from the great number of vagrants passing thro' the Prison ... that they are frequently sent in the most filthy and diseased state, [and] that every possible attention is paid to them'. As for the accusations of extortion made against him and his children, naturally he could explain these away, too, as mere misunderstandings or lies. Webbe had also been called before the committee and, with hand on heart, had declared the prison to be 'perfectly healthy'.

Predictably, this report made Burdett furious. Of what possible relevance was the poverty of the girl's parents, he demanded: 'Is this any excuse for the barbarity of depriving her, when sick, of her only covering, and leaving her to lie [in] a cold and damp cell?' The Prison

Committee made much of the fact that she didn't complain: but to whom would she make such a complaint? Perhaps to the nurse 'who afterwards trumps up the infamous and contemptible story of the child's improper conduct; who tore away from her the blanket with which she was covered'?[17] And who did the Prison Committee interview regarding the multiple failings in the prison's management? Why, those responsible: the gaoler, the surgeon and the parson – 'the very men who could not speak the truth without criminating themselves ... The very nature of the prison was such that a man might be murdered in it, and no one know anything about the matter'. It was a melancholy reflection, he observed, 'that Magistrates should be found in this country to sanction, by their approbation, such infamous cruelty, such infamous injustice, so gross a violation of every law of feeling and humanity', and concluded by moving, once again, that the entire House of Commons should resolve itself into a committee in order to fully investigate the Coldbath Fields House of Correction – a motion passionately and ably supported by Sheridan.

Just as he had on 11 July, Burdett had begun the debate by declaring that he did not anticipate success. While an inquiry seemed to him to be a natural consequence of the evidence laid before the House, he admitted that conversations he had held before entering the chamber had induced him 'to look forward with less confidence of support than he had once expected'.[18] But, on this occasion, his pessimism proved misplaced: seemingly against the odds, his long campaign was about to experience a remarkable reversal in fortunes.

Although the attorney general followed the well-trodden path of denying the need for Parliament to become involved, even going so far as to declare that 'Persons in charge of prisoners were forced sometimes to be a little arbitrary' in order to preserve peace and good order, he was almost immediately wrong-footed when William Dundas, the well-connected MP who had given the prison a clean bill of health in April 1799, agreed with Sheridan that the Prison Committee's report was 'utterly indefensible', though he still doubted the appropriateness of a parliamentary intervention. Even worse for the flabbergasted Mitford, Pitt himself now intervened, admitting that 'there were circumstances in the case which no man could see without dissatisfaction' and agreeing with George Tierney, his erstwhile duelling opponent, that instead of a parliamentary inquiry the House should prepare an address to the king, requesting that a Royal Commission should investigate the state of the prison. To the bewilderment of Mainwaring, who had supported the

Prime Minister through thick and thin, he went still further, observing that 'No man would think of *justifying* the *conduct of the Magistrates*, who had shewn a *want of that feeling* and circumspection so essential to form the genuine character of a *wise, upright*, and *humane* Magistracy ... *the Magistrates were to blame*'.[19]

Burdett must have been as surprised as Mitford and Mainwaring at this unexpected turn of events but, with the one proviso that the House should not 'think it enough to redress grievances, but to prevent the like in future', he immediately withdrew his original motion, and moved instead 'That an humble Address be presented to His Majesty, praying that he would be pleased to order an inquiry to be made into the state and management of His Majesty's Prison in Coldbath Fields', the motion being carried unanimously. For his part, Sheridan was delighted, telling his wife that the debate had 'turn'd out more to my satisfaction than almost anything I ever took a Part in since I have been in the House of Commons. I made the Speaker *bitter* – and I really think I smote Pitt's conscience. In short we carried our Point ... the Good is done'.[20]

Of course, Pitt's consent had been given only grudgingly, and the government might easily have delayed the inquiry's prosecution. However, the events of August 1800 would help to generate for the first time a genuinely shared sense of urgency: those events demonstrating that, unless its defects were remedied, the prison threatened to become a focus not merely for parliamentary debate, but for much more dangerous and widespread popular unrest.

As John Courtenay had made clear in his speech of 21 December 1798, the prison's reputation for brutality and neglect had spread far and wide in the preceding years, at least among those in the lower echelons of society. Burdett's campaign in Parliament had substantially increased awareness, with newspapers of all stripes carrying reports of the debates, often in great detail. And, as he had hoped, the story of Mary Rich's suffering had engendered genuine outrage, with some papers beginning to run articles overtly critical of both the prison and its defenders. On 25 July, for instance, the *Albion & Evening Advertiser* observed that 'the public at large will rejoice to find that its Representatives are alive to the honour and reputation of the nation, and individual Members will take a pride in contributing to rescue it from the foul imputation of almost unheard-of cruelty'. It went on to note ironically, if inaccurately, that when 'Mr Pitt visited the prison at Coldbath-fields, he found there, in irons, two persons who had been his most strenuous supporters when he was the advocate of Parliamentary Reform'.

Besides the accounts of Mary Rich's experiences, perhaps the testimony that generated the strongest reaction was that of the Nore mutineers immediately before and after their release at the beginning of August – testimony that almost certainly possessed an enhanced resonance because of the recent revelations in Parliament. On 26 July, just days after Burdett shared Rich's story with his fellow MPs, the prison became the scene of a second coroner's inquest into the death of Luke Early (or Eardley), a Royal Marine mutineer from HMS *Saturn*, who had died in the prison's infirmary on the 14th. Held 'in consequence of a request to the Coroner, that sufficient evidence had not been produced on the former inquest',[21] the purpose of this second hearing was to determine whether the original verdict of death 'by the Visitation of God' had been appropriate.

The mutineers who had asked for the second inquest were not permitted to give evidence, the nature of their crime having rendered them ineligible, but the coroner found other witnesses.* Predictably, Webbe, the surgeon, claimed that Early had been in poor health when first imprisoned; that, in consequence, he had been given extra allowances of bread, beer and milk; that he had been prescribed an 'acid medicine which was much used' – presumably the ubiquitous vitriol and water; and that he had himself visited the prisoner practically every day when he remained in his cell, and two or three times a day after his removal to the infirmary ten days prior to his death. 'Being questioned if he had ever heard the deceased say he died through cruel treatment, and for want of food', Webbe declared that 'he had not'.

In contrast, a prisoner named Hawkins, who had been a patient in the infirmary when Early was admitted, told the jury that the mutineer had complained of a fever, 'and told him, that if ever a man was murdered by cruel treatment, he was, as he had been ironed and locked up a long time,

---

*   According to the Lord Chief Baron, Sir Jeffrey Gilbert, 'there are several Crimes that so blemish, that the Party is ever afterwards unfit to be a Witness, as Treason, Felony, and every *Crimen falsi*, as Perjury, Forgery, and the like'; however, Gilbert also notes that 'the King's Pardon restores the reputation', enabling its recipients to once again become credible as witnesses. See Gilbert, *The Law of Evidence* (London: Rivington et al., 1777), pp. 139-41.

and kept short of provisions, and his meat had been repeatedly kept from him'. William Price, a turnkey, corroborated this evidence, stating that when the mutineers had placed a tin-can on a fire to heat its contents, the governor had objected to the smoke and called their actions an offence. He had then forbidden their use of a fire and ordered that the meat allowance for three prisoners, including Early, should be stopped, 'and sometimes it had been stopt two and three days as a punishment'. When questioned about the frequency of the surgeon's visits to Early, Price answered that Webbe had certainly seen him between 28 April and 4 June, but he could not recollect whether Early had requested more frequent visits. Pressed on the matter, the turnkey reluctantly admitted that 'the deceased might have asked him once or twice, or perhaps oftener'. Another prisoner, bravely or recklessly, also contradicted the surgeon's evidence, stating that, despite innumerable requests, he had not visited the mutineer more than twice in the thirty-seven days between the end of April and the beginning of June. Finally, he noted that Early had found his meat allowance inedible, being 'very hard and black'.

According to John Impey, a noted eighteenth-century legal commentator and expert on coronial duties, 'If a prisoner's death be owing to cruel and oppressive usage on the part of the gaoler, or any officer of his, it will be deemed wilful murder'.[22] In addition, Dr Michael Ryan, another subject-matter expert, would later observe that, though murder by 'inanition or hunger ... seldom happens ... it is well known that cruel and unnatural parents, step-fathers and step-mothers, occasionally destroy children and young persons by famine or starvation'.[23] Given that such murders were not unknown, in cases such as Early's he believed it 'important to inquire whether life has been extinguished by cold, hunger, poison &c', and went on to enumerate the symptoms of starvation that a corpse might be expected to exhibit, including emaciation, red and open eyes, dryness of the tongue and throat, empty stomach and intestines, and an absence of feculent matter in the bowels. Though Ryan was writing some thirty years after Early's death, his comments and methods of diagnosis were current in 1800, and not the product of later developments in forensic medicine or medical jurisprudence. And yet, no post-mortem was conducted on Early's corpse, and no second medical opinion sought. Instead, despite the evidence of neglect by the prison's surgeon, and of arbitrary cruelty and starvation by the governor, the coroner's inquest upheld the earlier verdict that the ex-marine had 'died a Natural Death by the Visitation of God'. Although the name of the coroner who conducted the inquest is unknown, Early had, it seems, received the same degree of justice as Coroner Edward Walter had dispensed in the case of Obaker Higgles in December 1798.

The second mutineer to attract particular attention was James Johnston, a seaman from the frigate HMS *Cyclops*. Johnston had met the Traverse jurors on their second visit to the prison on 4 June, when they had found him 'unable to stand on his weak limbs'.[24] He told them that he had been cruelly treated and starved, and that when he had applied to the surgeon for aid, Webbe had accused him of shamming; 'but you see, Gentlemen,' he had continued, 'I do not sham it; the gaol allowance I cannot eat ... my weak state denotes my situation'.[25]

Johnston had been one of the mutineers denied a voice at the inquest into Early's death, but by smuggling a letter out of the prison he was at least able to state the cause of what he knew to be his own imminent demise. And in J.S. Jordan and John Smith – the same John Smith that Courtenay, Burdett and Bosville had visited in the prison in November 1798 – he found radical members of the book trade more than willing to publish his account, which they included in their *Impartial Statement of the Inhuman Cruelties Discovered! in the Coldbath-Fields Prison*. 'In the presence of God,' wrote the mutineer:

> I solemnly declare that the principal, and I really believe only, cause of my present sickness has been occasioned by the severity of my confinement, want of food to support nature, and bad attendance when first afflicted. I have not the strength nor ability to enumerate the many instances of cruelty I have experienced, but suffice it to say (and it is not possible at this awful moment, I should belye my dying soul) that my death has been occasioned by the above stated reasons, the truth of which I call God the Almighty to witness.[26]

After his discharge from the prison on 4 August, Johnston would make a sworn public statement regarding the abuses practised in Coldbath Fields. Although the *Albion & Evening Advertiser* considered the accusations in his affidavit to be 'of too serious a nature' to be published during the course of the formal investigation, it did release some of the less contentious facts: that Johnston was clearly in 'a most melancholy condition'; that he and his friends believed him to be dying; that he spoke out in order to 'bring to Justice the man whom he accuses of having been instrumental in reducing him to his present deplorable condition'; and that he had lost 70lb in weight during his incarceration.[27]

Crucially, as well as enumerating the already familiar stories of beatings, starvation and neglect, Johnston outlined the tactics that Aris had used to conceal his activities: how he had told the mutineer that he would be moved to a room 'where there was always a good fire and should have double allowance of provisions with a pint of Beer daily, provided he would impeach his fellow prisoners ... and promise to report to the Magistrates or any Gentlemen that visited the gaol that [he] was well treated by the Governor!'[28] Courageously, Johnston had refused to falsely accuse his fellow prisoners in order to obtain better treatment for himself — but he knew that other inmates had not been so strong-minded, and that they had been persuaded to lie regarding their condition. He also related how, when the parliamentary Select Committee had inspected the prison in March 1799, he had been locked in a bare cell known as 'the Stone Jug', so that he would be hidden from Wilberforce, Dundas and the other MPs tasked with undertaking the investigation. Despite the reticence of the newspapers when reporting the details of his affidavit, Johnston could now rest easy in the knowledge that he had done everything possible to expose Aris's cruelty; unfortunately, he would not live to witness the effects of his denunciation: he died in St Bartholomew's Hospital on 24 September, aged just 27, with the subsequent inquest presided over by coroner Thomas Shelton finding that he had expired, like Higgles and Early before him, as a result of the 'Visitation of God'.[29]

Perhaps inevitably, the surfacing of these disturbing cases, when added to the prison's already dark reputation and the widely publicised criticisms made by Burdett and his supporters — to say nothing of the government's equally well-publicised opposition to reform — acted as a catalyst for popular, if very localised, unrest. The trouble erupted inside the house of correction itself on the evening of 14 August. *The Times* reported that 'a refractory spirit' had been discernible among the prisoners for some days, and at around 7.30 p.m., as the turnkeys began to lock their charges in their cells for the night, the prisoners resisted and had to be forced inside, where they began hissing, groaning and shouting loudly enough to be heard by passers-by outside. Well aware of the stories emanating from within the gaol's walls, and with word passing swiftly from door to door, and from tavern to tavern in the immediate neighbourhood, a large mob soon gathered, possibly numbering as many as 6,000.[30]

Anxious to understand the cause of the disturbance, some in the crowd called to the prisoners, who replied by yelling 'Murder! Murder!' and 'Starving alive!' and abusing the magistrates 'in the grossest terms'.[31] According to one breathless report:

As some particular whistles were heard on the outside, and answered from within, a fear arose that the whole was the effect of concert; that the Prisoners had agreed to make a tumult; that their partisans should assemble without, and collecting a mob, whose feelings might be worked upon, the Prison gates should be assailed on both sides, destroyed, the Prisoners released, and the Prison pulled down.[32]

Sir Robert Baker, the chief magistrate at Hatton Garden, agreed that the crowd, 'being worked upon by the apparent distress of those within, showed symptoms of a readiness to assist them if they could have made a violent effort to escape'.[33] Only too well aware that during the Gordon Riots of June 1780 the mob had demonstrated a powerful enmity towards all the institutions of criminal justice, attacking many of London's prisons, including Newgate and the Fleet, as well as Clerkenwell's New Prison and old Bridewell, Baker was in no mood to take any chances. With smouldering resentment threatening to burst into full-scale rioting, he called out a large contingent of policemen and volunteer militiamen, the latter being equipped with a small field gun, which they positioned at the prison's main entrance, ready to be swung in any direction.

The advent of these forces proved decisive, and by 10 p.m. the crowd – 'fearing from appearances that firearms might be used'[34] – had been dispersed and the prisoners silenced without any overt acts of violence being perpetrated by either side. However, Baker and his fellow magistrates remained nervous, and they maintained the presence of the volunteer corps for the next few days, while the twenty felons identified as ringleaders or active participants were kept in irons pending further investigations. Police officers outside the prison also arrested a man named Williams, whom they believed to be 'very active in promoting the disturbance', though he was released after providing sureties of £600;[35] whether he had any connection, familial or otherwise, with the H. Williams who had been identified as one of the prime movers inside the prison is unknown.

Despite the fear that the nascent riot had been orchestrated, the evidence suggests that the events of the 14th had not been planned in advance. When interviewed the following day, a convicted felon named John Nicholson told the magistrates that he had overheard a conversation between some of the leading rioters just minutes before the unrest began. According to Nicholson, these prisoners 'proposed last night to make the alarm, to gather a Mob round the Prison to rescue them out and make it as a free

Gaol ... some of them asked how they should make the alarm and it was agreed they should call out "Starving alive in the Bastille"'.³⁶ He also heard them vow that they would no longer pick oakum, and that 'their allowance was not sufficient to keep them in Existence'. At this juncture, two of the prisoners clambered up to peer from their cell windows and, seeing pedestrians passing by below, said 'then was the time to make the alarm ... we should give them three Huzzas and say "Starving alive" ... we'll call out "Bloody Murder" three times, which was done. We heard the clashing of Tongues without but could not hear what was said'. By no stretch of the imagination does this sound like a carefully planned demonstration or prison break.

The Times claimed that some, at least, of the prisoners had been inspired by reading *An Impartial Statement of the Inhuman Cruelties Discovered! in the Coldbath-Fields Prison* – copies of which were later found in the prison – and the publication may have encouraged them to believe that their plight had become a focus for popular indignation which they might turn to their advantage, but that is all. Nor was there any truth to the rumour that the recently liberated mutineers might have been responsible for rabble-rousing. In fact, 'by some very good management', all bar Johnston and one other man had been seized by a press gang as soon as they left the prison[37] – an act that at least one observer thought the product of 'some underhand work to get those men out of the way', and thereby prevent them from giving evidence about their treatment.[38]

Whatever the immediate causes of the riot, there is no doubt that the government believed in the existence of a genuine risk of popular unrest, and that this belief helped to expedite the inquiry that had been agreed to in the House of Commons on 22 July. It probably also recognised that any attempt at delay would be met with resistance, even within its own ranks. Certainly, the popular press supported the inquiry, with the *London Packet or New Evening Post* declaring its hope that it would be conducted 'with impartiality and vigour'. At the same time, it opined that prison governors should be:

> men worthy of the trust, and who are qualified to reconcile humanity with the discharge of their duty. We do not think, upon the information now authentically before the Public, that the Keeper of Coldbath Fields does so; and it is the necessary effect of oppression and cruelty to beget revenge and violence.

The conservative *Morning Post* agreed, expressing the hope that the riot would 'not prevent the strict and active inquiry into the general conduct of that place ... If it should, the disturbance will be as fortunate an occurrence as those who may be blameable could wish'.[39]

By 20 August, the *Albion & Evening Advertiser* could report not only that 'perfect tranquillity' had been restored in the prison as a result of the 'cautious and spirited' conduct of the magistrates, but also that the Royal Commission had been appointed. At its head, the Duke of Portland had placed the well-known prison reformer Sir George Onesiphorus Paul.

Like John Howard, Paul had first become interested in prison reform when he served as High Sheriff for his county. Having inspected the tumbledown and pestilential Gloucester Prison in 1783, he had begun a campaign for the building of a new prison and county Bridewells, and in 1785 succeeded in obtaining a special Act of Parliament to ensure that sufficient funding was made available. Designed by William Blackburn – the same William Blackburn who had accused Aaron Henry Hurst, the architect of Coldbath Fields, of plagiarism – Gloucester's new prison had opened in July 1791 and boasted a chapel, two infirmaries and workrooms for debtors, making it a model for future institutions.

To many on the government benches, Paul must have seemed an inspired choice. On the one hand, he enjoyed great credibility as a committed prison reformer second in repute only to Howard himself. On the other, as a magistrate, a member of the establishment and a regular guest at St James's Palace, he might also be expected to temper any criticisms of Pitt's administration. The rest of the Commission were also broadly sympathetic to the government, and included Sir Robert John Buxton, abolitionist and MP for the pocket borough of Great Bedwyn in Wiltshire; Sir Christopher Willoughby of Baldon House, Oxfordshire; John Spranger, one of the Masters in Ordinary of the Court of Chancery; William Morton Pitt, MP for the County of Dorset and a distant kinsman of the Prime Minister; John Berkeley Burland, a conscientious Somerset magistrate and future Tory MP for Totnes; Charles Shaw-Lefevre, the MP for Newtown on the Isle of Wight; and William Baker, the independently minded and humane MP for Hertfordshire, who had nonetheless opposed the lifting of the suspension of habeas corpus and denied that the Act had been abused.

There could be no doubt, then, that so far as the government was concerned the deck had been stacked in its favour. However, given the nature of the disclosures in the Commons and Pitt's surprise denunciation of the Middlesex magistrates, William Mainwaring, Thomas Aris, Dr Webbe and others must have awaited the Commission's findings with considerable unease; after all, less than a month earlier the Prime Minister had, in the most public fashion imaginable, indicated precisely where convenient scapegoats might be found.

9

'An Improper Place of Confinement'
THE ROYAL COMMISSION

In accepting the role of chairman of the Royal Commission, Sir George Onesiphorus Paul had complained that high summer was 'certainly not a time of year when it can be supposed that a journey to town and an attendance on an important Object of Inquiry can well accord with the other engagements of the Season',[1] and he had successfully petitioned for a slight delay in beginning the inquiry. As a result, it was not until Monday 22 September that he and his fellow commissioners made their first visit to Clerkenwell. Having obtained this concession, all the evidence suggests that whatever their political allegiances, he and his colleagues approached their new task conscientiously. Certainly, their 112-page report, which was laid before the House of Commons on 18 December 1800, was far from being the whitewash that many had anticipated, and some had undoubtedly hoped for.

The commissioners admitted that they could find no general grounds for complaint regarding the buildings' cleanliness, but they also pointed out that their inspection had been advertised well in advance and that any deficiencies might, therefore, have been addressed prior to their arrival. Suspicions on this score were underpinned by the condition of the prisoners themselves, many of whom they considered to be unacceptably dirty as a result of bathing being widely neglected and 'the washing and cleansing of Prisoners at entrance' having been 'entirely laid aside'.[2] Nor could they locate a single bath 'except a Tin portable one', to be shared by more than 200 prisoners.

Their findings were also heavily caveated on the subject of the inmates' health. On the one hand, the annual mortality rate had been satisfactorily low at a little below 3 per cent since the opening of the gaol. On the other, typhus had become widespread since 1799 – a development which Webbe attributed to the disease having been brought in by newly admitted prisoners. The Commission did not include a physician, but Paul's wide experience left him in no doubt that Webbe was obfuscating and that, in reality, the spread of gaol-fever must be attributed to a combination of factors: overcrowding; cleanliness and ventilation not being properly attended to; and the prisoners often being cold and still dressed in the filthy rags in which they had been admitted. However clean the prison might appear, the evidence clearly suggested that it was no stranger to squalor.

The commissioners believed that, overall, the low incidence of sickness furnished 'decided Proof of [Webbe's] Ability as well as of his Attention to the Sick',[3] but they also noted that, on investigating a suggestion that the surgeon had contrived, 'from corrupt Motives', to engineer the early release of a prisoner named Crowder, they thought the accusation 'so far substantiated as to be deserving Investigation before Magistrates competent to call for legal Evidence'.[4] While Webbe's skill might be obvious, his integrity remained deeply questionable.

When the commissioners interviewed the prisoners, they recorded that the 'Two prominent and general Complaints, and which indeed followed us through the Prison, were the Insufficiency of the Bread Allowance, and the Want of Warmth during the Day Time, in the Winter Season'.[5] So far as the cold was concerned, this seemed to be due entirely to faults in the prison's design and construction: the fact that the cells were unheated and their ventilation wholly dependent upon the shuttered but unglazed windows meant that 'the prisoners must either suffer extremely from cold, if they open the doors ... or from bad air if they keep them shut'.[6] As for the bread ration, during their visit the commissioners weighed twenty-eight loaves, and found seventeen over the stipulated weight, and eleven below – this variation being caused by the manner of baking and then separating them. 'This Inequality should be avoided', they observed, because 'a Prisoner estimates his Claims positively, and can never be led to consider the Injury done him by short Weight on One Day, as compensated by the Addition which may accidentally fall to his Share on another'.[7]

The vagrants and debtors, in particular, thought their prison allowance inadequate, especially when their circumstances rendered them unable to supplement their rations with food brought from outside the prison – and 'when they have not any Benefaction from the accidental Attention of the Cook'. Inequalities of this nature became a particular focus for the commissioners, who noticed that the situation was exacerbated by the written rules of the prison, which, as a result of frequent additions and revisions, had become confused and contradictory. To this confusion, they contended, and, above all, 'to the uncontrouled and seemingly unquestioned Operation of the Surgeon's Power to supersede both Rules and Orders, may not only be traced the Distinctions, but to such Distinctions may be attributed much of that Restlessness and Insubordination which has lately marked the Conduct of Prisoners confined in this House'.[8]

They also thought the timings of food distribution problematic. With the prisoners' first spartan meal served at 8 a.m., and their second at around midday, and with no facilities to save any of their food until a later hour, most fasted for a substantial portion of each day. 'As the Lower Classes accustom themselves to eat frequently', noted the report, 'in the Case of a long Term of Imprisonment, this Circumstance may be Injurious to Health; it may however be considerably relieved by fixing a later hour for the Delivery of the Dinner Meal'.[9]

Besides the shortage in the prisoners' rations and the issues relating to distribution, perhaps the commissioners' single greatest cause for concern was the potential for extortion and bribery. As well as finding means by which to encourage the 'benefactions' of Joseph Ballard, the cook – a man who, they noticed, 'appears to us to act a more considerable Part in the Management of this Prison than belongs to his peculiar Office'[10] – wealthier prisoners could pay to wear their own clothes, rent better rooms and even, 'by permission of the Surgeon … purchase Liquors forbidden by the General Regulations'.[11] This last breach of regulations they thought particularly reprehensible, as it involved the whole hierarchy 'in Criminality: the Surgeon, by his Permission to admit Liquors, which are sold for other than Medical Purposes, and without any Order in Writing … ; the Cook, in selling the several Liquors … ; and the Governor, by knowingly permitting these Acts to be done'.[12]

Overall, the commissioners believed that those inmates supplied with ready cash could procure almost anything they wanted, meaning that 'a pennyless and friendless Man, and one who has Friends and Money at command' would have very different experiences, despite being imprisoned for identical offences. Under such a system, they concluded, 'there cannot fail to arise a Competition in the Means of Bribery, which must end, if not in the Corruption, at least in the most dangerous Temptation, of him who has the Decision in his Power'.[13] A later commentator, but one familiar with the management of the prison, put it rather more bluntly, claiming that the 'first question addressed to a prisoner on his arrival, was, "had he money, or aught convertible into money, or would any friend, if apprised of its utility, supply him with money?'"[14] If the answer to this all important question was 'yes', then the prisoner might be protected, to some degree, from the worst excesses of gaol life. But that protection would last only as long as his cash, and with spoliation and trickery everywhere, he would soon find himself reduced to dire straits, the weakest being defrauded even of their daily ration of bread.[15]

Extraordinarily, given the obvious balance of power within the prison, the commissioners placed the blame for this systemic corruption not at the feet of Thomas Aris and his staff, but at those of the prisoners themselves, suggesting that they 'have but too well known how to suit their Proposals to the Wants of the Governor, and that in fact he has been sometimes tempted beyond what he has had Fortitude to resist'.[16] According to this interpretation, any demand for bribes on Aris's part was due not to his cupidity, but to simple – even excusable – human frailty.

Due to an excessive number of commitments by the magistrates, the governor not only omitted to strictly segregate the different types of prisoner, he also failed to obey regulations regarding the single occupancy of cells. The dimensions of these cells, the commissioners wrote, 'is certainly not greater than is necessary for the healthful Respiration of the One Person intended to be lodged in it; to lodge Two Persons in this Space is to counteract the Principle and subvert the Intentions of the Law'.[17] An analysis of the throughput of prisoners revealed that:

> within the present Year, Three Hundred and Twenty Prisoners have at one and the same Time been confined in this Prison, and that the Average through the Year has been Two Hundred and Sixty-five: It must then have happened, that One Hundred and Forty Persons have been so confined, as to sleep and live Two in a Space, provided and adapted to One person; and that, on an Average, Thirty Persons have so slept and lived.[18]

Moreover, since the prison contained only 248 bedsteads, 'Half of these Numbers have certainly slept without separate Bedsteads, and most of them probably without separate Bedding'.[19] Questions of hygiene aside, given that Howard had described solitude and silence as being critical to the encouragement of reflection and repentance, these failings could hardly be more damning of the prison's management.

Again in direct contravention of Howard's recommendations, the commissioners considered that Aris had been 'very deficient in point of obedience to those rules which enjoin him to execute the duties of his office in person, and by no means to be possessed of the requisite knowledge of what is passing in the prison'.[20] However, they do not appear to have considered whether the governor's pleas of ignorance were genuine, or merely a means by which to deny direct knowledge of, and complicity in, systematic rule-breaking.

Like the Grand and Traverse juries before them, the commissioners were at pains to point out that they had given every prisoner an opportunity to articulate his or her concerns, acknowledging on the one hand their awareness of the 'Caution and Reserve' that should be used when considering 'the Testimony of Persons suffering under the Restraints of a Prison, against those whose Duty it is to impose them', while on the other giving prisoners an opportunity to speak 'without Constraint from the Presence of the Governor or other Officer of the Prison'.[21] Overall, they thought it 'Much to the credit of the prisoners in general' that:

> we did not find them disposed to loose and unreasonable Complaints. Amongst the Convicts, particularly, we found Men ready to distinguish between Circumstances which necessarily follow a State of Imprisonment, intended to be their Punishment, and those which arise from Misrule and Neglect; the Points they felt as Grievances were few and specifically stated, so that it was not difficult to enquire into and satisfy ourselves of their Reality.[22]

In making such a statement, had the commissioners read the affidavit of James Johnston, in which he claimed not only that prisoners had been bribed to lie about their treatment in the gaol, but also that those who refused to be bribed were hidden from the inspectors?

Of course, stories regarding the regime's brutality had been reported widely, and the commissioners considered it 'impossible not to observe, and highly to blame, the irregular Facility with which the Punishment of refractory Behaviour has been inflicted'.[23] They noted that 'On Occasions of important Outrages ... we remark some Instances of Reference to the Authority of Magistrates', but they could find no trace of the formal log of disciplinary action that the prison's statutes required; 'nor does it appear', they continued, 'that any Regard has at any Time been paid to those Limits in Point of Time, and Circumstances of Punishment, which the Law has specifically directed'.[24] In addition, given that Paul had no authority to safeguard prisoners by ordering their removal to other gaols, what possible confidence could any witness have that they would be protected from the governor's wrath should they dare to tell the unvarnished truth? Being questioned without prison staff in attendance would grant a degree of anonymity, but would it be enough? In the event, it seems that no one dared to criticise the governor because the commissioners recorded that 'With regard to Mr Aris's general Character for Humanity, amongst the Prisoners in his Custody, we found it unimpeached',[25] and they did not recommend his dismissal.

Ironically, it was perhaps this 'general character for humanity' that saved Aris, because the commissioners made no bones about the fact that they had found his administration of the prison to be very seriously flawed in almost all respects. So flawed, indeed, that in their conclusion they condemned it as 'an improper Place of Confinement for … several Descriptions of unconvicted Persons'. They went further still, declaring that 'until its Discipline, Regulations, and Arrangement, shall have undergone considerable Alterations' it could not be considered any more suitable 'for Prisoners convicted for Misdemeanours on Indictments at Common Law'.[26] In other words, just six years after its completion at a cost of £80,000, the Royal Commission had found Coldbath Fields House of Correction wholly unfit for its intended purpose.

What of Aris's employers: Mainwaring and his fellow magistrates? In his *Considerations on the Defects of Prisons*, published in 1784, Paul had made it clear that he believed that the inadequacies of the original Gloucester Prison were due not to wilful neglect on the part of the county magistrates, but to 'Ignorance of the melancholy Facts, with, perhaps, an indolent Dread of meeting the Difficulties attending the Execution of extensive Reform'.[27] An examination of conditions at Coldbath Fields had led to a rather more damning suspicion. While it was possible that the Middlesex magistrates had, like their colleagues in Gloucester, 'neglected to inspect or otherwise to inform themselves of the real Situation in which Prisoners are placed by their Commitments',[28] there was clear evidence that regular inspections had been made by the Prison Committee. This fact suggested that the infractions identified by the commissioners had been perpetrated '*under the eye of the magistrates visiting the prison*',[29] meaning that they had deliberately winked at the prison's manifold failings.

To make matters still worse, by continuing to commit to the prison persons detained on suspicion, for trial and to give evidence, the magistrates had wilfully and repeatedly acted in direct contravention of the 'Orders for Magistrates' of December 1799, which instructed them 'not to send to the House of Correction in Coldbath Fields, any prisoners committed for re-examination'.[30] These findings were a very far cry from those of the Select Committee of 1799, which had reported that 'the attention of the

'An Improper Place of Confinement': The Royal Commission

Magistrates, to the general management of the Prison, has been exemplary and meritorious'.[31]

Burdett had spent two gruelling years investigating and publicising the squalid, degrading, and sometimes life-threatening conditions in which the inmates of the prison had been kept. In the process he had been attacked repeatedly, both in the House and by certain sections of the press, much as if he had been a dangerous revolutionary intent on destabilising the established order: 'held up to the world as an object of odium, stigmatised by a Secretary of State, my conduct condemned unheard'.[32] But now, with the publication of the Royal Commission's report, he had been completely, and very publicly, vindicated.

And yet he remained far from satisfied; after all, personal vindication without remediation meant nothing. Having had an opportunity to digest the report, on New Year's Eve he told the House of Commons that, while he thought Sir George Onesiphorus Paul and his colleagues had completed their task in a 'highly creditable' fashion, in effect they had been obliged to make the best of a bad job, their commission being 'so limited in its powers, that it gave them no opportunity to do what they should have done'.[33] Most damning of all, the commissioners had been denied the right to administer the oaths that would have rendered their examination of witnesses 'full and effectual'. By so tightly circumscribing the powers of a commission voted for by a majority in the Commons, he argued, Pitt had defied the will of the House and thereby insulted every one of its members.

Beginning in December 1798, Burdett had brought forward a catalogue of charges against Thomas Aris. Many of these charges had now been proved, but Aris remained in his post. Why? 'The Report,' he continued:

> limited as it is, states that in this Prison no rules of protection are observed – no limits set to the arbitrary will of the Ruler – that the cells are of stone, and damp, and that persons confined in them can have no warmth communicated to them; and that the allowance of bread is not sufficient for the sustenance of man ... Such were the actual and secret abuses of the Prison.[34]

Read the Commission's report, he told his fellow MPs: 'if they had bowels of compassion they would make up their minds'.[35]

Furthermore, since the Commission's investigations, additional abuses had come to light, including the treatment of a Nore mutineer named William Redfern, who had served as surgeon's mate on HMS *Standard*. Despite a lack of evidence against him, the Admiralty had decided to make an example of Redfern because of his rank, and he had been sentenced to death by his court martial; however, this sentence had been commuted to a term of solitary confinement in Coldbath Fields, to be followed by transportation to the penal colonies of Australia 'for and during the Term of his natural Life'.[36] Although the details are scanty, it seems that Redfern had become sick while in prison and that during his illness he had been fed a piece of cow's udder 'so bad that the milk was found in it, and proved to be in a state of putrefaction'.[37] When challenged, Aris had initially denied Redfern's claims, but he had been forced to acknowledge their truth when Webbe, 'who had humanity', supported them.

Unlike Early and Johnston, Redfern had recovered, and by order of the Duke of Portland in November 1800 he had been moved to a prison hulk moored off Portsmouth to await transportation.[38] But, again Burdett demanded, 'what was the consequence of such complaint and remonstrance?' Redfern had been transferred from his dank cell to a pestiferous and rotting hulk to await a voyage he might not survive, while Aris remained in full possession of his job, his house, and his salary.*

On 5 February 1801, Burdett tried a different tack, moving that a record of the income and expenditure of the house of correction for the last three years should be laid before the House. It seems that this motion was in the nature of a fishing trip rather than being based upon any certainty of financial malfeasance because he declined to answer when William Dundas asked him his reasons for requesting the accounts, and while the motion was ordered the matter appears to have progressed no further.

Burdett was on his feet again just four days later – and this time with much greater confidence. He wished, he told his peers, to call their attention 'to a transaction which ... had just come to his knowledge, and which he should deem it a criminal neglect of his duty not to mention':

> It was marked with such peculiar circumstances of atrocity as imperiously demanded the immediate interference of the House – nothing short of an instant and effectual remedy could serve to vindicate the

---

* William Redfern (1775–1833) would not only survive his voyage to New South Wales, he would thrive, eventually becoming one of the colony's most successful medical practitioners and a pioneer in public health reform.

character of the country where such an act of unparalleled cruelty was committed. It had occurred in Coldbath Fields prison; that notorious scene of persecution, where the most inhuman practices had too long been suffered to prevail; where, even while the Committee appointed to enquire into the state and conduct of that prison, were supposed to be actively employed in the exercise of their duty, the same barbarous treatment was continued towards the unfortunate prisoners, and with increased virulence.[39]

The incident in question bore a strong resemblance to the brutal assault on James Jones some two years earlier. According to Burdett's account, at around 8 a.m. on Sunday 8 February, an unnamed turnkey had approached a prisoner named Joseph Hudson in one of the prison's yards and demanded that he surrender a 'public paper' in his possession. When Hudson refused, the turnkey had kicked him in the stomach and then attempted to strike him with a broomstick. A scuffle had ensued, other prisoners and staff became involved, and by midday the prison yard had become the scene of a tense stand-off.

At this juncture, one of Aris's sons appeared on the scene and ordered all the prisoners except Hudson back to their cells, a command which they reluctantly obeyed. Once the other inmates were once again under lock and key, Aris junior and another of the turnkeys pinioned Hudson's arms and frogmarched him up and down the yard until he was provoked to resist. This, Burdett told the Commons, was all the gaoler's son wanted: 'He took a large bludgeon and so unmercifully beat the poor man as to give him several contusions, which had produced a burning fever, in which state he now was confined in his dungeon, loaded with bolts, refused medical aid, and without any other relief than cold water'.[40] Surely, he asked, this criminality could not be allowed to pass 'unnoticed or unredressed'?

He believed that an appeal to the Middlesex magistrates would be futile; instead, he suggested, the House should submit an address to the king requesting the immediate removal of Thomas Aris, and the appointment of another governor 'pro tempore until an enquiry into this affair should take place'. The parliamentary correspondent for the *Morning Post* reported that, at this juncture, '*The Hon Baronet was silent for a time, but no Member offered to speak*',[41] and the uncomfortable silence was broken only when Black Rod appeared with a message requesting the presence of the Commons in the Upper House in order to hear the Royal Assent given to a Bill relating to the use of barley and oats in the manufacture of flour.**

** The Sale of Bread Act (1801).

Burdett could hardly take the silence as being indicative of support for his recommendation.

The matter was raised again on 12 February, when the wealthy Tory MP for Plymouth, Sir William Elford, told the House that he had visited Coldbath Fields to satisfy himself regarding the facts behind the story, and that he now considered it 'extremely important that the public should be undeceived'.[42] Although Elford boasted that he was 'as independent of the favour or rewards of ministers' as the most self-righteous of Whigs,[43] in reality he had relentlessly petitioned Portland and Pitt for the baronetcy that he had been awarded in November 1800, and he could be relied upon to toe the government line enthusiastically. Burdett, he claimed, had been naïve in allowing himself to be persuaded to publicise the complaints 'of such a worthless character as this mutineer'. And, while he accepted that Aris had 'misconducted himself in various instances' and 'should be dismissed from his office', in this particular instance he had been 'falsely accused'.[44]

During his visit to the prison Elford had interviewed the governor, the turnkeys, Hudson, and Dr Webbe, and their testimony, he assured the House, had convinced him that it was Hudson, not Aris junior, who was to blame for the events of 8 February. He had 'behaved very ill' to two other inmates, and when Aris had intervened, he 'had beat him too'. The blows the mutineer received in return had been 'very light' and the fever which succeeded had been the result of a severe cold, and not of an assault. Elford did not, he said, accuse Burdett of wilfully misleading the House, but he believed that he had 'too easily believed the factious and interested assertions of Hudson'.[45] The possibility of Aris and the turnkeys' testimony being equally 'factious and interested' seems not to have occurred to him. Instead, to prove the truth of his assertions, he moved that Aris – a man whose dismissal from office he had advocated only moments before – should be called to give evidence at the bar of the House.

Much to Elford's embarrassment, at this juncture his motion was enthusiastically seconded not by a member on the government benches, but by Burdett, who could probably hardly believe his luck. Benjamin Hobhouse, James Martin and Evelyn Pierrepont all supported him, with Pierrepont condemning Aris's conduct as 'infamous, scandalous, and shocking', and Martin declaring that the governor's continued employment 'was a disgrace to the country'.[46] Despite this passionate advocacy the result of the debate was, once again, a defeat for the government's opponents, the motion being quashed by forty votes to twenty-one – no doubt to the immense relief of the humiliated Elford.

Although, in the aftermath of the debate, *The Times* expressed its surprise 'that no change has taken place both in the Executive Authority and the Constitution of that Gaol', and quipped that 'for our own part ... we think its *Aris*-tocracy is much too violent and intolerable',[47] *Bell's Weekly Messenger* perhaps came closer to summing up the general weariness with the subject when it described the recent exchanges in the Commons as a 'long, desultory, and uninteresting conversation'.[48] After all, while Burdett had campaigned tenaciously within Parliament, and had eventually obtained the long-sought-for Royal Commission, in reality, what had been achieved in terms of genuine change? With the prison still operational, with Aris still in post, with the same body of magistrates overseeing its functioning and with Pitt's government more than ever content with the status quo, even Burdett's most sanguine supporters would struggle to point to any truly meaningful achievements. In these circumstances, how could he hope to continue the fight and, more importantly, continue it with sufficient backing to enjoy even the remotest prospect of success?

10

'The Ambition of an Honest Man'
THE MIDDLESEX ELECTIONS

The answer to the question of how Burdett would continue his campaign came in the unexpected form of a letter addressed to him from a group of Middlesex freeholders, headed by two erstwhile members of the Society for Constitutional Information, Michael Pearson and William Tooke.

Originally from Cumbria, as a young man Michael Pearson had trained as an apothecary and surgeon in Hatton Garden before establishing a successful practice at No. 34 Spital Square. But, as well as being 'ever ready to assist with his advice the needy and the destitute, and to afford them every relief that the nature of their case might require',[1] Pearson was highly active politically, being a champion of John Wilkes during the Middlesex election dispute of 1769 and a founding member of the Revolution Society eleven years later. He also became a close friend of John Horne Tooke who, in his *Diversions of Purley*, described him as 'my steady and uniform accomplice and comforter in all my treasons; equally devoted with myself to the rights and happiness of our countrymen and fellow creatures'.[2]

For his part, William Tooke had made a substantial fortune as a factor dealing in woollen cloth at Blackwell Hall on Basinghall Street in the City of London. He, too, had championed Wilkes and had helped to found the Society of Gentlemen Supporters of the Bill of Rights. He had also been a patron of John Horne Tooke, who had adopted his surname in acknowledgement and also, probably, in the hope of a generous legacy. However, like William Wilberforce, the reactionary abolitionist, Tooke demonstrated a distinctly confused, and confusing, code of ethics. As well

'The Ambition of an Honest Man': The Middlesex Elections

as being a champion of constitutional reform in Great Britain, he was a co-owner of the Diamond Estate, a 500-acre sugar plantation on the east coast of the island of Grenada – an estate entirely reliant for its productivity on the use of slaves – and a signatory of the 1783 address to George III from the profoundly anti-abolitionist London West India Committee.

In their letter, which Burdett received on 26 June 1802, three days before the dissolution of Parliament for the forthcoming general election, Pearson and Tooke told him that:

> Having heard, from various quarters, of an intention in many freeholders to offer you their vote at the general election, as a fit person to represent the county of Middlesex in the next Parliament, we are anxious to know whether, in such event, you will stand forward, in compliance with their wishes. Our own votes, as well as our exertions among friends, depend on your answer; for, assure yourself, we feel as you feel, with respect to the late ministers and their measures.
>
> As Englishmen, we concur in your abhorrence of the use and management of such a prison as that in Coldbath Fields. As freeholders, we desire an occasion to express the sentiments we entertain of your manly opposition to the establishment in Middlesex.
>
> In any case, we trust a majority of our fellow freeholders will agree with us, that Sir Francis Burdett is more worthy than Mr Mainwaring to represent the interests, deliver the sense, and support the rights of the first county in England.[3]

According to his father-in-law, Thomas Coutts, recent experiences had left Burdett so disenchanted with national politics that he had actually contemplated 'transferring his fortune and residence to some foreign country'.[4] Nonetheless, he replied to Pearson and Tooke's overtures the same day, telling them that, though disenchanted, he did not despair, and he remained convinced that 'our country may still be saved; but by one means only: by a fair representation of the people in Parliament'.[5] And, in 1802, few counties epitomised the unfairness of existing parliamentary representation better than Middlesex. With a population of a little over 818,000,[6] it sent only two MPs to the House of Commons, with the electorate made up of around 6,000 men who owned property or land with a rental value of 40s or more per annum.*

---

* For the purposes of comparison, according to the Office for National Statistics in 2017 the average population of a parliamentary constituency was 72,200 in England, 67,200 in Scotland, 68,300 in Northern Ireland and 56,000 in Wales.

Certain that constitutional reform was absolutely essential if the British were to 'obtain the restoration of those invaluable rights which have been ravished from us', Burdett agreed to stand as a candidate for Middlesex, and to 'chearfully and zealously' devote himself to the service of its people. He believed the county's electorate to be 'more free, informed, and independent' than any other, but he knew, too, that the election would be hard-fought. After all, given that Middlesex was represented by just two MPs, and that one of the two seats had been held since 1790 by George Byng of Wrotham Park – a popular Foxite and, with an annual income of £20,000, one of the wealthiest of Whig commoners – the real contest would be between himself and the Tory candidate, who was none other than that stalwart of the establishment, chairman of the Middlesex Sessions, and champion of Thomas Aris, William Mainwaring, who had held the seat since 1784.

Riot, the French philosopher and historian Elie Halévy memorably observed in his *History of the English People in the Nineteenth Century*, 'belonged to the English political tradition'.[7] The truth of this assertion was never more apparent than during a contested election, when the enfranchised and disenfranchised alike poured onto the streets to cheer or deride the would-be representatives of the freeholders of each constituency, their antics fuelled by gin and ale paid for by the candidates, and all too often descending into brawling and the hurling of brickbats, which the parish officers struggled to contain or, deeming discretion the better part of valour, allowed to run their course unimpeded.

One contemporary French observer, who watched the mayhem in a state of fascinated revulsion, later remarked that there was 'an entire absence of dignity and greatness' in English electoral proceedings, and that he found in their place nothing but 'mean parody and wretched farce'.[8] Painting in the middle years of the eighteenth century, William Hogarth seems to have thought much the same thing, because in the four canvases of his *Humours of an Election* we see a depiction of unalloyed venery, corruption, drunkenness and violence. Not that the English system was entirely without its champions. 'Cockades,' the Irish John Courtenay told the House of Commons, 'and the liberty of huzzaing are things which every Englishman admires, and they contribute to give him an idea of the rights he enjoys, and on the possession of which he prizes himself [sic]'.[9] All of these characteristics would be displayed in spades on the streets of London during the Middlesex campaign of 13 to 29 July 1802.

Naturally enough, Burdett's supporters took as their rallying cry 'Burdett and no Bastille!' and the abuses attributable to the Habeas Corpus Suspension Act, to Thomas Aris and by association to William Mainwaring, would loom large throughout his campaign, despite the fact that the short-lived Treaty of Amiens of 27 March 1802 had brought a temporary end to the war with France, and the release of the vast majority of prisoners held under the Act.

The three candidates dined together at the White Hart Inn, Uxbridge on 8 July, but a discordant note was struck almost immediately. Toasts were drunk, cordially enough, to Byng and Burdett, but when the health of Mainwaring was proposed, one of the baronet's supporters provocatively suggested that the health of Governor Aris should be drunk at the same time. In reply, a reporter for the Whig-leaning *Morning Chronicle* noted, 'Mr Mainwaring complained of the practice of coupling this man's name with his', which then prompted Burdett to remark that 'you confess you are ashamed of your friend'. 'No, Sir,' answered the magistrate, 'I always considered him an honest, humane, and upright character!'[10] Mainwaring's humiliation continued later that day when in the north Surrey town of Staines the church bells rang out for his opponent, 'and continued their festive peals for about half an hour'; he, in contrast, and despite the fact that he owned a country seat in the neighbourhood, was 'very unfavourably received throughout. With him hisses, groans, and no Bastilles were the order of the day'.[11]

The conservative *Morning Post* immediately recognised the power of Burdett's sloganeering, acknowledging at the very beginning of the campaign that he and his friends 'have made a very active and successful canvass; and the populace are almost universally enthusiasts in his favour, exclaiming, "Burdett and no Bastille"'.[12] Mainwaring's supporters were no less aware, and the same reporter noted that they wished, most ardently, 'to set the Coldbath Fields prison wholly out of the question, denying the fairness of mixing it with Mr Mainwaring's eligibility as a Candidate'.[13] Of course, their wishes counted for nothing and on the first day of polling, 13 July, Burdett's cavalcade, consisting of some fifty coaches, accompanied by outriders, a band and 'about twenty butchers in white jackets, with marrow-bones and cleavers',[14] started for the hustings at Brentford with his dark blue and gold banners flying and his battle cry seemingly on everyone's lips along the way.

In time-honoured fashion, all three candidates' coaches were stopped en route, and their horses replaced by enthusiastic (or hired) supporters who dragged them the last part of the way. Once again, however, 'neither popularity or populace' attended Mainwaring and, despite the best efforts of his entourage, 'he was received with hisses instead of huzzas'.[15] Nor would there be any respite for the discomforted magistrate when the speeches began. Alderman Harvey Combe, a past Lord Mayor of London and Whig MP for Westminster, proposed Burdett, his nomination being seconded by William Breton of Forty Hall in Enfield, who, in 1792, had served as a committee member of the Society of the Friends of the People,[16] an organisation designed to encourage lower and middle class demands for parliamentary reform, but made up, like the SCI, almost exclusively of wealthy and aristocratic members.

Combe limited himself to a relatively anodyne summary of Burdett's merits as a politician and as a man. Breton, on the other hand, launched into a vitriolic attack on the recent administration in general, and on the Tory candidate in particular. 'Brother Freeholders', he began:

> Among the few privileges that remain to us, is that of calling to account our former Representatives, on occasions like the present. It is in virtue of that privilege that I arraign the conduct of one of your late Representatives ... Gentlemen, I did accuse, I was accusing, and I do still accuse Mr Mainwaring of being a uniform supporter of all the wicked measures of the late accursed Administration which brought the country into intolerable distress, and nearly into irrecoverable destruction ... I ask, Gentlemen, whether Mr Mainwaring did not vote for the Act which renders you liable to be treated as felons, in case of the petitioning Parliament in the manner conformable to the constitution, and the very essence of that constitution. I ask whether he did not sanction the Bastille, and whether he did not defend Governor Aris? Gentlemen, I have in my hand evidence of enormities committed in that Bastille, that could only be countenanced by a Robespierre. The only difference between the tyranny of Robespierre, and that which now provokes my censure, and which cannot fail to call down your detestation, is, that the victims of Robespierre were publicly and violently put to death when sent out, but here life was exhausted by slow and cruel means, amidst the darkness of the dungeons of the place, in order to afford a pretext for saying they perished by a natural death.[17]

Burdett took up the same theme, telling the assembled masses that his principal reason for offering himself as a candidate was his abhorrence at the conduct of Mainwaring respecting the house of correction, and that he 'could not think that a man who abetted the system on which that place was regulated, who countenanced, authorised, and defended all the cruel practices that prevailed in it, was a fit or proper person to represent you in Parliament'.[18] He then called on the father of Mary Rich to give eyewitness testimony regarding the barbarous treatment of his daughter, but at that point the county sheriffs intervened, calling the proposal too irregular to be permitted.

Over the coming days, the contest grew increasingly acrimonious with the rhetoric on both sides becoming ever more provocative, Burdett accusing Mainwaring of calling upon government influence to subvert the will of the people, while his opponent charged the baronet with treasonous practices and called his supporters 'unfit for society'.[19] There could be no uncertainty, however, regarding their respective popularity with the people as a whole. With his effigy openly paraded and mocked, his coaches pelted with mud and dung, and his supporters' windows broken, the magistrate found himself reduced to travelling 'with Police Officers, Magistrates, &c. having, at the same time, Patroles as outriders, on horseback'.[20] It was obvious, the *Morning Post* declared, that the 'populace were universally devoted to Sir Francis'.[21]

In Hammersmith, one imaginative householder hung out a sign showing a quart of water and a small piece of bullock's liver, surmounted by the caption 'Mainwaring's Hotel', while another displayed in contrast a sirloin of beef bedecked with Burdett's colours, and 'Burdett for ever' inscribed beneath. In a further demonstration on 27 July, two men paraded on the roof of a coach, one stripped to the waist, and the other flogging him, 'in imitation of the Bastille'.[22] Inevitably, violence increased in proportion to the amount of alcohol consumed, and on at least one occasion the local constables resorted to the use of cutlasses as well as their tipstaffs to disperse the mob.

Of course, while general demonstrations of popularity must be pleasing to any candidate, what really mattered were the votes of the tiny number of freeholders and, as one of Burdett's supporters observed, Mainwaring's 'long connection ... with his constituents, and his influence with his brother magistrates, afforded him not only great strength, but every means of knowing the electors and their residences'.[23] To make matters worse, Pearson and Tooke had written their letter of invitation less than three weeks before the election began, meaning that their candidate had very little time to establish and test his campaign machinery, let alone to obtain early commitments.

Given these disadvantages, Burdett had good cause to be pleased when, at the first poll, his count was only 350 or so below Mainwaring's. With the vocal support of leading Whigs including Fox, the Duchess of Devonshire and Lord William Russell, he continued to make bullish statements regarding his prospects and, as the days passed and more electors made their way across the county to the hustings, his numbers increased steadily. On the thirteenth day, Fox and Russell invited Burdett's supporters to a giant meeting at the Crown and Anchor on the eastern side of Arundel Street. Reputedly, the great room of the inn could hold upwards of 2,000 people, but still the crowd overflowed onto the streets and by 10 a.m. the traffic on the Strand, Pall Mall, St James's Street and Piccadilly had been forced to a virtual standstill.

Fearing a fiasco for the Tory candidate, the panic-stricken government mouthpiece, *The Sun*, denounced what it called the '*monstrous Coalition* between the Jacobins and the Whigs', and implored 'every friend of the Constitution who has a vote for the County of Middlesex, and remains yet unpolled ... to join in routing the Phalanx which has made so shameless an attack on public honour and public principle'.[24] But its call did little to stem the tide. By the fourteenth day, only fourteen votes separated the contenders, and on the final day of the election Burdett's euphoric supporters could claim victory, with 3,207 votes for their candidate against Mainwaring's 2,936.

Prior to being carried triumphantly back to London in a chair bedecked with laurel, the baronet told the cheering crowds that, though the election had been 'tedious and protracted',[25] it had given the freeholders an important and welcome opportunity 'deliberately to declare their sentiments of the present system of torture in the dungeons of Coldbath Fields and their opinion of Mr Justice Mainwaring and his humane friend, "The Steeled Gaoler, who seldom is the Friend of Man"'.* The Middlesex election, opined a measured editorial in the *Morning Post*, 'as a trial of the popular opinion respecting the Prison, is ... a complete triumph to Sir F. Burdett'.[26] The question now on everyone's lips, was how would Burdett capitalise on his victory – and what would it mean for both the inmates and the management of Coldbath Fields?

---

* Shakespeare, *Measure for Measure*, Act 4, Scene 2: 'This is a gentle provost; seldom when / The Steelèd gaoler is the friend of men.'

There could be no denying the significance of Burdett's electoral triumph. Nor could there be any doubt regarding the mainspring of his victory. It arose, declared the *Morning Post*, 'out of the grounds on which he placed the contest, namely, the prison of Coldbath Fields'.[27] More importantly, despite its Tory sympathies, the paper did not attempt to deny the justice of Burdett's complaints, or to refute the need for reform in both the prison and in the government's attitudes towards political dissent:

> It is admitted by candid and intelligent men of all parties that this prison is —; we must not attempt to describe it. Truth might be deemed a libel, and since truth may not be spoken we must be silent. We know by various persons disagreeing from Sir Francis in politics the character of the prison, and if we do not prove it to be a national misfortune, it is from motives of safety. The prison is known to the public; general report has not misrepresented it; and the opinion of the country respecting it has been expressed fairly in the course of the Middlesex Election. Let Ministers take warning. The people do not approve their acts of oppression, though they submit.[28]

The administration did take warning, but it responded in a manner very different from that envisaged by the editor of the *Morning Post*. In October, the Home Secretary, Lord Pelham, was credited 'with a laudable attention to the public feeling' when he announced that new regulations would be introduced to the prison, with the intention of removing 'every ground of complaint'.[29] But, in reality, far more attention was paid to overturning Burdett's electoral victory, than to addressing its causes.

On 29 July, in a manner not without modern parallels, Mainwaring had conceded defeat only with the greatest reluctance, accusing the sheriffs of partiality and telling his supporters that he intended to 'vindicate your Rights before a superior Tribunal'.[30] On the same day, William Pitt told his successor as Prime Minister, Henry Addington, that he was impatient to hear 'the result of Burdett's triumphal entry, though I think it will end without his being proclaimed first consul ... as to his being member for Middlesex, I do not suffer myself to think there is any chance of it, unless his mob decrees the repeal of Grenville's bill'.[31] The 'bill' in question was the Parliamentary Elections Act of 1770, which placed the power of deciding disputed elections in the hands of a small committee of MPs, selected by lot, thereby suggesting that from the outset Burdett's victory would be contested.

More than four months later, on 7 December, a petition from 'certain freeholders of Middlesex' was at last presented to the House of Commons, accusing Burdett and his agents of bribery and corruption during the election and asserting that Mainwaring had been unfairly denied his seat. Of course, this was a case of 'the pot calling the kettle black', and both sides had employed precisely the same unscrupulous but customary tactics, as Burdett made clear in an opposing petition. However, not content merely to let the formal parliamentary process run its lengthy course, and to allow the candidates' cases to stand or fall on their own merits, in the interim the government decided to call upon the services of one of its most effective and loyal hacks to discredit the baronet and undermine his continuing popularity.

A barrister and, during the early 1790s, a leading member of John Reeves's now defunct Association for Preserving Liberty and Property against Republicans and Levellers, John Bowles was a prolific and fiery pamphleteer, whose work was funded in part by secret service payments.[32] In his *Thoughts on the Late General Election, as Demonstrative of the Progress of Jacobinism*, he launched into a wide-ranging attack on all who had viewed the 1802 contest as an opportunity to champion constitutional reform. Such individuals, he declaimed, had been infected by the 'malignant distemper' of Jacobinism, which 'unless judiciously and powerfully counteracted ... might yet corrupt our system, infect our vitals, and, at length, prove fatal to our very existence'.[33]

Chief among Bowles's targets were John Horne Tooke and his 'pupil and friend', Burdett. Seemingly oblivious to the irony, he accused the baronet's supporters of using 'inflammatory advertisements' and 'atrocious means' in his campaign, and declared himself disgusted by their endeavour 'to concentrate the rays of popular fury against a prison in the metropolis', and, by doing so, 'consume a worthy magistrate, who had long represented the county'.[34] The frequent use of the word 'Bastille' in Burdett's campaign, he argued, proved that the prison's critics were intent on its destruction not as an end in itself, but as a prelude to full-scale revolution – just as the storming and demolition of the Parisian fortress had been 'pre-eminent among the causes which produced the subversion of the French Monarchy; so much so, indeed, that the day on which that demolition took place, became the anniversary of the French Revolution'.[35]

Having defended the suspension of habeas corpus, claiming that every committal made during the suspension had been 'with the exception only of the factious, generally approved', Bowles went on to examine and refute, in time-honoured fashion, every charge levelled against the prison's management, all of which he declared 'destitute of foundation in truth'. Once again, he implied, quite spuriously, that any criticism of the prison's regime must also be a condemnation of 'the benevolent Mr Howard', quoted selectively from the Royal Commission's findings to prove Aris's 'general character for humanity', and shamelessly used the discredited report of the Middlesex magistrates' Prison Committee to scoff at the 'most pathetic tale' of Mary Rich's alleged sufferings.

Undaunted by such flagrantly partisan attacks, at the end of July 1803 Burdett marked the first anniversary of his election with a stirring and undoubtedly provocative speech to the freeholders of Middlesex at the Crown and Anchor. Constitutional reform and a full and fair representation in Parliament remained essential, he told his audience, because without them 'Such streams of bitterness must issue forth, as would tend to unnerve every arm, to stifle every honest feeling of patriotism, and render it impossible for an honest man to know, in what way to move so as to do the least injury to his country'.[36] He went on to again condemn the now abandoned suspension of habeas corpus, which had been introduced 'under the cloak of canting morality', but expressed optimism when he cast his eyes about the room, knowing that those gathered before him 'had assembled solely upon the principles which he had just now laid down ... It had been the axiom of those in power, "Divide and govern." – Let it be their axiom, "Unite and be free."'[37]

As one commentator had wryly predicted, the inquiry into malpractice during the Middlesex election provided 'a harvest of employment'[38] for the committee appointed to investigate Mainwaring and Burdett's competing claims, and it did not report its findings until 9 July 1804 – nearly two years after the original contest. According to Lord Marsham, the committee's chairman, Burdett's return must be overturned because the sheriffs, Robert Albion Cox* and Sir William Rawlins, had 'wilfully, knowingly, and corruptly' counted fraudulent votes in his favour: a charge taken so seriously that the sheriffs would be severely reprimanded by the Speaker of the House of Commons and sentenced to two months in Newgate – a particularly humiliating experience for men who, as magistrates, had previously presided over the prison's management. However, since it had also been proved to the committee's satisfaction that Mainwaring had been

---

* In 1824–25, Cox would be held up to very public ridicule after suing the actor Edmund Kean for criminal conversation with his wife, the case being widely caricatured by George Cruikshank and others.

guilty of 'certain acts of bribery', the election as a whole should be declared void and a new contest ordered.³⁹

Substantial changes had occurred in the country between the Middlesex elections of July 1802 and July to August 1804. The peace brought about by the Treaty of Amiens had collapsed in the spring of 1803, Britain was once again at war with France, and on 10 May 1804 William Pitt replaced the ineffectual Addington to once again become Prime Minister. More importantly, perhaps, for Burdett's campaign, following the end of the suspension of habeas corpus and his subsequent release in May 1802, Edward Despard – whose case the baronet had so vocally championed during his attacks on Coldbath Fields – had demonstrated an unerring talent for self-destruction by becoming embroiled with Robert Emmet's attempts to revive the Society of United Irishmen.

Arrested at a public house in Lambeth on 16 November 1802, the colonel had been linked, albeit obliquely, with a planned assassination attempt on the king and had been charged with High Treason. Despite the testimony of defence witness Horatio Nelson, now Viscount Nelson of the Nile and a national hero, Despard had been found guilty at his trial at the Sessions House, Newington, on 7 February 1803, and on the 21st he and his six co-defendants had been publicly hanged and decapitated on the roof of Horsemonger Lane Gaol. Although Burdett knew that Despard had remained popular with the masses – so popular, indeed, that the government had feared his execution would provoke a riot – his association with the Irish rebels and his execution for treason rendered him a figurehead of doubtful utility with the all-important Middlesex freeholders.

Potentially of the greatest significance, though, was the decision of the 68-year-old William Mainwaring to withdraw from the contest, and to pass the baton to his son, George Boulton Mainwaring, a graduate of St John's College, Cambridge, and student member of Lincoln's Inn, who, thanks to his father's influence, had recently been appointed as treasurer to the County of Middlesex – a post for which he would, in due course, prove himself to be wholly, even criminally, unsuited.⁴⁰ If the blatant nepotism of the treasury appointment had dismayed many on both sides of the political divide, the nomination of George Boulton Mainwaring for a seat in the House of Commons left them stunned. The general disgust increased still further when the new candidate announced that he would not stand unless the costs of his campaign – which he estimated at £10,000 – were defrayed in full by his supporters. It was a declaration that prompted one erstwhile ally of his father's to exclaim that he, for one, would not agree to the forcing forward of 'a young man on a trading voyage with a borrowed capital to deal in politics'; it was, he thought, 'an insult on the County to fit out such a man to be their Representative', and he would vote, instead, for Burdett.[41]

Together, these factors might have produced, among Burdett's supporters, a desire for a change in the emphases of his campaign for re-election, with the abuses of Coldbath Fields, the suspension of habeas corpus, the plight of the Nore mutineers and that of the LCS prisoners being pushed to the periphery while the need for constitutional reform and the unsuitableness of the young Mainwaring for elected office were brought to the fore. But it was not to be. Believing that some, at least, of these issues might weaken Burdett's chances now that the country was again at war, his opponents focused on them to the exclusion of all else. It was a strategy that caused an angry, if unsurprised, Burdett to declare that 'it has been industriously spread by my opponents, that I am hostile to England, and the Constitution':

> During every day we have been engaged in this struggle, handbills have appeared, and it has been stated to Freeholders, that whoever voted for me, must be a friend to perjury, treason, mutiny, and revolution ... Such are the slight insinuations they throw out against my character, and think they are mere election squibs; the scurrility and vulgarity are so gross, that it only rebounds and injures themselves.[42]

He was right, because at the hustings the baronet continued to be treated as a conquering hero, while George Boulton Mainwaring and his supporters found it increasingly difficult to make themselves heard above the shouted abuse and hisses of the crowds. More broadly, the Middlesex election once again became the focus of national attention, and William Pitt, whose opposition to Burdett remained unabated, was reported to have the polling numbers brought to him each day.[43]

Of course, support for Burdett was not universal. In 1803, the moderately Tory *Morning Post* had changed hands and its new owner and editor, the hawkish Nicholas Byrne, whose political allegiances were indicated by his decision to name his son William Pitt Byrne, had quickly made it clear that his opinion of Burdett was very different from that of his predecessor, Daniel Stuart. Writing on 1 August 1803,

Byrne had described Burdett's speech to the Middlesex freeholders on 29 July, as 'the object of the execration of all who have read it, except of those few who wish to see the destruction of this kingdom by any means',[44] and Burdett himself as the champion of mutineers, rebels and traitors. But, in the face of the overwhelming demonstrations of public support for the radical ex-MP, even Byrne conceded that, by the end of the polling for the 1804 election, 'there is a moral certainty of the Baronet being returned'.[45]

Recognising their weakness, Mainwaring's electoral committee now adopted the strategy of objecting to every vote cast for Burdett, thereby substantially delaying proceedings and obliging every freeholder whose vote had been tendered but not ratified by the time polling closed to return the following day. Given that the same performance was repeated day after day, it was inevitable that some of Burdett's supporters would be prevented by press of business from returning, while others would grow weary of the farce and fail to register their votes altogether – all of which would be to Mainwaring's advantage.

By the last day of the election, 6 August, these tactics had done such damage that it became, in the words of the *Morning Chronicle*, 'an imperious duty on the Counsel of Sir Francis Burdett to demand a categorical answer from the Sheriffs as to the line they would ultimately pursue with regard to these deferred votes'.[46] Surely, the newspaper argued, all disputed votes must be assessed and ratified or rejected before the results of an election could be declared. Thomas Erskine, a leading expert on legal precedent and the barrister who had so brilliantly defended Thomas Hardy, John Horne Tooke and John Thelwall during the 1794 treason trials, agreed. According to his written opinion, if an individual had presented himself at the hustings 'to vote *for any of the candidates* during the legal continuance of the Poll, and the Sheriff has not rejected them, but has put them aside for consideration, he ought to decide upon their rights, by admitting or rejecting them before he makes his return'.[47] In the face of such authority – to say nothing of the growing restiveness of the huge crowds gathered around the hustings – the sheriffs eventually announced that, despite the vociferous complaints of Mainwaring's counsel, they would indeed examine every vote tendered prior to making their return. The result was a victory for Burdett, who was duly proclaimed the winner of the 1804 Middlesex election with a majority of just one.

Of course, the matter did not end there. Mainwaring protested, and the following day the sheriffs and the electoral assessor, Judge Newman Knowlys, the unpopular and reactionary Common Sergeant of London, once again went into conclave with lawyers from both sides. Mainwaring's counsel, supported by John Bowles, maintained that the sheriffs had acted beyond their powers by counting disputed votes after the deadline and, in support of their argument, cited the Parliamentary Elections Act of 1785, which stipulated that polling should close at 3 p.m. on the fifteenth and final day of an election. The unambiguous language of this legislation, they contended, utterly discountenanced any further examination of votes cast but not ratified prior to 3 p.m.

Predictably, Burdett's legal counsel, Thomas Plumer, took an opposite view. While he agreed that the legislation clearly stipulated that no votes could be *cast* after the 3 p.m. deadline, it did not forbid the continuing *analysis* and *counting* of votes cast prior to that time. If it were discovered, for instance, that a man had illegally voted twice, the polling would be duly amended – even if the fraud were discovered after the deadline. The principle of review and amendment after 3 p.m. had therefore been established. If a freeholder had appeared at the hustings within the stipulated period and had cast his vote, the sheriffs were morally bound to count that vote, so long as its validity had been proved. The time taken to establish that validity should not be used as a means by which to deny a freeholder his legal franchise.

Having listened to the competing arguments, it took Knowlys and the sheriffs just 15 minutes to make their final determination. Without any further discussion, the sheriffs climbed onto the hustings platform to make their announcement: they had agreed to overturn their previous decision, to discount all disputed votes not decided upon by the end of polling and as a result to declare that George Boulton Mainwaring was the duly elected MP for Middlesex, with a majority of five.

The sheriffs' declaration provoked widespread disgust. According to *Cobbett's Weekly Political Register*, 'loud and long continued hissing' discouraged the victor from attempting any speechifying, and instead he retreated ignominiously with a police escort, the same observer commenting that 'they seemed to carry him away as a set of thieves convey a piece of stolen goods',[48] while another imagined him 'seated between the humane Mr Aris and the witty and incorruptible Sir W. Curtis'* creeping home 'assisted by a regiment of constables, if not a party of military ... through back lanes and corners, greeted everywhere with the hisses and execrations of his constituents'.[49]

---

*   Sir William Curtis (1752–1829), banker and Tory politician, who served as MP for the City of London from 1790 to 1818.

In contrast, a loud cry was taken up for Burdett to be chaired from the hustings, in spite of his defeat, but it was an exhibition which he naturally preferred to avoid in the circumstances, using the excuse that, if he 'should hereafter be declared the legal representative of the county, which he had no doubt but he must be, the chairing would then be infinitely more glorious, as their victory would be quite complete'.[50] In like fashion, he dissuaded his supporters from unhitching the horses from his carriage, proceeding to town instead flanked by six horsemen carrying banners of imperial purple, with the words 'Burdett and Independence' embroidered in gold thread, and greeted on all sides by 'uninterrupted plaudits and acclamations'.[51]

But the Middlesex freeholders would never again enjoy the opportunity to chair Burdett through the streets, or to drag his horseless, banner-bedecked carriage. Though protests and counterprotests would be made by both sides, on 6 May 1805 a declaration from Burdett was read before the House of Commons in which he formally withdrew from the contest, leaving Mainwaring to claim the field. Burdett's biographer, Melville Patterson, has suggested that during the 1802 and 1804 elections Burdett had spent between £56,000 and £100,000 – roughly equal to between £4.7 and £8.4 million in today's terms* – and he had neither the appetite nor resources for yet another campaign.[52]

In the immediate aftermath of his defeat, Burdett told the Foxite MP, Thomas Creevey, that, morally, he regarded the election as 'a subject of great triumph and not of mortification ... I have done my duty and the Public acknowledge it – surely this is sufficient to satisfy the ambition of an honest man'.[53] In assessing the importance of his campaign against the management of Coldbath Fields, Patterson, too, has emphasised the baronet's altruism and nobility of character, arguing that 'it should not be forgotten that the first conspicuous action of this rich young man in Parliament was to secure elementary concessions to justice and humanity for the oppressed'.[54] More recently, Michael Ignatieff has taken a rather more nuanced view, seeing Burdett as a political opportunist who used the prison as 'a convenient but temporary issue',[55] noting that he did not raise the subject again after 1804, despite his election to Parliament as MP

---

* Source: Bank of England inflation calculator.

for Westminster in 1807, and that the restoration of habeas corpus and the liberation of the last prisoners detained during its suspension removed the impetus to use Coldbath Fields for political ends.

Both assessments hold more than a grain of truth. On the one hand, Burdett deserves every credit for his humanitarian zeal and determination. Enduring constant attacks on his character and reputation from the government and its supporters, for over five years he stuck to his chosen course, gathering and publishing evidence from multiple sources, including his own visits to the prison and his interviews with its inmates, in order to support his demands for a full inquiry into the prison and its management. And there can be no doubt that he achieved a great deal in bringing the prison's failings to widespread public attention. On the other, whether as a result of cynicism, despair or exhaustion he did abandon the subject after 1804, only alluding to it again in February 1808 when he backed Sheridan's call for a fresh inquiry into continuing abuses. In the final analysis, if his success is to be measured — as surely it must — in terms of his having secured 'elementary concessions' for the inmates of the house of correction, his campaign had been a dismal failure.

11

'He Never Did Feel Shame'
THE FALL OF THOMAS ARIS

There could be no better indicator of the extent of Burdett's ultimate failure than the fact that Thomas Aris remained in his post as governor of Coldbath Fields House of Correction, seemingly immune to all attacks and accusations, and obviously confident in the continued approbation of the Middlesex magistrates and the tacit support of government ministers.

Just weeks before Burdett's party first rapped on the prison's iron-studded gates in November 1798, Aris had welcomed the Duke of Clarence to the gaol and taken obvious, indeed justifiable, pleasure in reporting to his employers that the royal duke had 'expressed great Satisfaction on the review of every part of it' and 'was much pleased to find the Prison so quiet and all the Prisoners so usefully employed'.[1] With the sanction of a future king of England still ringing in his ears, Aris could afford to be dismissive of the criticisms of a mere baronet and, no doubt taking a lead from the offended magistrates and from the Duke of Portland's decision to ban Burdett's 'disruptive' visits, he told one witness that he would willingly have kicked the baronet out, and another that he 'would not come there any more till he came a prisoner, which would be soon, for he was a damned rascal'.[2]

In the succeeding months and years, the Middlesex magistrates' inquiry of March 1799 had found Aris guiltless of any serious misconduct, as had the subsequent parliamentary Select Committee report of April the same year. Even the highly critical Royal Commission of December 1800 failed to demand his dismissal and went on to acknowledge his 'general character for humanity', while the coroners' verdicts of death 'by the Visitation of God' were upheld in the cases of Obaker Higgles in December 1798, Luke Early in July 1800 and James Johnston two months later. Finally, in May 1801, when prosecuted for the alleged mistreatment of a prisoner named Joseph Heron, Aris had obtained sufficient support from the Middlesex magistrates to convince the Court that 'there was no just imputation whatever on the conduct of Aris, either for his general government of the prison, or his treatment of this particular person'.[3] Of course, it helped that the judge in the case was Lord Kenyon, a strong supporter of the Tory administration, who called the prosecution 'shameful in all its parts'.[4] William Garrow, KC, Aris's highly regarded defence barrister who is famed for having coined the phrase 'presumed to be innocent till proved guilty',* went even further, suggesting without any visible trace of irony that 'The persons appointed to superintend this prison would in future ages rank with the greatest benefactors of mankind'.[5]

Aris's burgeoning self-confidence is perhaps best evidenced by his decision, in the spring of 1803, to prosecute for slander William Dickie, the one-time foreman of the Traverse Jury for Clerkenwell. Ever since he had visited Coldbath Fields to investigate the details of Mary Rich's treatment in May 1800, Dickie had remained a vocal critic of both the prison and its governor. According to Edward Page, the foreman of the Traverse Jury for July 1800, when he and his colleagues toured the prison and found 'everything much to their satisfaction', Dickie had told them that 'they had not examined the prison so minutely as they ought to have done'.[6] In September, he had approached the jurors again to ask whether they had demanded to inspect particular rooms in the prison; when they replied 'no', Dickie had exclaimed 'Ha! Mr Aris has gammoned you, for you have not seen that place which you ought to have seen, nor have you seen the man who was obliged to drink his own urine for want of being supplied with water'.[7]

Another juryman, George Lever, described how Dickie followed the jurors every day from the Sessions House to the Crown Tavern on Clerkenwell Green to present them with affidavits from prisoners who claimed to have been mistreated, while a Mr Braine related how Dickie had stationed himself at the door of the coach carrying jurors home, telling

---

* Garrow first used the phrase on 14 September 1791 during the trial of George Dingler for the brutal murder of his wife, Jane. Dingler was found guilty and hanged at Newgate five days later.

those inside that they 'had not seen the worst part of the Prison'.[8] Perhaps the jurors would have been more tolerant of Dickie's maggoty-headedness had they found any evidence to support his accusations, but they claimed to have found everything in the prison 'perfect ... clean and decent' and the prisoners entirely content with their lot. One juryman even went so far as to quip 'that he found everything as good as at his own House, only that the Prisoners' places have Iron Bars and his house has Sashed Windows'[9] – an unconscious echo of the claim made by a magistrate in December 1798 that the prison's inmates 'were allowed as good food as ever he had at his own table'.[10]

Eventually, so persistent did Dickie become that, not content to dismiss him as 'a troublesome fellow' who 'came there to make mischief', some jurors decided to report him to the Middlesex Sessions. The chair of the sessions, William Mainwaring, would come to bear his own grudge against Dickie when, during the Middlesex election of 1802, the stationer actively supported Burdett's candidacy, even raising a triumphal laurel arch and a medallion inscribed '*Vox Populi*' outside his premises at No. 120 The Strand – much to the chagrin of his neighbours, the arch-Tory *Sun* and *True Briton* newspapers, who were mischievously reported by their competitors as being the erectors of the offending arch.[11] Even before the stationer committed this personal offence, however, Mainwaring would tolerate no criticisms of his favourite, and he began to collate a file of Dickie's unguarded declarations – a file that, in due course, would be used against the unwitting stationer when Aris chose, or was persuaded, to prosecute.

By the time Aris made his decision in the spring of 1803, Dickie had been declared bankrupt and it was almost certainly this misfortune that convinced the usually pugnacious stationer not to fight the prosecution – a surrender that would otherwise seem inexplicable given the publicity that Aris's alleged mismanagement of the house of correction had attracted since December 1798 and the number of witnesses willing to testify against him.[12] Instead, Dickie accepted an 'interlocutory judgement' pending a judge-led jury hearing to determine costs.* That hearing took place beneath the medieval hammer-beam roof of Westminster Hall on 2 June 1803 before Lord Ellenborough, Lord Kenyon's successor as Lord Chief Justice of the King's Bench.

Once again, Aris was represented by William Garrow and from the outset it was clear that Dickie could expect no mercy. The governor,

---

* Since April 1999, interlocutory judgements have been superseded by judgements 'for an amount and costs to be decided by the court'.

declared his legal team, 'was, and always had been, from the time of his nativity, a good, true, honest, just, humane, and faithful subject of our Lord the King'.[13] He had never been suspected of 'any felony, murder, manslaughter, cruelty or oppression, whatsoever', and was instead 'always held, esteemed, and reputed to be a person of good fame, credit, and reputation, and of a merciful and humane disposition'. Naturally, no mention was made of the many accusations made against Aris prior to those articulated by Dickie, or to Aris having been charged with assaulting Thomas Stone in 1773. Instead, Garrow declared, this fine, upstanding public servant, this paragon of all the virtues, had been wilfully and repeatedly traduced by just one man, the defendant, who had never apologised for his actions and now offered absolutely no justification for his calumnies.

Such behaviour, Garrow told the jury, merited substantial damages. 'They tell me', he continued, 'Mr Dickie has twice been a bankrupt, and therefore he has no means to pay, nothing in the world. But you will not find small damages, because it may be inconvenient for Mr Dickie to pay them ... if he has no purse to pay, he must go to gaol'.[14] In reply, Dickie's defence barrister, Thomas Erskine, argued that Aris had suffered no significant inconvenience as a result of his client's allegations: he had never been charged with murder, so at no point had his life been at stake, and since he remained in his post it could not be argued that he had suffered any material loss. But Ellenborough was having none of it.

A stalwart conservative known for his displays of political bias when on the bench, Ellenborough had been the presiding judge at Edward Despard's trial for High Treason four months earlier and had summarily dismissed the jury's plea for clemency 'on account of his former good character, and the services he has rendered his country'.[15] Now he left the jury in no doubt as to his opinion regarding the size of the damages they should award. After all, he declaimed in his characteristically hectoring fashion, with 'the most malignant of purposes' Dickie had accused Aris of murder: an accusation which, 'if it had excited credit, would have deprived him at once of every ray of character in the estimation of persons, whose estimation is at all valuable'. Inquests had been held into the deaths of the prisoners whom Dickie accused Aris of murdering – and in every instance a verdict of death 'by the Visitation of God' had been given. And yet, Ellenborough went on, Dickie:

> still endeavours to insist on that course, and to make it manifest he aimed at the destruction of this man's office, nay more for the

destruction of his life, aiming at it through the medium of the destruction of the house of correction. He threw out that intelligible hint of certain mischief, of another sort, by razing from the ground, the prison itself; and as a probable consequence of that, it will be for you to say, whether he did not contemplate the destruction of the gaoler himself. The single question is, what damages a person so injured ought to receive?[16]

In an extraordinary interpretation of the evidence, Ellenborough was instructing the jury not merely to determine suitable damages for defamation but for an entirely unproven, indeed entirely imaginary, attempt on Aris's life. Of course, Dickie had never been charged with any such offence and Ellenborough's egregious suggestion was based on nothing more substantial than Dickie's ill-judged assertion that the prison should be destroyed. According to Ellenborough, the expression of such a wish must, as a matter of course, involve the death by violence of the prison's governor.

Ellenborough was so unaccustomed to having his instructions ignored that it has been suggested that his death in 1818 was precipitated by a later jury's decision to acquit the satirist William Hone of blasphemy after he had instructed them to find him guilty;[17] but he had no cause for dissatisfaction on the present occasion. Having apparently taken his recommendation as a direct command the jury duly set damages at an extraordinarily punitive £700, plus a further £52 of costs.*

Unsurprisingly, Aris proved as little inclined to mercy as Ellenborough. When, after more than a year in prison, Dickie sought to obtain his release under the terms of the Insolvent Debtors Relief Act of July 1804, Aris attended the hearing in person to oppose his petition, 'upon the ground that the damages given to a plaintiff for malicious slander were excepted from the debts to which the Insolvents' Act referred'.[18] Of course, in so doing, he knew full well that, as a prisoner, Dickie would be unable to earn money with which to repay him, so his actions were dictated by malignity rather than pragmatism. No longer benefiting from the advice of a lawyer, and unable to argue his own case, Dickie had no option but to return to what Charles Dickens would describe in *The Posthumous Papers of the Pickwick Club* as the 'damp and gloomy stone vaults' of the Fleet, no doubt sharing Mr Pickwick's 'depression of spirit and sinking of heart, naturally consequent upon the reflection that he was cooped and caged

---

* Roughly £65,000 today. Source: Bank of England inflation calculator.

up without a prospect of liberation'.[19] Unlike Dickens's hero, who was imprisoned in the Fleet for his refusal to pay damages to Mrs Bardell for breach of promise, Dickie would never regain his liberty: he died on 24 September 1808 after nearly five years of imprisonment, leaving 'a distressed widow and four children still to lament his unfortunate offence and unhappy death'.[20]

Despite his foolhardiness in publicly repeating his allegations against the advice of his well-wishers, there can be very little doubt that Dickie was as much a victim of political repression as the radicals imprisoned after the suspension of habeas corpus. Although there is no documentary evidence to reveal who appointed or paid William Garrow, one of the most eminent barristers of his day, it seems improbable that it was Aris himself. In addition, there can be little doubt that Ellenborough's insistence on exorbitant damages resulted from his conviction that Dickie was a political radical intent on subverting the established order, as personified by Aris and the Tory-leaning Middlesex magistracy. Either way, though Burdett and John Horne Tooke offered to stand bail,[21] and may even have paid for Erskine's services, no wealthy Whigs or radicals stumped up the money necessary to ensure Dickie's release from the Fleet prison, nor was any subscription for his relief launched. Perhaps, in the end, his monomania had simply become too eccentric, and too extreme, for him to be championed as a radical martyr.

Almost incredibly, Aris would go on to survive yet another high-profile inquiry into the prison: an inquiry that once again had its origins in the findings of a Grand Jury for the County of Middlesex, led by its foreman, Alexander Stephens. A member of the Middle Temple, a regular contributor to *The Monthly Magazine*, and author of a history of the French Revolutionary Wars, Stephens was a man of radical sympathies distinguished, according to one admirer, for 'the manliness and zeal with which he supported measures which to him appeared likely to prove beneficial'.[22] Presumably alerted to continuing abuses by an unknown third party, and driven by this 'manliness and zeal', on 3 November 1807 Stephens led a party of nine jurors into the house of correction to conduct a tour of inspection. They listed their findings in a petition to the House of Commons, which was read to the assembled members by Sheridan on 18 February the following year.

Stating that he did not present the Grand Jury's petition 'for any party purposes whatever', and strongly supported by Burdett, Sheridan began by deploring the fact that the previously reported abuses 'had not been done away or remedied' but, instead, 'had been rather encouraged and increased'.[23] The most recent inspection had revealed that, in spite of the recommendations made by Sir George Onesiphorus Paul over six years earlier, a substantial portion of the loaves of bread served to the prisoners were underweight, and the prison's weights and measures defective; some of the inmates' accommodation remained inadequate; one prisoner, a Frenchman, had been driven insane by his treatment; some prisoners continued to be inappropriately shackled, including some who were sick; and, perhaps worst of all, 'a female prisoner had been debauched by the son of the Gaoler, and [had] brought forth a child, which was chargeable to the parish'.[24] Such discoveries, Sheridan declared, could only 'bring odium on his Majesty's Government and our excellent Constitution', and something must be done.

After the customary parliamentary wrangling, that 'something' took the form of a second Royal Commission, chaired not by the disillusioned Paul whose past experiences had led him to declare that the prison system as a whole was 'so deformed, cankered, and disordered'[25] as to render any future service futile, but by his erstwhile deputy, William Morton Pitt. Crucially, the commission's remit was broad enough to satisfy even the most vocal of the prison's critics, with Pitt and his colleagues empowered to investigate each and every element of the prison's management, including the role played by the visiting magistrates. Moreover, unlike the earlier commission, that of 1808 would have the authority to summon and examine upon oath 'all and every person and persons who could give evidence upon all or any of the matters therein referred to us',[26] including the gaoler and his turnkeys, the magistrates, the surgeon, clerk and chaplain, and, of course, the prisoners themselves. Unfortunately, despite its extensive powers, the report of the second commission, dated 1 August 1808, displayed none of the independence, critical acumen and investigative zeal that had distinguished Paul's efforts. Instead, it absolved the prison's staff of any wrongdoing, and found that nearly every issue raised by Alexander Stephens could be dismissed, excused or easily remedied.

Having questioned the prison's bakers, the commissioners found, not unreasonably, that it was impracticable to guarantee that each of the 200 to 300 loaves baked every day would weigh the 1lb dictated by the statutes and that the rule would not have been laid down had the magistrates responsible fully understood the implications of what they were asking.

'We conceive', they wrote, 'that such a deviation is not contrary to the spirit and meaning of [the regulations], provided a proper limit to the excess or deficiency in weight of each loaf is specified'.[27] As to the defective weights and measures, Aris had neglected his duty to ensure their accuracy but the situation had been resolved since the Grand Jury made its submission, and no further action was deemed necessary.

Despite the lapse of years since the publication of the first commission's recommendations, many prisoners were still denied access to a fire, their cell windows remained unglazed and the reliance on wooden shutters meant that, all too often, they must choose between cold and darkness. Some prisoners remained in irons, but the commissioners accepted Aris's statement that he removed them if he thought it safe to do so, and that 'he does not put irons on such prisoners as are brought without irons, unless he knows them to be notorious thieves, and that it would be dangerous to let them remain without irons'.[28] As to sick prisoners being restrained, once again the commissioners expressed themselves as being satisfied that their condition was 'unknown to the officers of the prison' – though they appear not to have explored the reasons for such ignorance, or to have challenged the turnkeys' assertion that the prisoners had never requested medical assistance. Tellingly, the commissioners noted that some prisoners were still expected to wait for up to 'eighteen or nineteen hours' between meals, meaning that the most basic and easily remedied of Paul's findings had not been addressed – though Pitt's report merely stated the fact, rather than commenting on it.

The Frenchman who had allegedly gone mad during his confinement turned out to be an individual of some rank, the Chevalier Charles de Blin, who had served as aide-de-camp and secretary to the royalist General Charles-François du Périer Dumouriez, then resident in England. Suspected of spying for Napoleon, de Blin had been arrested on 30 April 1807 under the terms of the Aliens Act of 1793,* and confined in Coldbath Fields from 3 May. According to Aris's testimony to the commission, at the time of de Blin's committal the chief

---

*   The Act for Regulating Immigration into Great Britain (1793) was the first of a series of acts passed between 1793 and 1826 which granted the government broad powers of regulation over the country's resident foreign population. The powers included the authority to expel resident aliens and to keep aliens from entering the country, and represented the first attempt on the part of the British government to regulate England's entire population of aliens. The legislation's primary driver was the mass emigration of French nationals fleeing France after the French Revolution and the government's concern that these might include Jacobin agents disguised as refugees.

magistrate at Bow Street, James Read, had instructed him that the prisoner should 'want for nothing', but that he must be prevented 'from conversing with Etienne Martelly (an alien committed on the same day) or any other person',[29] and he had therefore placed the chevalier in one of the 'state rooms' on the ground floor previously occupied by the state prisoners arrested during Pitt's 'reign of terror'. The government allowed one guinea per week for de Blin's upkeep, and his cell benefited from a glazed window looking out into the prison yard, and a fireplace which was regularly supplied with coals; he was also permitted to exercise in the yard under the supervision of a turnkey.

After some four months of this solitary confinement, homesick and melancholic, missing his wife and children, unable or unwilling to speak English, and prevented from communicating with anyone other than his gaolers, de Blin had begun to reveal clear signs of mental derangement. He 'attempted to get over the wall which separates this yard from the female prisoners,' Aris told the commissioners, 'throwing his money, linen, clothes and provisions over that wall'.[30] Dr Webbe, who spoke some French, concurred, adding that, as well as attempting to climb the chimney in his cell, the chevalier had begun 'tearing his linen and writing upon it, and talking incoherently with respect to his wife and children'.[31]

The authorities' response to de Blin's deteriorating condition was to permit occasional visits from his wife. Sensibly, Webbe also sought the opinion of Dr Thomas Monro, principal physician of the Bethlem Royal Hospital for the Insane and an acknowledged expert who would later be consulted during King George III's second bout of madness in 1811–12. After further observation, the two agreed that de Blin should be removed from the prison and taken, instead, to the nearby St Luke's Hospital for Lunatics on Old Street, Islington. Despite its grandiose architecture and its supposed superiority to Bedlam, this hospital had a poor reputation. Patients were confined in cells with small windows set high in the walls, with no heating and loose straw strewn on wooden bedsteads (those deemed incurable were denied bedsteads). As for the treatment regime, this consisted of cold-water baths as shock therapy, and the usual antispasmodics, emetics and purgatives to be found in the arsenal of all contemporary apothecaries.[32] How de Blin subsequently fared is unknown, but given that the conditions in St Luke's were, if anything, worse than those in Coldbath Fields, where he at least had a fire, there seems little reason to hope that his condition improved.*

---

* The baptismal record for de Blin's daughter, Louisa, confirms that he was dead by 1827. Louisa was baptised as an adult aged 20 at the parish church of St Mary's, Lambeth, on 24 January 1827. The baptismal record describes her father as an army officer, deceased.

Having taken the opportunity to interview de Blin themselves, the commissioners saw no reason to question the diagnosis of the country's foremost mad-doctor. Nor did they challenge Thérèse de Blin's statement that her husband had never evidenced the slightest indication of insanity prior to his incarceration. This being the case, they had little choice but to accept that his derangement had 'arisen during his confinement',[33] though they 'did not see any ground for supposing that his insanity arose from any treatment which he experienced in this prison'[34] – an astonishing conclusion given that the chevalier had been utterly deprived of company, stimulation and conversation for four months.** Perhaps not entirely convinced by their own assertions, the commissioners went on to state that, if madness had been caused by his treatment, 'the same effect would have followed from his being kept in custody in any other prison'. If this were the case – and assuming that Aris accurately described the relatively comfortable conditions in which de Blin was kept – then his illness arose from the terms of his confinement, as dictated by James Read, the magistrate, and was not due to the conduct of the governor and his staff which, the commissioners concluded, 'has been proper and undeserving of censure or reproach'.[35]

The final and equally shocking case examined by the Royal Commission was that of Elizabeth Kew, who, in January 1803, had been sentenced to a month in the house of correction for an unknown misdemeanour. It was Kew who, according to the accusations heard by Alexander Stephens, 'had been debauched by the son of the Gaoler, and brought forth a child'. When interviewed, Aris informed the commissioners that, on her conviction, the magistrates of the Middlesex Sessions had asked that Kew be kept separate from the other inmates: a tacit acknowledgement that the corruption of younger prisoners – the 'devoting them to destruction'[36] that Howard had so deprecated – was still very much a feature of life in Coldbath Fields. Upon her admission to the prison, he had 'conversed with her, and finding her a meek well-behaved woman, I sent her into my house to act as a servant'.[37] Asked whether he often employed female prisoners in this fashion, he admitted that he did, if 'given a direction similar to that I received in favour of Elizabeth Kew, or if I have found amongst the female prisoners one that appeared to me deserving to be kept apart

---

** For a review of recent scientific studies into the serious and often long-lasting psychological impacts of solitary confinement, see: Craig Haney, 'Restricting the Use of Solitary Confinement', *Annual Review of Criminology*, 1 (2018), pp. 285–310. doi.org/10.1146/annurev-criminol-032317-092326.

from prisoners of the same class. I have no doubt the magistrates know that I do so'.[38]

The governor went on to declare that, after her discharge on 10 February, he had continued to employ Kew in the same capacity until August, when her mother had asked her to return to the family home at Kensington Gravel Pits to help with a sick sister. It was there that, a year later, on 22 August 1804, she had given birth to a baby girl. She had named the child Esther Maria Aris,* and when, in May 1807, she had sought relief from the parish overseers she had named the governor's son, Thomas, as the father. Aris junior had not denied the claim and he, his father and another unnamed individual had given the necessary sureties to the parish to maintain the child, now aged nearly 3.

In their summing up of the case, the commissioners noted that Kew's lodging with the governor:

> gave his son Thomas, who resided with him, an opportunity of becoming acquainted with her; but it does not appear that their acquaintance had proceeded to criminality before she left the service of Mr Aris ... or that Mr Aris ever knew his son had been connected with her until the warrant issued against the son as the putative father of the child, which was not born until eleven months at least after she had quitted the service, and eighteen months after she had ceased to be a prisoner.[39]

Of course, the date of the child's birth confirms that conception must have occurred after Kew left Thomas Aris's service but without the evidence of either Kew or Aris junior there could be no certainty regarding the nature of the relationship, when it began or in what circumstances. The failing of the commissioners was that, despite the powers granted to them by the Crown, they chose not to conduct those interviews or to examine in any way the balance of power between the governor, his sons and the female prisoners: a failing that seems little short of criminal in the light of later revelations. Instead, having noted that they found 'nothing censurable' in the governor employing female prisoners in his house, they concluded their remarks on the case by stating that 'We are of opinion that the whole

---

*   Esther Maria Aris was christened at St Mary Abbots Church, Kensington, on 21 October 1804, the daughter of Thomas and Elizabeth Aris [sic]. Elizabeth was the daughter of Thomas Kew, gardener to Sir George Baker, physician to George III.

of the charge in this section is unfounded, so far as it imputes misconduct to Mr Aris the governor'.[40]

In the final paragraph of their report the commissioners would go even further, observing that during their inspection of the prison they 'heard no complaint whatever against [Aris]; that in our opinion he is a man of great humanity; that his general management of the prison, with very few exceptions, is extremely creditable to him, and that he is a most useful servant to the public'.[41] Thomas Amos, the storekeeper and taskmaster, they thought 'extremely active and intelligent', and Webbe 'very assiduous in the discharge of the duties of his office'. They did not mention, however, that in order to make their report they, like the magistrates of the Prison Committee and the parliamentary Select Committee, had not thought it necessary to interview a single current or former prisoner, with the exception of the prison's in-house baker, and that their opinions on the management of the prison were, therefore, based almost exclusively upon what they had been told by the governor and by those who depended upon his favour. Once again, Aris had emerged unscathed and could look to the future with unalloyed satisfaction, more convinced than ever of his own invulnerability.

In the event, it was not brutality, neglect, exploitation or incompetence that brought about Aris's spectacular downfall, but his corruption. In the summer of 1810 the prisoners in Coldbath Fields included two men of very different criminal pedigrees: at one end of the scale, Harper (alias Smith), a small-time crook serving a sentence of six months for theft; at the other, Robert 'Bob' Roberts, a notorious fraudster who was believed to have obtained substantial sums in the north of England by impersonating Hugh, Earl Percy, the heir to the Duke of Northumberland.[42] A man of considerable daring and panache more than capable of convincing others of his bogus wealth and breeding, in recent years Roberts had progressed from impersonation to embezzlement and the forging of banknotes – 'the cream of the counterfeit money-trade' according to Kellow Chesney[43] – and was now being held at Coldbath Fields pending 'a final examination on the charge of forgery on the Bank of England'.[44]

The two men were supposed to be unknown to one another, and yet, in the early hours of 28 August, when Harper succeeded in breaking through his cell's wall into an unoccupied and unlocked cell next door, his first act was not to find his way over the boundary walls as quickly as possible, but to somehow unlock no fewer than six gates and doors in order to liberate Roberts, before both men made their way to a new but only partly completed lodge built against the prison's outer wall. Climbing onto the building's roof, they let down a rope and, following in the footsteps of the seven Nore mutineers who had escaped in April 1798, disappeared into the silent streets and alleys of Clerkenwell.

There could be very little doubt that Roberts, facing a capital charge, had used a combination of his considerable personal charm and promises of monetary reward to evade justice. The question now facing the embarrassed Middlesex magistrates was how far did the corruption spread? Unfortunately for the Aris family, a prisoner in a cell next to Roberts's had overheard a number of conversations between him and Daniel Aris, another of the governor's sons, which clearly implicated the latter in the escape. During a course of interviews undertaken by the magistrates, Michael McNamara revealed that as well as seeing the two walking together in the garden of the governor's lodge after lock-up time – an indulgence granted to no other inmate – on the day before the escape, he had listened to an exchange between Roberts and Aris junior in which the latter had said 'Be sure to be awake at my hollow [sic]'. Roberts had replied, 'Be sure to come, for you know what risk I shall run if you do not', and the exchange had concluded with Aris declaring, 'Never fear me, you know I always stick to what I say'.[45] McNamara also claimed to have heard Aris's voice in the corridor at around 1 a.m., the presumed time of the escape.

During the hearings, it quickly became clear that Thomas Aris had no more endeared himself to his staff than to the inmates because turnkeys as well as prisoners lined up to give damning evidence against him and his sons. Thomas Amos, the storekeeper and taskmaster who was also Aris's son-in-law,* agreed that Daniel 'used to walk in the garden with Roberts, and he was a good deal with him ... There was no other prisoner permitted the indulgence of walking in the garden but Roberts, and the Governor knew of these favours'.[46] For his part, Paull, one of the prison's watchmen, deposed that 'Governor Aris frequently conversed with Roberts, and he went out in his (Roberts's) chaise on the 18th of August'. Paull then went on to assert – irrelevantly, perhaps, but damningly – that another of Aris's sons, Charles, who was nominally employed by the governor, 'had 23s a week, but he had not done any duty in the prison for two years'. Another

---

* Thomas Amos married Sarah Aris on 29 November 1800, at St Andrew's, Holborn.

turnkey, Samuel Winsell, observed that on the night of the escape Aris had appeared at locking-up time to wish Roberts goodnight – an attention that he had never paid to any other prisoner, or even to Roberts, except on this one occasion. Finally, the combined evidence of McNamara and Haswell, the prison clerk, proved that, after the escape, Aris had been told of his son's conversation with the prisoner, but that he had concealed this information when questioned by the magistrates.[47]

During the hearings, the thuggish Daniel Aris – an amateur boxer and of 'considerable note as a setter-to'[48] – did little to attract sympathy, 'biting his lip, and alternately boxing the palm of his hand with his fist', until he was reprimanded for his indecorous behaviour. Nor did his father, once the darling of the Middlesex magistrates, obtain a more lenient hearing. One magistrate accused him of 'supineness',[49] and even Mainwaring, once Aris's most outspoken champion, called his behaviour 'shameful'. When Aris replied that 'he had never done an act in his life of which he was ashamed', another of his inquisitors took the opportunity to express his belief that 'Aris never did feel shame'.[50]

At the end of the proceedings the chief magistrate informed Daniel Aris that he would be committed 'for feloniously aiding and abetting in the escape of Roberts and Harper' and the scowling amateur pugilist was taken away in chains. As for Aris senior, he had been found guilty of favouritism towards certain prisoners, presumably in return for bribes, and neglectful of his duties; he was also suspected of complicity in the escape – or at the very least of attempting to hide his son's involvement. In the circumstances there could be no alternative to immediate dismissal.

Bewildered by the swiftness of his fall, stripped of his generous annual salary, of his home, the governor's lodge, and of all the perquisites of his post, legitimate and otherwise, over the coming weeks Aris continued to petition the magistrates, pleading that:

> After devoting the last seventeen years of my life to the superintendence of the House of Correction ... and conscientiously discharging the duty of Governor of that prison, I find myself removed from my situation at 66 years of age, which renders me incapable of obtaining other employment, without any charge having been made against me, or even [being] heard in my own defence ...
>
> Nor had I, on this trying occasion, the advice or consolation of a friend; for those who before treated me with kindness and attention, were the first to desert me without a cause ...

> I do most respectfully appeal to your justice and humanity for that protection and support, which I humbly conceive I am entitled to, upon this occasion; and I beg to assure you, that should I be restored again to the situation of Governor of the House of Correction, I will, by the most assiduous and unremitting attention to the duties of the office, endeavour to prove myself once more worthy of the confidence which was heretofore reposed in me.[51]

Crucially, as well as alluding to the unwarranted vilification and prejudice of his accusers, in his letter Aris referred to 'subsequent discoveries', which 'fortunately for public justice, my injured character, and for my poor son's safety' would absolve him of any complicity in Roberts's escape.

The discoveries he mentioned had been made by a 'meritorious servant of the late governor',[52] and consisted of a 'voluntary confession' from a prisoner named John Taylor, then serving a sentence of two years in Coldbath Fields. According to Taylor's deposition, Roberts had approached him soon after being committed and had asked whether he, as a sweeper who enjoyed a greater degree of freedom and access than most prisoners, could assist him to break out, 'for if he did not escape he was sure to die'.[53] After pocketing the expected bribe, Taylor had agreed that he would obtain the key to the prison's interior gates, if Roberts could find the means to copy and return it before it was missed. In line with this plan, a week or so before the escape, Taylor had passed the key to Roberts who 'made an impression with it on a piece of soap about two inches thick, in Taylor's presence, by striking it with a boot-jack'.[54] Taylor had also procured a padlock from an empty cell, 'all being made to open with one key', and, on Roberts's instructions, he then passed the soap and the lock to 'a trusty friend of Taylor's (a servant in the prison)' who conveyed them to one of Roberts's contacts on the outside.

A few days later, after further letters had been passed to and fro between Roberts and his confederates to hammer out the details of the plan, the duplicate keys were conveyed to him in a similar manner, and Tuesday 28 August was set for the attempt. Only one further matter needed to be arranged. It had been decided that in order to facilitate his exit over the prison's high outer wall Roberts would need the assistance of a second prisoner, who would escape at the same time. This man was Harper, to whom Taylor gave the counterfeit keys, being a man whose cell was less likely to be searched.

Taylor's story elicited different responses in different quarters. The *Morning Post* expressed itself as being entirely satisfied that there could be 'no doubt whatever of this being the real statement relative to the escape', and went on to suggest that the investigations conducted by Aris's meritorious (but curiously anonymous) servant entitled 'him to the greatest praise for the zeal he has manifested in tracing the thing from its origin'.[55] *The Times*, on the other hand, was altogether less convinced: 'This deposition', it declared, 'contains so many inconsistencies and improbabilities, that we feel very much inclined to believe that it is brought forward for some particular purpose'[56] — that purpose being, of course, the complete exculpation of the Aris family. But, whatever doubts might be entertained regarding its truthfulness, Taylor's statement clearly gave Aris's erstwhile employers pause for thought. At a meeting on 20 September, Aris had been dismissed from his post as governor 'by the unanimous consent of the Bench',[57] but at a further meeting on 8 November, originally convened to select his replacement, the magistrates decided, after 'considerable discussion', to suspend the recruitment process until the next Sessions, to allow time for further investigation into the conduct of the late governor, 'who appears to have been dismissed without being regularly heard in his defence, and in whose favour circumstances, apparently of considerable weight, had come out'.[58]

The delay would prove to be only a stay of execution for Aris and on 21 November the magistrates proceeded to the selection of a new governor, appointing in his place William Adkins, an 'indefatigable officer' of Bow Street.[59] And yet ambiguities remain. Though it is clear that Aris's dealings with Roberts were highly questionable and tended to raise doubts regarding his integrity and judgement, the evidence of his, and his son's, collusion in the forger's escape was circumstantial at best, with some of it provided by individuals whose motives must be questioned. In addition, what reason could Taylor have for voluntarily implicating himself in the escape? Aris no longer possessed the authority to coerce him, and if he resorted to bribery this was never proved.

The waters are muddied still further by the events following the recapture of Roberts. Instead of fleeing the capital after his escape, the forger had demonstrated his usual sangfroid by taking rooms at the Royal Oak public house near Vauxhall, where he claimed to be an Oxford attorney named Sydney visiting London on Chancery Court business, but recommended to take the Vauxhall air by his physician.[60] Roberts had claimed that 'fifty men would lose their lives' before allowing him to be harmed,[61] but with a 300-guinea reward offered for his apprehension, his luck could not last forever and he seems to have been betrayed by one of a party of four men whom he entertained on the evening of Thursday 27 September.

Two days later, two Bank of England investigators and four Bow Street Runners, led by John Foy, surprised him in his rooms and arrested him before he could draw the brace of loaded pistols later found in his pockets, along with £200 of forged banknotes. According to one account, Roberts appeared 'much agitated' at the moment of his arrest, 'but after having been securely ironed, he recovered himself, and inquired who had betrayed him' before making the philosophical observation 'that he had placed too much confidence in man'.[62]

Roberts's equanimity did not desert him, and when transferred to the 'State side' of Newgate Prison he is reputed to have told the man riveting the irons to his ankles that 'Though you have caught me you shall not hang me'.[63] In this he would prove quite correct because, rather than stand trial, he saved his neck by turning King's evidence and it was his testimony that hanged his accomplices, Richard Armitage and Charles Thomas, on 24 June the following year. Roberts would appear at the Old Bailey on his own account in September 1811, to face the charge of 'unlawfully escaping from and out of the House of Correction, at Coldbath Fields'.[64] But once again he eluded justice. Only one witness was called, the magistrate Nathaniel Conant, who confirmed that he had written a document shown to him by a clerk of the Court. On receiving this confirmation, the judge, Mr Justice Bailey, instructed the jury to find the defendant 'not guilty', and the trial had ended almost as soon as it began.

Described by the *Gentleman's Magazine* as being possessed of 'a very clear understanding and promptness in decisions', Conant had proved himself a keen servant of the government and the law and a willing employer of spies and informers. In this instance, the archives of the Bank of England reveal that the document which served as Roberts's 'get out of gaol free card' had been prepared in part payment for his services in ensuring the break-up of the larger counterfeiting ring in which he had been such a key player. While imprisoned in Newgate, Roberts had written a series of letters to John Pearse, the Governor of the Bank, in which he provided full details not only of his counterfeiting career, but also of his escape from Coldbath Fields, naming his accomplices in both endeavours.

According to Roberts's affidavit, Daniel Aris, Taylor, William Folkard, a member of his forgery gang, and Haswell, the clerk, had all played their part in his midnight flit: Aris and Taylor had obtained the keys and padlocks; Folkard had made the arrangements for the copying of the keys by a blacksmith named Brooks; and Haswell had ensured that Roberts and

Folkard could speak together unsupervised so that their plans could be finalised and the keys handed over. The one person whom Roberts did not implicate was the governor, telling Pearse in a letter of 16 September 1811, that 'I acquit him of all knowledge or connivance'.[65] But even here there are uncertainties because, in June, Roberts had told Pearse that he knew Aris intended to have him tried for his escape, and that he greatly feared the 'dreadful life' he would lead on the prison hulks prior to transportation, 'as it would be known I had given evidence'. Could it be, then, that Aris and Roberts had come to a mutually beneficial agreement: Aris would not pursue Roberts, if, in return, Roberts denied his involvement in the escape? We will never know for sure. What we do know, however, is that, as Charles Thomas piteously declared at his trial for forgery, Roberts's word 'cannot be taken' for anything.[66]

Whatever the truth of the matter, the fact remains that Thomas Aris and his son had been condemned for aiding and abetting Roberts in the commission of a crime of which he had subsequently been found 'not guilty'. Taken together, these facts make it impossible for us not to ask the question: in losing his post as governor of the house of correction, had Thomas Aris – a man previously accused of fraud, brutality, neglect, incompetence, sexual exploitation, and murder – actually been the victim of a miscarriage of justice? Certainly, Aris never gave up proclaiming his innocence and one of his successors, Captain George Laval Chesterton, would recall that, 'Many years subsequently to those transactions, Aris and his sons, would come and importune me for assistance, and the former never failed to aver that he was unjustly sacrificed to popular clamour'.[67] Though clearly no admirer of Aris as a man, or as a type, even Chesterton would eventually admit that the ex-governor 'may possibly have been not a whit more guilty than his compeers'.

Guilty or not, details of his later career make it extremely difficult to maintain even the slightest sympathy for Thomas Aris. In April 1813, nearly three years after his dismissal, he appeared as a witness at the Old Bailey where a young woman named Sarah Evans was on trial for her life, the indictment against her being that she, 'not having the fear of God before her eyes, but being moved and seduced by the instigation of the Devil', had drowned her illegitimate 4-year-old son, George, in the New River, near Sadler's Wells.[68]

Initially, Evans denied that the badly decomposed body was that of her child, insisting that he had been placed in the St Pancras Workhouse. Under sustained questioning, however, and in fear for her life, she eventually admitted that the boy was hers – and that its father was Thomas Aris. She went on to assert that her earlier lies were the result of 'the threats of Mr. Aris' and that he 'has threatened to shoot me three times'. Gradually her whole sorry tale tumbled forth: she had first met Aris in 1799, when she was a prisoner in Coldbath Fields. On her release he had employed her, as he had employed Elizabeth Kew, as a chambermaid. At some point during her employment, though it is unclear whether this was when she was a prisoner or a free woman, the two had begun a sexual relationship, and Aris had gone on to father five of her children, whom he had supported with irregular subsidies. Given that he had been 56 when they met, and Evans just 18, he the all-powerful prison governor and she, in all probability, poor and anxious not to be returned to the cells, it is all too easy to imagine the circumstances in which their liaison began.

After fourteen years, having lost his post as governor, and in straitened circumstances – so straitened, indeed, that he was then a prisoner in the King's Bench Debtors' Prison, and allowed out only on Sundays – Aris could no longer afford the children's upkeep. The solution to this problem, he had told Evans, was to send little George to Buckinghamshire, to Aris's widowed sister-in-law. In compliance with his instructions, on 21 February in Gray's Inn Lane, Evans had delivered the boy into the hands of a woman sent by him. She had not seen the child again until his body was fished out of the New River on 14 March, a ligature made from a handkerchief around his neck and his body weighed down with half a brick. After the discovery, Aris had again spoken with her and had coached her in the story she was to tell if questioned:

> I was to say that I had sent him to my own relations in the country. He said, if ever I told any person that he had taken the child he would surely be the death of me; and so he certainly would. He had threatened me many times.[69]

It was these threats, and Evans's conviction that Aris would carry them out, that had made her lie, 'and that only'.

When called to the witness box Aris acknowledged that George Evans was his son – or, at least, that Sarah Evans had named him as the father. At first he denied meeting the child more than once, when George had been in his mother's company, but then acknowledged that he had seen the boy 'half a dozen times'. He claimed to have been astonished when he read of the drowning in a newspaper: 'I think it was the *Daily Advertiser*, and seeing Sarah Evans in the paper, it struck me, good God, it cannot be this woman that I have known'.[70] Under examination, Aris admitted that, since his dismissal from Coldbath Fields, he had been in want of money and that he had been obliged to support eleven children, including at least three of Evans's – though he piously declared that 'I do not call it a burthen'. He also reminded the Court that he was 'not under recognisance to appear' and that he 'came here voluntary today'. However, when questioned about the handkerchief, which Evans had sworn was one in his possession, his self-assurance began to waver: 'I never,' he declared, 'in all my existence, was possessed of such a handkerchief as that ... I will swear it five hundred times.'[71] Finally, when asked whether he had met Evans, as she claimed, on Sunday 21 February, Aris replied 'Never ... I passed that day with my family ... It is my practice never to go out on Sundays'.

The next witness to be called was a Mrs Simpson who, herself a prisoner of the King's Bench, had washed clothes for Aris. In particular, Simpson had laundered a number of handkerchiefs for him and had no hesitation in identifying the one that had been tied around the child's neck as being his. Simpson was followed by a policeman named John Matthews, who when asked whether he ever saw Aris out on a Sunday flatly contradicted Aris's earlier statement, replying, 'I did, about a quarter or ten minutes before ten in the morning. I spoke to him. It was about a month or six weeks before this affair [the discovery of the body] happened.'

And there, astonishingly, the matter ended. Evans, whom a number of witnesses described as a loving mother, was found 'not guilty', but when the jury foreman declared that he and his colleagues were 'unanimously of opinion that Aris was deeply implicated in this charge' and that 'some immediate judicial notice should be taken of him',[72] the trial judge replied that, while the jury 'had done their duty in making this representation', he could take 'no judicial notice of any person except those before the Court for trial'. Of course, in reality, while he could not take immediate action against Aris, there was no reason why the judge should not direct the attention of the magistracy, prosecutors and law officers towards the evidence that had come to light implicating Aris in the murder of his son. That he did not suggests that, once again, Aris was benefiting from the exertion of powerful influences, or at the very least prejudice, in his favour – a suggestion that is reinforced by the fact that the trial judge was no less a person than Lord Ellenborough, the reactionary Lord Chief Justice whose words had done so much to inflate the damages awarded to Aris in 1803.

Aris's escape from prosecution divided opinion. Calling him 'a wretched old man' who could 'derive neither consolation from his past, nor comfort from his future prospects', *The Examiner* condemned his profligacy as 'highly reprehensible' and opined that his actions merited 'the poverty and disgrace into which he has fallen'. Surprisingly, however, given the radical sympathies of the editor, Leigh Hunt, it declared that it did not believe that 'the ends of justice would be forwarded by his prosecution'.[73] This suggestion provoked astonishment among some of the paper's readers, with one correspondent writing under the pseudonym 'Vindex' asserting that it was unworthy of the most popular journal in the country to suggest that 'because vice and misconduct have produced ... their usual effects ... he is to be exempted from the consequences of any future crimes that may be imputed to him'.[74]

Surely it was more than enough, Vindex continued, that over the course of his iniquitous career Aris had enjoyed the 'singular good fortune' of finding continued protection 'under every circumstance of accusation and complaint'.[75] It is a judgement with which few who have surveyed his career could disagree; and yet the ex-governor continued to be 'exempted'. Though we have practically no information regarding how he eked out the remaining years of his long life, we do know that, in April 1840, some anonymous benefactor put forward the name of the 97-year-old Aris to be one of the 168 persons, all of them 'descended from comparative affluence', to receive Gate Alms of 13s from the young Queen Victoria.[76] This would be his last public appearance, as he died in December of the same year – but it seems to indicate that, up to the very moment he drew his last breath, Aris continued to benefit from a patronage that had never been entirely lost to him, no matter what his crimes.

12

After Aris

It should come as no surprise to learn that opinions regarding Coldbath Fields House of Correction varied as widely in the years immediately after the fall of Thomas Aris as they had during the period of his unchallenged sway. His immediate successors were both ex-Bow Street Runners, William Adkins, who served as governor from 1810 until his death in December 1822, and John Vickery, George IV's favourite royal protection officer, who assumed the role in January 1823, but was forced to retire in 1829 after a magistrates' inquiry found that his incompetence or collusion had enabled the escape of two prisoners.[1] Neither man had a reputation for brutality but, despite a generous annual salary of £400, a twelve-room lodge, and complimentary candles and coals (all provided tax-free), there can be little doubt that they, like Aris, indulged in peculation and extortion, with one (albeit biased) commentator claiming that the two men 'held that their primary obligation consisted in feathering their own nests'.[2]

Adkins and Vickery also failed – as did their masters, the Middlesex magistrates – to address many of the fundamental criticisms repeatedly made of the prison. Although the reformer James Neild reported in 1812 that certain alterations had been made, including the installation of a stove in the chapel,[3] such improvements have to be placed in the context of the admissions made by Adkins in 1818 – nearly twenty years after Burdett's first revelations, and eight since the governor had taken up his appointment.

Interviewed by a parliamentary Select Committee in September of that year, Adkins acknowledged that he had never been issued with any written rules or orders regarding his own conduct, that many of the cells were still ventilated and lighted by unglazed windows, and that the prisoners' meals continued to be served at 8 a.m. and 2 p.m., meaning that they ate nothing for some eighteen hours each day. Astonishingly, he even proved unable to confirm the exact number of cells in the prison, estimating that there were between 280 and 290.[4] There were, in fact, 354 at the time of Neild's inspection.[5] Finally, the perpetual problem of overcrowding meant that regulations concerning the strict separation of different types of offender continued to be ignored, with a committee of the Quakers' Society for the Improvement of Prison Discipline and the Reformation of Juvenile Offenders noting in December 1822, that the 'prison is very full; there being occasionally above double the number of prisoners in confinement that the Building was originally designed to contain'.[6]

However, conditions were not universally poor. Samuel Bamford, the Lancashire weaver, poet and radical, who was arrested on suspicion of High Treason in 1817 and spent some days in Coldbath Fields prior to his release, shared a room with five other radicals but 'saw nothing to complain about', except the fleas:

> When our place was ready, a turnkey conducted the six of us who remained together, through a number of winding passages to a flagged yard, into which opened a good room, or cell, about ten yards in length, and three in width. On each side of the room were three beds, placed in what might be termed wooden troughs; at the head of the room a good fire was burning; and we found a stock of coal and wood to recruit it at our pleasure. There were also a number of chairs, a table, candles, and other requisites; so that, had it not been for the grating at the window above the door ... we might have fancied ourselves to be in a comfortable barrack.[7]

The food, too, he thought both excellent in quality and generous in quantity – so generous, indeed, that he and his companions routinely smuggled their leftovers to the women prisoners whose cells abutted their own, and who, 'poor, lost, cut-off and world-despised' (in Bamford's estimation), fared far less well.[8] It was the women that the Society for the Improvement of Prison Discipline thought particularly badly affected by the overcrowding, observing five years after Bamford's release that the situation still called 'earnestly for immediate attention', with 'all descriptions of bad characters' confined together, and with 'no matron, nor any female officers to attend them'.[9]

Although Adkins and Vickery would both be praised for their humanity – by prisoners as well as by the authorities – mortality rates in the prison remained more or less static. Based upon the figures provided by Thomas Webbe in 1800, Sir George Onesiphorus Paul had calculated that 'Mortality will be as Two and something more than an Half in the Hundred in the Year'.[10] In comparison, Thomas R. Forbes estimates that for the period from 1822 to 1829 the death rate was approximately 3.5 per cent,[11] and therefore over double the average annual mortality rate for ninety-three English prisons in the period 1826 to 1831.[12] Inevitably, given that death registration (as distinct from burial registration) did not become mandatory until 1838, the documented causes of death remain as ambiguous as ever, with almost a third having no recorded cause, and a further fifth ascribed to the 'Visitation of God'; moreover, the figures reveal, predictably given the prison's flaws, that prisoners were still far more likely to die in the colder months – just as they had a quarter of a century earlier.

Scandals, too, could still draw unwelcome attention to the prison, though not on the scale of those of the 1790s and early 1800s. On 28 December 1811, for instance, the inadequate surveillance of Adkins and his staff enabled John Williams, the prime suspect in the shocking Ratcliff Highway murders, to evade justice by using a neckerchief to hang himself from a peg in his cell prior to his trial, and without any admission of his guilt – an act which, one outraged newspaper declared, 'should not have been left in the power of such a wretch'.[13]

More shocking still were the events of Friday 21 February 1823, when a negligent turnkey permitted an 11-year-old girl named Ann Thomas to enter the prison without the necessary magistrates' pass. She had brought a gift of food from her parents to Samuel, or 'Little', Waddington, a publisher of diminutive stature and doubtful reputation, held on a charge of having distributed works by the radical campaigner Richard Carlile. Having admitted her to the prison without the required documentation, the turnkey, or one of his colleagues, then allowed the child to enter Waddington's cell unsupervised where, according to her testimony, he raped her, 'stopping her mouth with the bed clothes to prevent her making a noise, and threatening her, if she said anything about it to her father or mother, he would have her confined in a solitary cell, or kept to work at the treadmill'.[14] Without the evidence of an independent witness, Waddington would be found 'not guilty' at his subsequent trials for rape and assault, but nobody denied that through a gross dereliction of duty on the part of the turnkeys an unaccompanied minor had been left with a prisoner.

Of course, many of the prison's inadequacies remained as invisible to casual observers in the 1820s as they had in the 1790s. In late August 1824, one such visitor was the Yorkshire landowner and diarist Anne Lister who, on a brief trip to London, declared her wish to 'see everything worth seeing', including the prison. Described by one journalist as 'A lady whose address and habiliments bespoke her of foreign extraction', she told the somewhat bemused Hatton Garden magistrates, to whom she applied for a pass, that 'in a metropolitan prison there is nothing indelicate or offensive – nothing, I presume, which a female might not, with the strictest regard to propriety or decorum, inspect'.[15] Whether or not they shared her confidence, the magistrates authorised Lister's admission, and she visited the same day, in the company of Dr Webbe, who would continue to serve as the prison's surgeon until his death, aged 77, in November 1831.*

Updating her diary immediately after her visit, Lister noted that she had been treated with 'the utmost civility' during her tour, that she had been able to view 'the whole interior' and that she had found it a 'most gratifying sight to see the prison so clean, and healthy, and orderly, and altogether in such excellent discipline'.[16] Though keen to inspect the prison as a whole, she acknowledged that the feature she had been most anxious to see – and, indeed, to try for herself – was one of the two notorious innovations, one mechanical and the other disciplinary, that have become a key facet in popular perceptions of the nineteenth-century British prison system: the treadwheel, or treadmill.

Invented in 1818 by William Cubitt, a talented civil engineer and inventor who would go on to earn a knighthood for supervising the erection of the Crystal Palace for the Great Exhibition of 1851, the first treadmill – called by its inventor a 'Discipline Mill' – had been designed in response to a commission from the Suffolk magistracy. The requirement was to identify an effective means by which to employ prisoners sentenced to hard labour and, in particular, to make use of 'the joint efforts of many, at one time, and in such manner, that although unwilling agents, each should be obliged to do his proper share of the work, without the power of throwing any part on his fellows'.[17]

Cubitt's simple but ingenious solution, which would be championed by the Society for the Improvement of Prison Discipline and by the prison reformers Elizabeth Fry and her brother Joseph John Gurney, consisted of an elongated version of the type of driving wheel commonly found in

---

*   Webbe was interred in the burial ground of St George the Martyr, Clerkenwell, on 29 November (now St George's Gardens).

watermills, but with the driving force provided by human muscle, rather than by hydropower. The effect for the prisoners, recorded an admiring report for the society, 'is simply that of ascending an *endless* flight of steps, the combined weight of the prisoners acting upon every successive stepping-board, precisely as a stream of water upon the float-boards of a water-wheel'.[18] In other words, the prisoners would be reduced to pure, unthinking motive power. Partitions would separate the individual prisoners to prevent conversation and, unable to stop, to pause or even to slow down because of the constant revolutions of the wheel, they would be expected to continue their gruelling task for up to 11 hours a day, equating to 12,000ft of ascent,** with breaks of 20 minutes in each hour. Admittedly, the mills would be costly to construct, but the power generated could be applied to a range of industries, from the grinding of grain in predominantly agricultural regions like East Anglia, to spinning textiles and driving lathes in the industrial north, so they would soon pay for themselves.

The first such treadmill was erected in Bury St Edmunds in November 1819, but their use spread so rapidly that within three years more than twenty could be found operating in penitentiaries and houses of correction across the British Isles, from Edinburgh in the north to Exeter in the south, and from Haverfordwest in the west to Ipswich in the east. In response to a survey conducted in January 1823 by the Home Secretary, Robert Peel, in response to complaints regarding multiple accidents and injuries, county magistrates were uniform in their praise of Cubitt's invention, claiming that it had actually resulted in improved health among the prisoners. An article published in the *Stamford Mercury* went further still, asserting that, following regular stints on the treadmill, a great many prisoners 'are generally discharged ... very beneficially reformed in their characters'. Fear of the machine also operated powerfully 'as a check to crime, by deterring those to whom its nature has been explained by their suffering companions'. Overall, the article concluded cheerily, the deterrent value of the treadmill was so great 'that ere long, the functions of the mill will be suspended for the want of *feet* to keep it in motion'.[19]

But enthusiasm for the treadmill was very far from being universal. Writing in the Tory newspaper *John Bull*, Theodore Hook called it 'barbarous and shameful' and mocked the Society for the Improvement of Prison Discipline for its advocacy, quipping that its members must surely define

---

** This was later reduced to 7,500ft, with the prisoners allowed an increased diet in order to sustain the labour.

prison discipline as 'hard work and hard whipping'.[20] At the other end of the political spectrum, the Whig magistrate and later Deputy Lieutenant for his county, John Ivatt Briscoe, addressed an open letter to Peel, stating that while he had originally supported the introduction of the treadmill, and had even tried it for himself, his observations over an extended period had convinced him that the 'labour is of a nature tending in all cases to injure the prisoner in a greater or less degree', both physically and psychologically.[21] Once described by George III, not entirely complimentarily, as 'that busy man', Sir John Cox Hippisley, diplomat, MP, and champion of Catholic emancipation, also became involved in the debate, describing the mechanism as 'highly mischievous in its principle and baneful in its effects' and 'an instrument which neither the Government nor the people of this Country can countenance, when its evils are fully laid before them'.[22]

There can be very little doubt regarding what the prisoners in Coldbath Fields thought of Cubitt's brainchild. By the beginning of July 1822, eight separate treadmills had been erected in the different yards of the prison and on the 2nd the first prisoners, both male and female, were introduced to the new machines. According to one newspaper, as with many novelties at the first trial 'it was looked upon as a mere matter of amusement',[23] but the relentless, grinding nature of the toil quickly became apparent. 'After some little time', reported *The Examiner*:

> the men in one of the wards, to the number of 40, declared they would not work any longer. The Governor (Mr Adkins) remonstrated with the mutineers in vain – one of the ringleaders, acting as spokesman, positively declared their intention not to work again. Mr Adkins, with becoming firmness (and he is as humane as he is firm) immediately ordered 16 of the most prominent to be double-ironed and locked up in their cells, declaring that they should remain in this state on bread and water, until they thought proper to show contrition. This had the desired effect. The whole of those who remained immediately set to work, and in the course of the day, 11 of the 16 who had been locked up begged to resume their occupation.[24]

Adding to the controversy over the introduction of the treadmill, at the time it first went into operation at Coldbath Fields the energy generated by the prisoners' labours served no profitable purpose, the mill being unconnected to grindstones or looms. But, while a flour-mill was planned for the future, its absence did not prevent the treadmill being operated: Cubitt had allowed for just such a contingency by fitting a regulating fly, meaning that 'the power derived from the action of about 240 prisoners is expended in the air'.²⁵ Lack of genuine productivity therefore became, a report for the Society for the Improvement of Prison Discipline blithely noted, 'a matter of no concern' to the prisoners.²⁶

The decision to order female prisoners onto the treadmill proved particularly contentious, with one impassioned critic writing of its 'barbarous impropriety', and citing numerous occasions when injuries had been sustained as a result of 'the effects of the discipline on the female frame'.²⁷ Following two visits made to Coldbath Fields during the autumn of 1823, this anonymous campaigner went on to describe how several women had fainted and fallen from the treadmill, while another, who had borne twelve children, appeared 'distressed ... to the very last degree' and declared 'she would sooner perform any conceivable task than tread'. Equally shocking was the decision to permit curious spectators, both men and women, 'to stare at the women in this their degraded attitude and condition', just as paying visitors had been allowed to gawp at the patients in Bedlam until the last quarter of the eighteenth century. 'I am assured', wrote the same campaigner, 'that the most abandoned characters complain bitterly at this exposure to strangers' eyes, and ask whether it is not enough for them to endure the drudgery, without being exposed to the gaze of others?'*

The second notorious penal innovation introduced to Coldbath Fields was adopted by Vickery's replacement as governor, Captain George Laval Chesterton. A former Royal Artillery officer who had served under Wellington during the Peninsular War, and with the British Legion in Colombia under Simón Bolívar, Chesterton was a man very different from his predecessors in terms of background and experience. Very different, too, in his views on how a prison should be run, writing that, on his appointment in July 1829, he found 'the whole machinery betokened the most appalling abuse ... everything around me stamped with iniquity and corruption', and the entire institution in desperate need of root and branch reform.²⁸

---

* Internal evidence suggests that the writer of this lengthy letter to the *Morning Chronicle* may have been the equally anonymous 'Student of the Inner Temple' who published in 1824, *Thoughts on Prison Labour*, a 480-page compilation of published criticisms of the treadwheel, and who also visited the prison. Women would continue to labour at the treadmills at Coldbath Fields until 1847, but would be removed from the prison altogether in 1850.

Chesterton would spend the first few years of his twenty-five-year stint as governor stamping out the multiple abuses that he had inherited, gradually replacing his entire staff of turnkeys and introducing reforms to everything from diet to divine service, and from security to sanitation. In the process he earned the hatred of those who had previously benefited from the laxity and corruption, but the admiration of many discerning observers, including Charles Dickens, that most vocal critic of the English penal system, who described him as 'enlightened and superior' and remarkable for his 'firmness, zeal, intelligence, and humanity'.[29] Aided by the growing interest in prison reform that had given rise to the Gaols Act of 1823,* and would subsequently result in the Prisons Act of 1835,** by the mid-1830s Chesterton had succeeded in resolving many of the prison's shortcomings, and he and the Middlesex magistrates agreed that the time had come to introduce a wholesale change to the prison's system of discipline. Two new models were available, both American in origin: the 'Separate System' and the 'Silent System'.

First trialled in the Eastern State Penitentiary in Philadelphia, the Separate System required the complete isolation of inmates, throughout their terms of imprisonment. They would eat, sleep and work in their cells, and exercise in individual yards, their only human interaction restricted to occasional exchanges with the prison guards. In contrast, the Silent System, developed during the 1820s in New York State's Auburn Prison, allowed prisoners to eat, work, pray and, if necessary, sleep together, but with complete silence rigorously enforced at all times. The practical advantages and disadvantages of each system were obvious: while the Separate System could be introduced only in prisons with a cellular design, prisoner management would require a relatively small number of guards; the Silent System, on the other hand, could be introduced without modifications to existing prison structures, but would rely upon significant numbers of guards to maintain the silence, 24 hours per day, and for 365 days a year.

Towards the end of 1834, Chesterton visited Wakefield Prison, where the Silent System had already been introduced, and the Duke Street Prison

---

* An Act for consolidating and amending the Laws relating to the building, repairing and regulating of certain Gaols and Houses of Correction in England and Wales. 4 Geo. IV. c. 64 (1823).

** An Act for effecting greater Uniformity of Practice in the Government of the several Prisons in England and Wales; and for appointing Inspectors of Prisons in Great Britain. 5 & 6 Will. IV. c. 38 (1835).

in Glasgow, where the Separate System had been adopted. On his return, he presented to the Middlesex magistrates a detailed report advocating the introduction of the former system to Coldbath Fields; the magistrates accepted his recommendations and, as Chesterton later recounted in his *Revelations of Prison Life*, 'on 29th December, 1834, a population of 914 prisoners were suddenly apprized that all intercommunication by word, gesture, or sign, was prohibited; and, without a murmur, or the least symptom of overt opposition, the silent system became the established rule of the prison'.[30]

Philip Collins has observed that the merits of the two disciplinary systems 'were hotly, often angrily, debated, with the devotees of each generally claiming every kind of incompatible virtue for his particular nostrum; it was healthier, more reformative, more deterrent, less cruel, less costly, and so on'.[31] The decision to adopt the Silent System in Coldbath Fields was almost certainly driven by practical considerations – specifically the prohibitive costs that would have been involved in converting the prison to a cellular design – but, over time, Chesterton became a vocal and determined champion of its merits, and an equally outspoken denigrator of the alternative. His voice would be just one of many, because arguments over the merits and demerits of the treadmill (and of hard labour more generally), and of the Silent and Separate systems – of their impacts, for good or ill, on prisoners' physical, mental, and spiritual wellbeing, and, crucially, on their potential for reoffending – would continue to rage throughout much of the nineteenth century, just as equally fraught arguments over the means by which to reduce prison populations, while at the same time punishing the guilty and preventing reoffending, rage to this day.

But these debates lie outside the ambit of this work because they were in no way unique to, or focused on, Coldbath Fields. For some sixteen years, however, the prison was unique – made so by the extraordinary conjunction of events and individuals in the years immediately before and after its construction. The burgeoning of British radicalism in response to George III's domination of politics and Parliament from the early 1760s, the eruption of the French Revolution in 1789, the repressive measures introduced in response by Prime Minister William Pitt and the appointment of Thomas Aris as governor of the newly built Coldbath Fields House of Correction, all coincided to ensure that a prison designed specifically to reflect the humane principles of John Howard would become not merely the foremost political prison of its age, but also the most notorious because of the abuses practised within its walls, and to which the government and the magistracy systematically turned a blind eye.

In the view of one later commentator, under Chesterton Coldbath Fields would become 'the best-managed of the Metropolitan Prisons',[32] but neither he nor his successors would ever succeed in removing the tarnish of its earliest years, and at the time of its closure in November 1885 – a result of the rationalisations brought about by the passing of the Prisons Act of 1877* – the prison was still commonly referred to as the Bastille, or 'Steel'. Today, 140 years after its gates closed for the last time, the prison is almost completely forgotten, its site entirely covered by Royal Mail's London Central Mail Centre, and with not a vestige of the original prison still standing. Almost entirely forgotten – but not quite; because to anyone interested in the history of British radicalism and electoral reform, and in the individuals who fought for and against it, Mount Pleasant, Clerkenwell, will always be remembered as the site of London's infamous Bastille.

---

*   An Act to amend the Law relating to Prisons in England. 40 & 41. Vict. c. 21 (1877).

Notes

Prologue
1. Although there is no record of the coach used by Bosville and Burdett on this occasion, Bosville is known to have employed his coach and four when visiting William Cobbett in Newgate Prison between 1810 and 1812. See John Sinclair, *Memoirs of the Life and Works of the Late Right Honourable Sir John Sinclair, Bart.* (London: Blackwood and Sons, 1837), vol. I, p. 187.
2. Richard King (ed.), *The Complete Modern London Spy, for the Present Year 1781* (London: Hogg, 1781), pp. 84–5.
3. William Ralph Douthwaite, *Gray's Inn: Notes Illustrative of Its History and Antiquities* (London: privately printed, 1876), p. 2.
4. Henry Mayhew and John Binny, *The Criminal Prisons of London: And Scenes of Prison Life* (London: Griffin, Bohn and Co., 1862), p. 279.
5. According to the historian of London, Jerry White, by 1797 approximately one-third of all Clerkenwell's residents earned a living by watchmaking, some 1,600 workers producing 120,000 watches annually. See Jerry White, *London in the Eighteenth Century: A Great and Monstrous Thing* (London: The Bodley Head, 2012), pp. 215–6.

1. 'The Cries of the Miserable': Howard's Call to Reform
1. John Howard, *The State of the Prisons in England and Wales, with Preliminary Observations, and an Account of Some Foreign Prisons* (Warrington: William Eyres, 1777), p. 1.
2. John Howard, *The State of the Prisons in England and Wales, with Preliminary Observations, and an Account of Some Foreign Prisons* (Warrington: William Eyres, 1777), p. 2.
3. See John Impey, *The Practice of the Office of Sheriff and Under-Sheriff* (London: Clarke, 1835), p. 50.

4. John Howard, *The State of the Prisons in England and Wales, with Preliminary Observations, and an Account of Some Foreign Prisons* (Warrington: William Eyres, 1777), p. 4.
5. John Howard, *The State of the Prisons in England and Wales, with Preliminary Observations, and an Account of Some Foreign Prisons* (Warrington: William Eyres, 1777), p. 488.
6. See *Journal of the House of Commons*, v. 34, 13 Geo. 3, Parl. 13, Sess. 6 (1772 & 1773).
7. John Howard, *The State of the Prisons in England and Wales, with Preliminary Observations, and an Account of Some Foreign Prisons* (Warrington: William Eyres, 1777), p. 4.
8. John Howard, *The State of the Prisons in England and Wales, with Preliminary Observations, and an Account of Some Foreign Prisons* (Warrington: William Eyres, 1777), p. 5.
9. Charles Lethbridge Kingsford (ed.), *A Survey of London by John Stowe, Reprinted from the Text of 1603* (Oxford: The Clarendon Press, 1908), vol. I, pp. 36–7.
10. Edward Hall, *Hall's Chronicle; Containing the History of England* (London: Johnson, Rivington, Payne et al., 1809), p. 632.
11. Thomas Coghan [sic], *The Haven of Health* (London: Roger Ball, 1636), p. 318.
12. Raphael Holinshed, *Holinshed's Chronicles of England, Scotland, and Ireland* (London: Johnson, Rivington, Payne et al., 1808), vol. IV, p. 868.
13. See John Lord Campbell, *The Lives of the Chief Justices of England* (London: Murray, 1874), vol. III, p. 75. For retention of the practice until the 1970s see sirhenrybrooke.me/2017/06/02/gaol-fever/.
14. John Howard, *The State of the Prisons in England and Wales, with Preliminary Observations, and an Account of Some Foreign Prisons* (Warrington: William Eyres, 1777), p. 39.
15. John Howard, *The State of the Prisons in England and Wales, with Preliminary Observations, and an Account of Some Foreign Prisons* (Warrington: William Eyres, 1777), p. 17.
16. See Vic Gatrell, *The Hanging Tree: Execution and the English People, 1770–1868* (Oxford: OUP, 1994), p. 7.
17. John Pringle, *Observations on the Diseases of the Army* (London: Strahan, Rivington, Johnston et al., 1775), pp. 287–8.
18. William Grant, *An Essay on the Pestilential Fever of Sydenham, Commonly Called the Gaol, Hospital, Ship, and Camp-Fever* (London: Cadell, 1775), pp. 7–8.
19. See, for example, A.L. Lincecum, 'Typhus Fever', *Buffalo Medical Journal*, 74, 2, September 1918, pp. 42–3.
20. John Howard, *The State of the Prisons in England and Wales, with Preliminary Observations, and an Account of Some Foreign Prisons* (Warrington: William Eyres, 1777), p. 5.
21. *Evening Post*, 5 March 1774.
22. John Howard, *The State of the Prisons in England and Wales, with Preliminary Observations, and an Account of Some Foreign Prisons* (Warrington: William Eyres, 1777), pp. 8–9.
23. John Howard, *The State of the Prisons in England and Wales, with Preliminary Observations, and an Account of Some Foreign Prisons* (Warrington: William Eyres, 1777), p. 12.

24. John Howard, *The State of the Prisons in England and Wales, with Preliminary Observations, and an Account of Some Foreign Prisons* (Warrington: William Eyres, 1777), p. 14.
25. Act 22 and 23, Charles II. Quoted in John Howard, *The State of the Prisons in England and Wales, with Preliminary Observations, and an Account of Some Foreign Prisons* (Warrington: William Eyres, 1777), p. 46.
26. John Howard, *The State of the Prisons in England and Wales, with Preliminary Observations, and an Account of Some Foreign Prisons* (Warrington: William Eyres, 1777), p. 16.
27. John Howard, *The State of the Prisons in England and Wales, with Preliminary Observations, and an Account of Some Foreign Prisons* (Warrington: William Eyres, 1777), p. 69.
28. Roy Porter, *Mind-Forg'd Manacles: A History of Madness in England from the Restoration to the Regency* (London: The Athlone Press, 1987), pp. 117–8
29. 'An Act for reducing the Laws relating to Rogues, Vagabonds, Sturdy Beggars and Vagrants, into one Act of Parliament; and for the more effectual punishing such Rogues, Vagabonds, Sturdy Beggars and Vagrants, and sending them whither they ought to be sent' [Vagrancy Act], Public Act, 13 Anne, c. 26, Parliamentary Archives: GB-061, Catalogue Ref: HL/PO/PU/1/1713/13An36.
30. See Roy Porter, *Mind-Forg'd Manacles: A History of Madness in England from the Restoration to the Regency* (London: The Athlone Press, 1987). pp. 117–8.
31. John Howard, *The State of the Prisons in England and Wales, with Preliminary Observations, and an Account of Some Foreign Prisons* (Warrington: William Eyres, 1777), p. 16.
32. Hansard, House of Commons, debate on pauper lunatics, 6 April 1808.
33. *Journal of the House of Commons*, v. 34, p. 469, 14 Geo. 3, Parl. 13, Sess. 7 (1774)
34. *London Chronicle*, 10 March 1774.
35. John Howard, *The State of the Prisons in England and Wales, with Preliminary Observations, and an Account of Some Foreign Prisons* (Warrington: William Eyres, 1777), p. 40.
36. John Roberton, *A Treatise on Medical Police, and on Diet, Regimen, &c.* (London: Thomas Bryce and John Murray, 1809), vol. I, p. 14.
37. John Howard, *The State of the Prisons in England and Wales, with Preliminary Observations, and an Account of Some Foreign Prisons* (Warrington: William Eyres, 1777), p. 43.
38. John Howard, *The State of the Prisons in England and Wales, with Preliminary Observations, and an Account of Some Foreign Prisons* (Warrington: William Eyres, 1777), p. 45.
39. Thomas Archer, *The Pauper, The Thief and the Convict: Sketches of Some of their Homes, Haunts, and Habits* (London: Groombridge, 1865), p. 158.
40. For an excellent analysis of the history of support for hard labour, I recommend Philippa Hardman's unpublished PhD thesis, *The Origins of Late Eighteenth-Century Prison Reform in England*, Department of History, University of Sheffield (2007).

41. John Howard, *The State of the Prisons in England and Wales, with Preliminary Observations, and an Account of Some Foreign Prisons* (Warrington: William Eyres, 1777), p. 50.
42. John Howard, *The State of the Prisons in England and Wales, with Preliminary Observations, and an Account of Some Foreign Prisons* (Warrington: William Eyres, 1777), p. 65.
43. John Howard, *The State of the Prisons in England and Wales, with Preliminary Observations, and an Account of Some Foreign Prisons* (Warrington: William Eyres, 1777), p. 187.
44. John Howard, *The State of the Prisons in England and Wales, with Preliminary Observations, and an Account of Some Foreign Prisons* (Warrington: William Eyres, 1777), p. 186.
45. [Anon.], *Reasons Offered for the Reformation of the House of Correction in Clerkenwell* (London: J. Scott, 1757), p. 5.

2. 'Some Alteration Should be Made': Design and Build

1. [Anon.], *Reasons Offered for the Reformation of the House of Correction in Clerkenwell* (London: J. Scott, 1757), pp. 7–8.
2. London Metropolitan Archives, Middlesex Sessions, General Orders of the Court, April 1783. London Lives ref. LMSMGO556070443.
3. London Metropolitan Archives, Middlesex Sessions, General Orders of the Court, April 1783. London Lives ref. LMSMGO556070442.
4. See London Metropolitan Archives, Middlesex Sessions, Sessions Papers – Justices' Working Papers, January 1783. London Lives ref. LMSMPS507630037.
5. See London Metropolitan Archives, Middlesex Sessions, Sessions Papers – Justices' Working Papers, January 1783. London Lives ref. LMSMPS507630040.
6. London Metropolitan Archives, Middlesex Sessions, General Orders of the Court, April 1783. London Lives ref. LMSMGO556070444.
7. London Metropolitan Archives, Middlesex Sessions, General Orders of the Court, April 1783. London Lives ref. LMSMGO556070443.
8. Simon Devereux, 'The Making of the Penitentiary Act, 1775–1779', *The Historical Journal*, 42, 2 (1999), pp. 405–33.
9. London Metropolitan Archives, Middlesex Sessions, General Orders of the Court, April 1783. London Lives ref. LMSMGO556070443.
10. London Metropolitan Archives, Middlesex Sessions, General Orders of the Court, April 1783. London Lives ref. LMSMGO556070449.
11. London Metropolitan Archives, Middlesex Sessions, Sessions Papers – Justices' Working Documents, February 1784. London Lives ref. LMSMPS507780086.
12. London Metropolitan Archives, Middlesex Sessions, Sessions Papers – General Orders of the Court, July 1784. London Lives ref. LMSMPS507840080.
13. *Morning Chronicle*, 26 October 1784.
14. *Morning Chronicle*, 26 October 1784.
15. *Post Boy*, 28 March 1700. Quoted in 'West of Farringdon Road', in *Survey of London*: Volume 47, Northern Clerkenwell and Pentonville, ed. Philip Temple

(London, 2008), pp. 22–51. British History Online www.british-history.ac.uk/survey-london/vol47/pp.22–51.
16. For the history of Bagnigge Wells see Walter Thornbury, 'Bagnigge Wells', in *Old and New London* (London, 1878), vol. II, pp. 296–8.
17. William J. Pinks, *The History of Clerkenwell*, second edition (London: Charles Herbert, 1881), p. 159.
18. Alexander Pope, *The Dunciad with Notes Variorum, and the Prolegomena of Scriblerus* (London: Lawton Gulliver, 1729), pp. 119–20.
19. James Ewing Ritchie, *Days and Nights in London: Studies in Black and Gray* (London: Tinsley Brothers, 1880), p. 261.
20. John Howard, *The State of the Prisons in England and Wales, with Preliminary Observations, and an Account of Some Foreign Prisons* (Warrington: William Eyres, 1777), p. 40.
21. London Metropolitan Archives, Middlesex Sessions, Sessions Papers – General Orders of the Court, 23 December 1784. London Lives ref. LMSMGO556090089.
22. William J. Pinks suggests that the owner of Gardiner's Field was Thomas Clarke Jervoise (1764–1809), the son of Jervoise Clarke Jervoise (1734–1808); however, the Middlesex Sessions papers identify the father as the landholder. See Edward J. Wood (ed.), William J. Pinks, *The History of Clerkenwell*, second edition (London: Charles Herbert, 1881), p. 82.
23. William III, 1698–9: An Act to enable Justices of Peace to build and repair Gaols in their respective Counties (Chapter XIX. Rot. Parl. 11 Gul. III. p. 3. n. 10.), in *Statutes of the Realm: Volume 7, 1695–1701* (1820), pp. 609–10.
24. *Whitehall Evening Post*, 17–19 August 1784.
25. London Metropolitan Archives, Middlesex Sessions, Sessions Papers – General Orders of the Court, 10 May 1785. London Lives ref. LMSMGO556090127.
26. London Metropolitan Archives, Middlesex Sessions, Sessions Papers – General Orders of the Court, 11 February 1786. London Lives ref. LMSMGO556090211.
27. London Metropolitan Archives, Middlesex Sessions, Sessions Papers – General Orders of the Court, 11 February 1786. London Lives ref. LMSMGO556090211.
28. London Metropolitan Archives, Middlesex Sessions, Sessions Papers – General Orders of the Court, 11 February 1786. London Lives ref. LMSMGO556090212.
29. London Metropolitan Archives, Middlesex Sessions, Sessions Papers – General Orders of the Court, 17 February 1786. London Lives ref. LMSMGO556090212.
30. London Metropolitan Archives, Middlesex Sessions, Sessions Papers – General Orders of the Court, 27 March 1786. London Lives ref. LMSMGO556090219.
31. London Metropolitan Archives, Middlesex Sessions, Sessions Papers – General Orders of the Court, 27 March 1786. London Lives ref. LMSMGO556090218.
32. London Metropolitan Archives, Middlesex Sessions, Sessions Papers – General Orders of the Court, 26 June 1787. London Lives ref. LMSMGO556090342.
33. *Gentleman's Magazine*, Supplement for the Year 1796, p. 1065.
34. London Metropolitan Archives, Middlesex Sessions, Sessions Papers – General Orders of the Court, 25 April 1789. London Lives ref. LMSMGO556090492.
35. London Metropolitan Archives, Middlesex Sessions, Sessions Papers – General Orders of the Court, 26 May 1790. London Lives ref. LMSMGO556100065.

36. London Metropolitan Archives, Middlesex Sessions, Sessions Papers – General Orders of the Court, 9 June 1791. London Lives ref. LMSMGO556100149.
37. London Metropolitan Archives, Middlesex Sessions, Sessions Papers – General Orders of the Court, 9 June 1791. London Lives ref. LMSMGO556100149.
38. London Metropolitan Archives, Middlesex Sessions, Sessions Papers – General Orders of the Court, 8 December 1791. London Lives ref. LMSMGO556100186.
39. London Metropolitan Archives, Middlesex Sessions, Sessions Papers – General Orders of the Court, 27 June 1793. London Lives ref. LMSMGO556100309.
40. London Metropolitan Archives, Middlesex Sessions, Sessions Papers – General Orders of the Court, 27 June 1793. London Lives ref. LMSMGO556100310.
41. *Morning Chronicle*, 19 July 1793.
42. London Metropolitan Archives, Middlesex Sessions, Sessions Papers – General Orders of the Court, 5 June 1794. London Lives ref. LMSMGO556100346.
43. London Metropolitan Archives, Middlesex Sessions, Sessions Papers – General Orders of the Court, 5 June 1794. London Lives ref. LMSMGO556100346.
44. *Whitehall Evening Post*, 8 October 1794.
45. Thomas Archer, *The Pauper, The Thief and the Convict: Sketches of Some of their Homes, Haunts, and Habits* (London: Groombridge, 1865), pp. 151–2.
46. George Laval Chesterton, *Revelations of Prison Life; with an Enquiry into Prison Discipline and Secondary Punishments* (London: Hurst and Blackett, 1856), vol. I, p. 16.
47. Leigh Hunt, 'The Prince on St. Patrick's Day', *The Examiner*, 22 March 1812.
48. J.E. Morpurgo (ed.), *The Autobiography of Leigh Hunt* (London: The Cresset Press, 1949), p. 240.
49. William Jones, *The Works of the Right Reverend George Horne, DD, Late Lord Bishop of Norwich; to which are Prefixed Memoirs of his Life, Studies, and Writings* (New York: Onderdonk, 1846), vol. II, p. 35.
50. Royal Society, EC – Certificates of election and candidature for Fellowship of the Royal Society, 1764, ref. EC/1764/25.
51. Samuel Glasse, *The Sinner Encouraged to Repentance: A Sermon, Preached at the Opening of the Chapel of the New House of Correction, for the County of Middlesex* (London: Rivington, Robinson and Gardner, 1794), p. 1.
52. London Metropolitan Archives, Middlesex Sessions, Sessions Papers – General Orders of the Court, 11 February 1786. London Lives ref. LMSMGO556090215.
53. London Metropolitan Archives, Middlesex Sessions, Sessions Papers – General Orders of the Court, 11 February 1786. London Lives ref. LMSMGO556090215.
54. London Metropolitan Archives, Middlesex Sessions, Sessions Papers – General Orders of the Court, 11 February 1786. London Lives ref. LMSMGO556090215.
55. Leslie Stephen and Sidney Lee (eds.), *Dictionary of National Biography* (New York: Macmillan, 1908), vol. VII, p. 1300.
56. Samuel Glasse, *The Sinner Encouraged to Repentance: A Sermon, Preached at the Opening of the Chapel of the New House of Correction, for the County of Middlesex* (London: Rivington, Robinson and Gardner, 1794).
57. London Metropolitan Archives, Middlesex Sessions, Sessions Papers – General Orders of the Court, 4 December 1794. London Lives ref. LMSMGO556100374.

58. *Oracle*, 9 October 1794.
59. *Oracle*, 9 October 1794.
60. London Metropolitan Archives, Middlesex Sessions, Sessions Papers – General Orders of the Court, 27 March 1786. London Lives ref. LMSMGO556090218.
61. London Metropolitan Archives, Middlesex Sessions, Sessions Papers – General Orders of the Court, January 1794 [sic]. London Lives ref. LMSMPS507770228.
62. Samuel Glasse, *The Sinner Encouraged to Repentance: A Sermon Preached at the Opening of the Chapel of the New House of Correction, for the County of Middlesex* (London: Rivington, Robinson and Gardner, 1794), pp. iii–iv.
63. Samuel Glasse, *The Sinner Encouraged to Repentance: A Sermon Preached at the Opening of the Chapel of the New House of Correction, for the County of Middlesex* (London: Rivington, Robinson and Gardner, 1794), p. 8.

3. 'Diversified in Disposition and Pursuits': The Governor and His Wards

1. William J. Pinks, *The History of Clerkenwell*, second edition (London: Charles Herbert, 1881), p. 169.
2. See Thomas Cromwell, *History and Description of the Parish of Clerkenwell* (London: J. & H.S. Storer, 1828), pp. 253–4; also 'New Wells', in *Survey of London*: Volume 47, Northern Clerkenwell and Pentonville, ed. Philip Temple (London, 2008), pp. 52–83. British History Online www.british-history.ac.uk/survey-london/vol47/pp.52–83.
3. Thomas Cromwell, *History and Description of the Parish of Clerkenwell* (London: J. & H.S. Storer, 1828), p. 255.
4. William J. Pinks, *The History of Clerkenwell*, second edition (London: Charles Herbert, 1881), p. 167.
5. London Metropolitan Archives, Middlesex Sessions Papers - Justices' Working Documents, April 1780. London Lives ref. LMSMPS507240042.
6. *Plan of the Finsbury Dispensary, St John's Square, Clerkenwell, for Administering Advice and Medicines to the Poor* (London: no publisher, n.d.), pp. 3–5.
7. *The Times*, 4 April 1792.
8. London Metropolitan Archives, Middlesex Sessions Papers – Justices' Working Documents, December 1782. London Lives ref. LMSMPS507610148.
9. Middlesex Sessions, Sessions Papers – Justices' Working Documents, May 1786, London Lives, 1690–1800, LMSMPS508100040 (www.londonlives.org), London Metropolitan Archives.
10. London Metropolitan Archives, MJ/SP/1793/10/215, Middlesex Sessions of the Peace, Court in Session, 25 September–23 October 1793.
11. London Metropolitan Archives, LMSMPS508890420, Middlesex Sessions of the Peace, Court in Session, October 1793.
12. London Metropolitan Archives, Middlesex Sessions Papers Justices' Working Documents, October 1793. London Lives ref. LMSMPS508890419.
13. London Metropolitan Archives, MJ/SP/1793/10/215, Middlesex Sessions of the Peace, Court in Session, 25 September–23 October 1793.

14. *The Evening Mail*, 10 December 1792. See also *Diary or Woodfall's Register*, 10 December 1792.
15. London Metropolitan Archives, Middlesex Sessions Papers – Justices' Working Documents, October 1793. London Lives ref. LMSMPS508890421.
16. Middlesex Sessions of the Peace, Court in Session, September 1773, London Lives, 1690–1800, MJ/SP/1773/09/016 (www.londonlives.org), London Metropolitan Archives.
17. William Lambard, *Archeion, or a Discourse Upon the High Courts of Justice in England* (London: Seile, 1635), pp. 85–6.
18. This sample list of misdemeanours is taken from Richard Burn, *The Justice of the Peace, and Parish Officer* (The Savoy: Lintot, 1766).
19. George Laval Chesterton, *Revelations of Prison Life; with an Enquiry into Prison Discipline and Secondary Punishments* (London: Hurst and Blackett, 1856), vol. I, pp. 4–5.
20. Anthony Babington, *A House in Bow Street: Crime and the Magistracy, London 1740–1881* (London: Macdonald, 1969), p. 32.
21. William Blackstone, *Commentaries on the Laws of England* (Dublin: Exshaw, Saunders et al., 1770), vol. IV, p. 278.
22. Old Bailey Proceedings Online (www.oldbaileyonline.org, version 9.0) 11 April 1804. Trial of John Lowrie and Thomas Lewis. Available at: www.oldbaileyonline.org/record/t18040411-74 (Accessed: 29 March 2024).
23. See convictrecords.com.au/convicts/lowrie/john/122127.
24. Old Bailey Proceedings Online (www.oldbaileyonline.org, version 9.0) 4 July 1804. Trial of Thomas Bucknell (t18040704-17). Available at: www.oldbaileyonline.org/record/t18040704-17 (Accessed: 29 March 2024). See also: www.capitalpunishmentuk.org/1800.html.
25. Old Bailey Proceedings Online (www.oldbaileyonline.org, version 9.0) 18 April 1798. Trial of Augustus Seaton and Thomas Clifton (t17980418-105). Available at: www.oldbaileyonline.org/record/t17980418-105 (Accessed: 29 March 2024).
26. Old Bailey Proceedings Online (www.oldbaileyonline.org, version 9.0) 27 October 1802. Trial of James Briscoe, John Denham, Jarvis Baker (t18021027-103). Available at: www.oldbaileyonline.org/record/t18021027-103 (Accessed: 29h March 2024).
27. *The World*, 6 June 1789.
28. *The World*, 8 October 1788.
29. *Morning Post*, 22 November 1796.
30. *Morning Post*, 22 November 1796.
31. *The Times*, 3 August 1796.
32. *Morning Post*, 22 November 1796.
33. *Johnson's British Gazette and Sunday Monitor*, 7 May 1797.
34. *True Briton*, 9 November 1797.
35. *True Briton*, 9 November 1797.
36. *True Briton*, 9 November 1797.
37. *Jackson's Oxford Journal*, 29 September 1810.

38. *Jackson's Oxford Journal*, 29 September 1810.
39. *Morning Chronicle*, 28 September 1810.
40. *Report from the Commissioners on the Coldbath Fields Prison* (House of Commons, 19 May 1809), p. 14.
41. *St James's Chronicle*, 15 September 1803.
42. *St James's Chronicle*, 15 September 1803.
43. *St James's Chronicle*, 15 September 1803.
44. London Metropolitan Archives, MJ/SP/1803/10/028, R. Ford to J. Stirling, 27 October [1803].

4. 'Our Jacks Will Grumble': Naval Mutinies at Spithead and the Nore

1. See John Sinclair, *Memoirs of the Life and Works of the Late Right Honourable Sir John Sinclair, Bart.* (London: Blackwood and Sons, 1837), vol. I, p. 183. The author was Bosville's great-nephew.
2. Anna M.W. Stirling, *A Painter of Dreams and Other Biographical Studies* (London: Lane, 1916), p. 75.
3. Anna M.W. Stirling, *A Painter of Dreams and Other Biographical Studies* (London: Lane, 1916), p. 75.
4. John Sinclair, *Memoirs of the Life and Works of the Late Right Honourable Sir John Sinclair, Bart.* (London: Blackwood and Sons, 1837), vol. I, p. 184.
5. 'Sir Francis Burdett', in [Anon.] *Public Characters of 1802–1803* (London: Richard Phillips, 1803), p. 500.
6. Burdett to Thomas Coutts, 28 January 1798. Quoted in Melville W. Patterson, *Sir Francis Burdett and His Times, 1770–1844* (London: Macmillan, 1931), vol. I, p. 33.
7. Burdett to Thomas Coutts, 28 January 1798. Quoted in Melville W. Patterson, *Sir Francis Burdett and His Times, 1770–1844* (London: Macmillan, 1931), vol. I, p. 40.
8. Quoted in Sir Lewis Namier and John Brooke (ed.), *The History of Parliament: The House of Commons 1754–1790* (Oxford: History of Parliament Trust, 1964), p. 261.
9. Sir Nathaniel W. Wraxall, *Historical Memoirs of his Own Time* (London: Bentley, 1836), volume II, pp. 352–3.
10. Quoted in Sir Lewis Namier and John Brooke (ed.), *The History of Parliament: The House of Commons 1754–1790* (Oxford: History of Parliament Trust, 1964), p. 262.
11. John Courtenay, *Philosophical Reflections on the Late Revolution in France, and the Conduct of the Dissenters in England, in a Letter to the Rev. Dr Priestley* (London: Becket, 1790), p. 2.
12. James Eason, University of Chicago, https://penelope.uchicago.edu/courtenay.
13. Melville W. Patterson, *Sir Francis Burdett and His Times, 1770–1844* (London: Macmillan, 1931), vol. I, p. 123.
14. Horatio Nelson to Fanny Nelson, 11 September 1793. See *The Despatches and Letters of Vice Admiral Lord Viscount Nelson with Notes by Sir Nicholas Harris Nicolas* (London: Chatham Publishing, 1997), vol. I, p. 325.
15. Mutineers of HMS *London* to Charles James Fox. Quoted in Conrad Gill, *The Naval Mutinies of 1797* (Manchester: University Press, 1913), p. 263.

16. *Regulations and Instructions Relating to His Majesty's Service at Sea* (London, 1790), p. 46.
17. Address from the crew of HMS *Winchelsea* to the Lords of the Admiralty, quoted in George E. Manwaring and Bonamy Dobrée, *The Floating Republic: An Account of the Mutinies at Spithead and the Nore in 1797* (London: Penguin Books, 1937), p. 18.
18. Admiral Bridport to the Lords of the Admiralty, 16 April 1797. Quoted in Conrad Gill, *The Naval Mutinies of 1797* (Manchester: University Press, 1913), p. 23.
19. Sir Evan Nepean to Admiral Bridport, 16 April 1797. Quoted in Conrad Gill, *The Naval Mutinies of 1797* (Manchester: University Press, 1913), p. 25.
20. Denver Brunsman, 'Men of War: British Sailors and the Impressment Paradox', *Journal of Early Modern History*, 14 (1–2), p. 31.
21. Conrad Gill, *The Naval Mutinies of 1797* (Manchester: University Press, 1913), p. 139.
22. Conrad Gill, *The Naval Mutinies of 1797* (Manchester: University Press, 1913), pp. 139–40.
23. *The Annual Register, or a View of the History, Politics, and Literature, for the Year 1797* (London: Rivington, 1797), p. 219.
24. *Evening Mail*, 19 April 1797.
25. *The Annual Register, or a View of the History, Politics, and Literature, for the Year 1797* (London: Rivington, 1797), p. 219.
26. See Conrad Gill, *The Naval Mutinies of 1797* (Manchester: University Press, 1913), p. 186.
27. Petition 'To the King's Most Excellent Majesty', *c.* 5 June 1797. Quoted in Conrad Gill, *The Naval Mutinies of 1797* (Manchester: University Press, 1913), pp. 216–7.
28. Quoted in Conrad Gill, *The Naval Mutinies of 1797* (Manchester: University Press, 1913), p. 241.
29. Joint memorandum from Aaron Graham and Daniel Williams at Sheerness, 24 June 1797. The National Archives ref. HO 42/41/38.
30. George E. Manwaring and Bonamy Dobrée, *The Floating Republic: An Account of the Mutinies at Spithead and the Nore in 1797* (London: Penguin Books, 1937), p. 245.
31. The number of Nore mutineers confined at Coldbath Fields is confirmed by London Lives, Middlesex Sessions, General Orders of the Court, 14 January 1796 to 18 September 1800, ref. LMSMGO556110158.

5. 'Disaffected Persons': The Advocates of Radical Reform

1. London Metropolitan Archives, Report on the escape of the mutineers, George Gainer, John Davis, Abraham Nelson, William Hooper, John Griffiths, John Wells and James Jones, from the Coldbath Fields House of Correction, April 1798, ref. MJ/SP/1798/04/130.
2. See London Metropolitan Archives, Report on the escape of the mutineers, George Gainer, John Davis, Abraham Nelson, William Hooper, John Griffiths, John Wells and James Jones, from the Coldbath Fields House of Correction, April 1798, ref. MJ/SP/1798/04/130.
3. *London Chronicle*, 3 May 1798.

Notes

4. Letter to fellow prisoners left in the cell of George Gainer, mutineer, 31 March 1798. London Metropolitan Archives, ref. MJ/SP/1798/04/133.
5. Duke of Portland to Sir William Mainwaring, 14 April 1798, Middlesex Sessions, General Orders of the Court, 19 April 1798, SM/GO, London Lives, ref. LMSMGO556110186.
6. Henry Selby to the Duke of Portland, 1 May 1798, Middlesex Sessions, General Orders of the Court, 19 April 1798, SM/GO, London Lives, ref. LMSMGO556110186.
7. Memorial of His Majesty's Justices of the Peace for the County of Middlesex to the Duke of Portland, 24 May 1798, Middlesex Sessions, General Orders of the Court, SM/GO, London Lives, ref. LMSMGO556110198.
8. *Morning Herald*, 9 April 1798.
9. *Morning Herald*, 9 April 1798.
10. See Melville W. Patterson, *Sir Francis Burdett and His Times, 1770–1844* (London: Macmillan, 1931), vol. I, p. 67.
11. *The Times*, 22 December 1798.
12. See Michael T. Davis (ed.), *The London Corresponding Society, 1792–1795* (London: Routledge, 2002), vol, V, pp. 147–76.
13. *The Times*, 22 December 1798.
14. 'Further Examination of Thomas Aris', in appendices to John Bowles, *Thoughts on the Late General Election, as Demonstrative of the Progress of Jacobinism* (London: Rivington, 1802), p. 91.
15. *The Times*, 7 January 1799.
16. *An Impartial Statement of the Inhuman Cruelties Discovered! in the Coldbath-Fields Prison, by the Grand and Traverse Juries for the County of Middlesex, and Reported in the House of Commons on Friday 11th June 1800 by Sir Francis Burdett, Bart.* (London: J.S. Jordan [1800]), p. 9.
17. See London Metropolitan Archives, Middlesex Sessions, General Orders of the Court, 6 December 1798. London Lives ref. LMSMGO556110244.
18. John Howard, *The State of the Prisons in England and Wales, with Preliminary Observations, and an Account of Some Foreign Prisons* (Warrington: William Eyres, 1777), p. 39.
19. Edmund Burke, *Reflections on the Revolution in France, and on the Proceedings in Certain Societies in London Relative to the Event in a Letter Intended to Have Been Sent to a Gentleman in Paris* (London: Dodsley, 1790), p. 7.
20. Edmund Burke, *Reflections on the Revolution in France, and on the Proceedings in Certain Societies in London Relative to the Event in a Letter Intended to Have Been Sent to a Gentleman in Paris* (London: Dodsley, 1790), p. 8.
21. Thomas Paine, *Rights of Man* (London: Jordan, 1791), p. 166.
22. Prospectus of the Society for Constitutional Information (Printed and distributed gratis by the Society for Constitutional Information; undated, but *c.* 1790).
23. 'Declaration of those Rights of the Commonalty of Great Britain, Without which they cannot be FREE (Printed and distributed gratis by the Society for Constitutional Information; undated, but *c.* 1790).

24. *The Correspondence of the Revolution Society in London, with the National Assembly, and with Various Societies of the Friends of Liberty in France and England* (London: no publisher, 1792), p. 2.
25. *The Correspondence of the Revolution Society in London, with the National Assembly, and with Various Societies of the Friends of Liberty in France and England* (London: no publisher, 1792), p. 3.
26. *Journal de Bordeaux*, 6 October 1790. Quoted in Micah Alpaugh, 'The British Origins of the French Jacobins: Radical Sociability and the Development of the Political Club Networks, 1787–1793', *European History Quarterly*, 44, 4 (2014), pp. 593–619.
27. *The London Corresponding Society to the Nation at Large* (no publisher, 1792), pp. 1–2.
28. *Narrative of the Proceedings at a General Meeting of the London Corresponding Society* (no publisher, 1795), p. 10.
29. Kenneth R. Johnston, 'The First and Last British Convention', *Romanticism*, 13, 2 (2007), pp. 99–132.
30. Kenneth R. Johnston, 'The First and Last British Convention', *Romanticism*, 13, 2 (2007), pp. 99–132.
31. Henry Cockburn, *Memorials of His Time* (New York: Appleton, 1856), p. 115.
32. *First Report from the Committee of Secrecy, Ordered to be printed 17th May 1794* (London: Debrett, 1794).
33. Habeas Corpus Suspension Act 1794 (34 Geo. 3. c. 54).
34. John Hostettler, *Thomas Erskine and Trial by Jury* (Chichester: Barry Rose Law Publishers Ltd, 1996), p. 126.
35. William Hague, *William Pitt the Younger* (London: HarperCollins, 2004), p. 354.
36. *Morning Post*, 27 October 1795.
37. *Morning Post*, 27 October 1795.
38. *Truth and Treason! Or a Narrative of the Royal Procession to the House of Peers, October the 29th, 1795* (no place of publication, or publisher, 1795), p. 2.
39. *Truth and Treason! Or a Narrative of the Royal Procession to the House of Peers, October the 29th, 1795* (no place of publication, or publisher, 1795), p. 3.
40. W.S. Hathaway (ed.), *The Speeches of the Right Honourable William Pitt in the House of Commons* (London: Longman, Hurst, Rees, et al., 1817), vol. II, pp. 101–4.
41. W.S. Hathaway (ed.), *The Speeches of the Right Honourable William Pitt in the House of Commons* (London: Longman, Hurst, Rees, et al., 1817), vol. II, p. 112.
42. John Wright (ed.), *The Speeches of the Right Honourable Charles James Fox, in the House of Commons* (London: Longman, Hurst, Rees et al., 1815), vol. VI, p. 8.
43. Mary Thale (ed.), *The Autobiography of Francis Place* (New York: Cambridge University Press, 1972), p. 179.
44. Mary Thale (ed.), *The Autobiography of Francis Place* (New York: Cambridge University Press, 1972), p. 177.
45. *The Parliamentary History of England, From the Earliest Period to the Year 1803* (London: Longman, Hurst, Rees et al., 1819), vol. XXXIV, p. 643.
46. *London Packet or New Evening Post*, 2 March 1798.
47. See *Bell's Weekly Messenger*, 4 March 1798. In this report, Coigly is referred to by the aliases Favey and Colonel Morris.

Notes

48. George T. Wilkinson, *The Newgate Calendar Improved; Being Interesting Memoirs of Notorious Characters, Who have been Convicted of Offences against the Laws of England* (London: Thomas Kelly, n.d.), vol. II, p. 566.
49. George T. Wilkinson, *The Newgate Calendar Improved; Being Interesting Memoirs of Notorious Characters, Who have been Convicted of Offences against the Laws of England* (London: Thomas Kelly, n.d.), vol. II, p. 566.
50. W.S. Hathaway (ed.), *The Speeches of the Right Honourable William Pitt in the House of Commons* (London: Longman, Hurst, Rees, et al., 1817), vol. II, p. 418.
51. W.S. Hathaway (ed.), *The Speeches of the Right Honourable William Pitt in the House of Commons* (London: Longman, Hurst, Rees, et al., 1817), vol. II, p. 421.
52. Mary Thale (ed.), *The Autobiography of Francis Place* (New York: Cambridge University Press, 1972), p. 175.
53. *The Atlantic Monthly*, vol. XIII, June 1864, no. LXXX.
54. John Diprose, *Some Account of the Parish of Saint Clement Danes (Westminster) Past and Present* (London: Diprose and Bateman, 1868), p. 100.
55. Mary Thale (ed.), *The Autobiography of Francis Place* (New York: Cambridge University Press, 1972), p. 176.
56. *The Sun*, 21 April 1798.
57. 'An Act to enable His Majesty more effectually to provide for the Defence and Security of the Realm during the present War, and for indemnifying Persons who may suffer in their Property by such Measures as may be necessary for that Purpose' (38 Geo. 3), 5 April 1798.
58. Mary Thale (ed.), *The Autobiography of Francis Place* (New York: Cambridge University Press, 1972), p. 177.
59. *The Sun*, 20 April 1798.
60. Christina Parolin, *Radical Spaces: Venues of Popular Politics in London, 1790–c. 1845* (Canberra: ANU E Press, 2010), p. 131.
61. Mary Thale (ed.), *The Autobiography of Francis Place* (New York: Cambridge University Press, 1972), p. 177.
62. *The Sun*, 21 April 1798.

6. 'The Heaviest Penalty': Radicals in the House of Correction

1. Mary Thale (ed.), *The Autobiography of Francis Place* (New York: Cambridge University Press, 1972), p. 181.
2. Mary Thale (ed.), *The Autobiography of Francis Place* (New York: Cambridge University Press, 1972), p. 181.
3. Sir Richard Phillips, *A Letter to the Livery of London, Relative to the Views of the Writer in Executing the Office of Sheriff* (London: Phillips, 1808), pp. 83–9.
4. John Thelwall, *Poems Written in Close Confinement in the Tower and Newgate under a Charge of High Treason* (London: printed for the author, 1795), p. 9.
5. Memorial of His Majesty's Justices of the Peace for the County of Middlesex to the Duke of Portland, 24 May 1798, Middlesex Sessions, General Orders of the Court, SM/GO, London Lives, ref. LMSMGO556110198.

6. Mary Thale (ed.), *The Autobiography of Francis Place* (New York: Cambridge University Press, 1972), p. 181.
7. For the details of John Kirby's career I am indebted to Alexander Wakelam's 'Mr John Kirby (1727–1804) – A Debtor Turned Gaoler and the Rise of Professional Prison Keeping', alexanderwakelam.com, 8 July 2020.
8. Alexander Wakelam, 'Mr John Kirby (1727–1804) – A Debtor Turned Gaoler and the Rise of Professional Prison Keeping', alexanderwakelam.com, 8 July 2020.
9. James Neild, *Account of Persons Confined for Debt in the Various Prisons of England and Wales* (London: Printed at the Philanthropic Reform, 1800), p. 32.
10. *Star and Evening Advertiser*, 3 January 1793.
11. *Oracle*, 20 June 1799.
12. *The Times*, 7 January 1799.
13. Mary Thale (ed.), *The Autobiography of Francis Place* (New York: Cambridge University Press, 1972), pp. 177–8.
14. Mary Thale (ed.), *The Autobiography of Francis Place* (New York: Cambridge University Press, 1972), p. 179.
15. Mary Thale (ed.), *The Autobiography of Francis Place* (New York: Cambridge University Press, 1972), p. 176.
16. *Bell's Weekly Messenger*, 22 Apr 1798.
17. Mary Thale (ed.), *The Autobiography of Francis Place* (New York: Cambridge University Press, 1972), p. 198.
18. [John Bone], *Reformers no Rioters* (London: LCS, c. 1794), p. 3.
19. See Michael T. Davis (ed.), *The London Corresponding Society, 1792–1799* (London: Routledge, 2002).
20. London Metropolitan Archives, Middlesex Sessions, General Orders of the Court, 14 January 1799. London Lives ref. LMSMGO556110296.
21. *The Times*, 7 January 1799.
22. Thomas R. Forbes, 'A Mortality Record for Coldbath Fields Prison, 1795–1829', *Bulletin of the New York Academy of Medicine: Journal of Urban Health*, 53, 7 (1977), p. 669.
23. London Metropolitan Archives, Middlesex Sessions, General Orders of the Court, 14 January 1799. London Lives, ref. LMSMGO556110274.
24. London Metropolitan Archives, Middlesex Sessions, General Orders of the Court, 14 January 1799. London Lives ref. LMSMGO556110274.
25. London Metropolitan Archives, Middlesex Sessions, General Orders of the Court, SM/GO, 14 January 1796–18 September 1800, ref: LMSMGO556110256-262, 10 January 1799.
26. *Mirror of the Times*, 30 June 1798.
27. Thomas Townshend to Archibald Campbell, 14 December 1782, quoted in James Bannantine, *Memoirs of Edward Marcus Despard* (London: Ridgway, 1799), p. 13.
28. Charles Oman, *The Unfortunate Colonel Despard and Other Studies* (London: Arnold, 1922), p. 3.
29. For the best modern account of the Nicaraguan campaign of 1780 see Clifford D. Conner, *Colonel Despard: The Life and Times of an Anglo-Irish Rebel* (Pennsylvania: Combined Publishing, 2000).

30. Charles Oman, *The Unfortunate Colonel Despard and Other Studies* (London: Arnold, 1922), p. 3.
31. Benjamin Moseley, *A Treatise on Tropical Diseases; On Military Operations; and On the Climate of the West-Indies* (London: Cadell, 1792), p. 136.
32. Benjamin Moseley, *A Treatise on Tropical Diseases; On Military Operations; and On the Climate of the West-Indies* (London: Cadell, 1792), p. 146.
33. Benjamin Moseley, *A Treatise on Tropical Diseases; On Military Operations; and On the Climate of the West-Indies* (London: Cadell, 1792), p. 143.
34. John Polson to Governor Dalling, 30 April 1780; quoted in Clifford D. Conner, *Colonel Despard: The Life and Times of an Anglo-Irish Rebel* (Pennsylvania: Combined Publishing, 2000), p. 53.
35. Archibald Campbell to Lord Townshend, 10 October 1782; quoted in *The London Gazette*, 26–30 November 1782.
36. Thomas Townshend to Archibald Campbell, 14 December 1782; quoted in James Bannantine, *Memoirs of Edward Marcus Despard* (London: Ridgway, 1799), pp. 13–14.
37. Charles Oman, *The Unfortunate Colonel Despard and Other Studies* (London: Arnold, 1922), p. 6.
38. Lord Sydney to Edward Despard, 26 June 1787; quoted in James Bannantine, *Memoirs of Edward Marcus Despard* (London: Ridgway, 1799), pp. 25–6.
39. Letter of the 'Committee of Honduras Settlers'; quoted in Clifford D. Conner, *Colonel Despard: The Life and Times of an Anglo-Irish Rebel* (Pennsylvania: Combined Publishing, 2000), p. 97.
40. Lord Sydney to Edward Despard, 6 February 1788; quoted in Clifford D. Conner, *Colonel Despard: The Life and Times of an Anglo-Irish Rebel* (Pennsylvania: Combined Publishing, 2000), p. 103.
41. See E.M. Trahey, *Free Women and the Making of Colonial Jamaican Economy and Society 1760–1834*. PhD thesis (2018), University of Cambridge, doi.org/10.17863/CAM.32469
42. James Bannantine, *Memoirs of Edward Marcus Despard* (London: Ridgway, 1799), p. 26.
43. James Bannantine, *Memoirs of Edward Marcus Despard* (London: Ridgway, 1799), pp. 27–8.
44. Mike Jay, *The Unfortunate Colonel Despard* (London: Bantam Books, 2004), p. 238.
45. Mike Jay, *The Unfortunate Colonel Despard* (London: Bantam Books, 2004), p. 264.
46. Mary Thale (ed.), *The Autobiography of Francis Place* (New York: Cambridge University Press, 1972), p. 178.
47. *Express* and *Evening Chronicle* and *The Times*, 13 March 1798.
48. John Despard to Andrew Despard, May 1796; quoted in Clifford D. Conner, *Colonel Despard: The Life and Times of an Anglo-Irish Rebel* (Pennsylvania: Combined Publishing, 2000), p. 151.

7. 'Everybody Knows the Bastille': Burdett's Campaign

1. *The Times*, 22 December 1798.
2. *Courier*, 22 December 1798.
3. *Courier*, 22 December 1798.
4. *Courier*, 22 December 1798.
5. *Courier*, 22 December 1798.
6. *Courier*, 22 December 1798.
7. *Courier*, 22 December 1798.
8. *The Times*, 22 December 1798.
9. *The Times*, 22 December 1798.
10. See Memorial of His Majesty's Justices of the Peace for the County of Middlesex to the Duke of Portland, 24 May 1798, Middlesex Sessions, General Orders of the Court, SM/GO, London Lives, ref. LMSMGO556110198.
11. *Courier*, 22 December 1798.
12. *Courier*, 22 December 1798.
13. Francis Bickley (ed.), *The Diaries of Sylvester Douglas (Lord Glenbervie)* (London: Constable, 1928), vol. I, p. 394.
14. *Courier*, 22 December 1798.
15. *Courier*, 22 December 1798.
16. *Morning Chronicle*, 27 December 1798.
17. [John Reeves], *Thoughts on the English Constitution. Addressed to the Quiet Good Sense of the People of England in a Series of Letters. Letter the First* (London: Owen, 1795), p. 15.
18. Valentine Lawless, *Personal Recollections of the Life and Times, with Extracts from the Correspondence of Valentine Lord Cloncurry* (Dublin: McGlashan, 1849), p. 47.
19. *Morning Chronicle*, 27 December 1798.
20. *Morning Chronicle*, 27 December 1798.
21. *The Times*, 27 December 1798.
22. *Morning Chronicle*, 27 December 1798.
23. *The Times*, 27 December 1798.
24. *The Times*, 27 December 1798.
25. *The Times*, 1 January 1799.
26. *Evening Mail*, 4 January 1799.
27. *Star and Evening Advertiser*, 7 January 1799.
28. *Star and Evening Advertiser*, 7 January 1799.
29. *Courier*, 12 March 1799.
30. *Courier*, 12 March 1799.
31. *Courier*, 12 March 1799.
32. *Acts of the Apostles*, King James Version, 8:7.
33. *Courier*, 12 March 1799.
34. *Courier*, 13 March 1799.
35. *Courier*, 13 March 1799.
36. See *Star and Evening Advertiser*, 6 April 1799.
37. *General Evening Post*, 20 April 1799.
38. *General Evening Post*, 20 April 1799.
39. *Observer*, 21 April 1799.

40. *Evening Mail*, 22 May 1799.
41. London Metropolitan Archives, Middlesex Sessions, General Orders of the Court, SM/GO, 14 January 1799. London Lives ref. LMSMGO556110286.
42. *Evening Mail*, 22 May 1799.
43. *Evening Mail*, 22 May 1799.
44. *Evening Mail*, 22 May 1799.

8. 'Disgraceful to Humanity': Debates and Inquiries

1. See 'British artists' suppliers, 1650–1950', National Portrait Gallery, www.npg.org.uk/collections/research/programmes/directory-of-suppliers/suppliers-c.
2. Samuel Taylor Coleridge, 'The Devil's Thoughts' (1799), stanza IX.
3. 'The Presentment of the Grand Jury for the County of Middlesex', in *An Impartial Statement of the Inhuman Cruelties Discovered! in the Coldbath-Fields Prison, by the Grand and Traverse Juries for the County of Middlesex, and Reported in the House of Commons on Friday 11th June 1800 by Sir Francis Burdett, Bart.* (London: J.S. Jordan [1800]), p. 7.
4. 'The Presentment of the Grand Jury for the County of Middlesex', in *An Impartial Statement of the Inhuman Cruelties Discovered! in the Coldbath-Fields Prison, by the Grand and Traverse Juries for the County of Middlesex, and Reported in the House of Commons on Friday 11th June 1800 by Sir Francis Burdett, Bart.* (London: J.S. Jordan [1800]), p. 7.
5. 'The Presentment of the Grand Jury for the County of Middlesex', in *An Impartial Statement of the Inhuman Cruelties Discovered! in the Coldbath-Fields Prison, by the Grand and Traverse Juries for the County of Middlesex, and Reported in the House of Commons on Friday 11th June 1800 by Sir Francis Burdett, Bart.* (London: J.S. Jordan [1800]), p. 7.
6. 'The Presentment of the Grand Jury for the County of Middlesex', in *An Impartial Statement of the Inhuman Cruelties Discovered! in the Coldbath-Fields Prison, by the Grand and Traverse Juries for the County of Middlesex, and Reported in the House of Commons Friday 11th June 1800 by Sir Francis Burdett, Bart.* (London: J.S. Jordan [1800]), p. 8.
7. 'Inspection of the House of Correction, Coldbath Fields, on the 30th May and 4th June 1800, by the Traverse Jury for Clerkenwell', in *An Impartial Statement of the Inhuman Cruelties Discovered! in the Coldbath-Fields Prison, by the Grand and Traverse Juries for the County of Middlesex, and Reported in the House of Commons on Friday 11th June 1800 by Sir Francis Burdett, Bart.* (London: J.S. Jordan [1800]), p. 8.
8. 'Inspection of the House of Correction, Coldbath Fields, on the 30th May and 4th June 1800, by the Traverse Jury for Clerkenwell', in *An Impartial Statement of the Inhuman Cruelties Discovered! in the Coldbath-Fields Prison, by the Grand and Traverse Juries for the County of Middlesex, and Reported in the House of Commons on Friday 11th June 1800 by Sir Francis Burdett, Bart.* (London: J.S. Jordan [1800]), p. 10.
9. 'Inspection of the House of Correction, Coldbath Fields, on the 30th May and 4th June 1800, by the Traverse Jury for Clerkenwell', in *An Impartial Statement of the Inhuman Cruelties Discovered! in the Coldbath-Fields Prison, by the Grand and Traverse Juries for the County of Middlesex, and Reported in the House of Commons on Friday 11th June 1800 by Sir Francis Burdett, Bart.* (London: J.S. Jordan [1800]), p. 11.

10. 'Inspection of the House of Correction, Coldbath Fields, on the 30th May and 4th June 1800, by the Traverse Jury for Clerkenwell', in *An Impartial Statement of the Inhuman Cruelties Discovered! in the Coldbath-Fields Prison, by the Grand and Traverse Juries for the County of Middlesex, and Reported in the House of Commons on Friday 11th June 1800 by Sir Francis Burdett, Bart.* (London: J.S. Jordan [1800]), p. 12.
11. 'Inspection of the House of Correction, Coldbath Fields, on the 30th May and 4th June 1800, by the Traverse Jury for Clerkenwell', in *An Impartial Statement of the Inhuman Cruelties Discovered! in the Coldbath-Fields Prison, by the Grand and Traverse Juries for the County of Middlesex, and Reported in the House of Commons on Friday 11th June 1800 by Sir Francis Burdett, Bart.* (London: J.S. Jordan [1800]), p. 13.
12. George Rudé, *Hanoverian London, 1714–1808* (Stroud: Sutton Publishing, 1971), p. 83.
13. *An Impartial Statement of the Inhuman Cruelties Discovered! in the Coldbath-Fields Prison, by the Grand and Traverse Juries for the County of Middlesex, and Reported in the House of Commons on Friday 11th June 1800 by Sir Francis Burdett, Bart.* (London: J.S. Jordan [1800]), p. 16.
14. London Metropolitan Archives, Middlesex Sessions, General Orders of the Court, SM/GO, 10 July 1800. London Lives ref. LMSMGO556110463.
15. *An Impartial Statement of the Inhuman Cruelties Discovered! in the Coldbath-Fields Prison, by the Grand and Traverse Juries for the County of Middlesex, and Reported in the House of Commons on Friday 11th June 1800 by Sir Francis Burdett, Bart.* (London: J.S. Jordan [1800]), p. 22.
16. Report of the Prison Committee, Middlesex Sessions, General Orders of the Court, SM/GO, 10 July 1800, London Metropolitan Archives, London Lives ref. LMSMGO556110464.
17. *St. James's Chronicle or the British Evening Post*, 24 July 1800.
18. *St. James's Chronicle or the British Evening Post*, 24 July 1800.
19. *A Further Account (Being Part II) of the Cruelties Discovered in the Cold-Bath Fields Prison* (London: Jordon [1800]), p. 21.
20. Sheridan to his wife [23 July 1800], in Cecil Price (ed.), *The Letters of Richard Brinsley Sheridan* (Oxford: Clarendon Press, 1966), vol. II, p. 135.
21. *Albion & Evening Advertiser*, 13 August 1800.
22. John Impey, *The Office of Sheriff, Showing Its History and Antiquity* (London: the Author, 1786), p. 79.
23. Michael Ryan, *A Manual of Medical Jurisprudence* (London: Renshaw and Rush, 1831), p. 219.
24. *An Impartial Statement of the Inhuman Cruelties Discovered! in the Coldbath-Fields Prison, by the Grand and Traverse Juries for the County of Middlesex, and Reported in the House of Commons on Friday 11th June 1800 by Sir Francis Burdett, Bart.* (London: J.S. Jordan [1800]), p. 11.
25. *An Impartial Statement of the Inhuman Cruelties Discovered! in the Coldbath-Fields Prison, by the Grand and Traverse Juries for the County of Middlesex, and Reported in the House of Commons on Friday 11th June 1800 by Sir Francis Burdett, Bart.* (London: J.S. Jordan [1800]), p. 11.
26. James Johnston to J.S. Jordan, 20 June 1800, in *An Impartial Statement of the Inhuman Cruelties Discovered! in the Coldbath-Fields Prison, by the Grand and Traverse Juries for the*

County of Middlesex, and Reported in the House of Commons on Friday 11th June 1800 by Sir Francis Burdett, Bart. (London: J.S. Jordan [1800]], pp. 11–12.
27. *Albion & Evening Advertiser*, 22 August 1800.
28. Affidavit of James Johnston, August 1800. Bodleian Library, MS Eng. Hist. C. 296 ff. 88–9, 90,114–15.
29. *Albion & Evening Advertiser*, 25 September 1800.
30. *The Times*, 16 August 1800.
31. *The Times*, 16 August 1800.
32. *The Sun*, 15 August 1800.
33. Sir Robert Baker to the Duke of Portland, 15 August 1800. The National Archives, ref. HO 42/50.
34. *The Sun*, 15 August 1800.
35. *London Packet or New Evening Post*, 18 August 1800.
36. London Metropolitan Archives, Evidence of John Nicholson, 15 August 1800, Middlesex Sessions, General Orders of the Court, SM/GO, 18 September 1800. London Lives ref: LMSMGO556110487.
37. *London Packet or New Evening Post*, 18 August 1800.
38. Patrick Duffin to John Horne Took, 8 August 1800. Bodleian Library, MS Eng. Hist. C. 296 ff. 88–9, 90,114–15.
39. *Morning Post*, 16 August 1800.

9. 'An Improper Place of Confinement': The Royal Commission
1. Sir George Onesiphorus Paul to the Duke of Portland, 20 August 1800. The National Archives, ref. HO 42/50.
2. *Papers Presented to the House of Commons, Relating to His Majesty's Prison in Cold Bath Fields*, Ordered to be printed 18th December 1800, p. 22.
3. *Papers Presented to the House of Commons, Relating to His Majesty's Prison in Cold Bath Fields*, Ordered to be printed 18th December 1800, p. 48.
4. *Papers Presented to the House of Commons, Relating to His Majesty's Prison in Cold Bath Fields*, Ordered to be printed 18th December 1800, p. 50.
5. *Papers Presented to the House of Commons, Relating to His Majesty's Prison in Cold Bath Fields*, Ordered to be printed 18th December 1800, p. 17.
6. *The Parliamentary Register; or, History of the Proceedings and Debates of the Houses of Lords and Commons* (London: Debrett, 1801), vol. XV, p. 603.
7. *Papers Presented to the House of Commons, Relating to His Majesty's Prison in Cold Bath Fields*, Ordered to be printed 18th December 1800, p. 19.
8. *Papers Presented to the House of Commons, Relating to His Majesty's Prison in Cold Bath Fields*, Ordered to be printed 18th December 1800, p. 22.
9. *Papers Presented to the House of Commons, Relating to His Majesty's Prison in Cold Bath Fields*, Ordered to be printed 18th December 1800, p. 19.
10. *Papers Presented to the House of Commons, Relating to His Majesty's Prison in Cold Bath Fields*, Ordered to be printed 18th December 1800, p. 50.
11. *Papers Presented to the House of Commons, Relating to His Majesty's Prison in Cold Bath Fields*, Ordered to be printed 18th December 1800, p. 16.

12. *Papers Presented to the House of Commons, Relating to His Majesty's Prison in Cold Bath Fields*, Ordered to be printed 18th December 1800, pp. 50–1.
13. *Papers Presented to the House of Commons, Relating to His Majesty's Prison in Cold Bath Fields*, Ordered to be printed 18th December 1800, p. 36.
14. George Laval Chesterton, *Revelations of Prison Life; with an Enquiry into Prison Discipline and Secondary Punishments* (London: Hurst and Blackett, 1856), vol. I, p. 46.
15. Details of the prisoners' rations are taken from James Neild, *State of the Prisons in England, Scotland, and Wales* (London: Nichols, 1812), p. 142.
16. *Papers Presented to the House of Commons, Relating to His Majesty's Prison in Cold Bath Fields*, Ordered to be printed 18th December 1800, p. 36.
17. *Papers Presented to the House of Commons, Relating to His Majesty's Prison in Cold Bath Fields*, Ordered to be printed 18th December 1800, p. 41.
18. *Papers Presented to the House of Commons, Relating to His Majesty's Prison in Cold Bath Fields*, Ordered to be printed 18th December 1800, p. 42.
19. *Papers Presented to the House of Commons, Relating to His Majesty's Prison in Cold Bath Fields*, Ordered to be printed 18th December 1800, p. 42.
20. *The Times*, 26 December 1800.
21. *Papers Presented to the House of Commons, Relating to His Majesty's Prison in Cold Bath Fields*, Ordered to be printed 18th December 1800, p. 17.
22. *Papers Presented to the House of Commons, Relating to His Majesty's Prison in Cold Bath Fields*, Ordered to be printed 18th December 1800, p. 17.
23. *Papers Presented to the House of Commons, Relating to His Majesty's Prison in Cold Bath Fields*, Ordered to be printed 18th December 1800, p. 47.
24. Papers Presented to the House of Commons, Relating to His Majesty's Prison in Cold Bath Fields, Ordered to be printed 18th December 1800, p. 47.
25. *Papers Presented to the House of Commons, Relating to His Majesty's Prison in Cold Bath Fields*, Ordered to be printed 18th December 1800, p. 48.
26. *Papers Presented to the House of Commons, Relating to His Majesty's Prison in Cold Bath Fields*, Ordered to be printed 18th December 1800, p. 43.
27. George O. Paul, *Considerations on the Defects of Prisons, and Their Present System of Regulation* (London: Cadell, 1784), p. 4.
28. *Papers Presented to the House of Commons, Relating to His Majesty's Prison in Cold Bath Fields*, Ordered to be printed 18th December 1800, p. 43.
29. Report of the Royal Commission into the management of Coldbath Fields House of Correction, p. 50. Quoted in *The Trial between Thomas Aris, Governor of the House of Correction for the County of Middlesex, Plaintiff, and William Dickie* (London: Stratford, 1803), p. 13.
30. Orders of the Magistrates, December Sessions, 1799, quoted in Sir Richard Phillips, *A Letter to the Livery of London, Relative to the Views of the Writer in Executing the Office of Sheriff* (London: Phillips, 1808), p. 43.
31. Select Committee report of 1799, quoted in the appendices to John Bowles, *Thoughts on the Late General Election, as Demonstrative of the Progress of Jacobinism* (London: Rivington, 1802), p. 97.
32. Quoted in Melville W. Patterson, *Sir Francis Burdett and His Times, 1770–1844* (London: Macmillan, 1931), vol. I, p. 72.

33. *The Times*, 1 January 1801.
34. *The Times*, 1 January 1801.
35. *The Times*, 1 January 1801.
36. King's Pardon, 4 September 1797. The National Archives, ref. HO 13/11, pp. 511–13.
37. *The Times*, 1 January 1801.
38. Duke of Portland to Thomas Aris, 25 November 1800. The National Archives, ref. HO 13/13, p. 203.
39. *The Times*, 10 February 1801.
40. *The Times*, 10 February 1801.
41. *Morning Post*, 10 February 1801.
42. *Morning Chronicle*, 13 February 1801.
43. Quoted in R. Thorne (ed.), *The History of Parliament: the House of Commons 1790–1820* (1986). See www.historyofparliamentonline.org/volume/1790–1820/member/elford-william-1749-1837.
44. *Morning Chronicle*, 13 February 1801.
45. *The Times*, 13 February 1801.
46. *Morning Chronicle*, 13 February 1801.
47. *The Times*, 14 February 1801.
48. *Bell's Weekly Messenger*, 15 February 1801.

10. *'The Ambition of an Honest Man': The Middlesex Elections*

1. *The Monthly Magazine; or the British Register*, vol. XXII, part II (London: Richard Phillips, 1806), p. 186.
2. John Horne Tooke, ἔπεα πτερόεντα, or *The Diversions of Purley* (London: J.W. Jackson, 1840), p. 445.
3. Michael Pearson and William Tooke to Sir Francis Burdett, 26 June 1802. Quoted in 'Sir Francis Burdett', in [Anon.] *Public Characters of 1802–1803* (London: Richard Phillips, 1803), p. 494.
4. Thomas Coutts to William Pitt, 25 July 1802. Quoted in Melville W. Patterson, *Sir Francis Burdett and His Times 1770–1844* (London: Macmillan, 1931), vol. I, p. 140.
5. Burdett to Pearson and Tooke, 26 June 1802. Quoted in 'Sir Francis Burdett', in [Anon.] *Public Characters of 1802–1803* (London: Richard Phillips, 1803), p. 494.
6. Middlesex population statistics are taken from 'Table of population, 1801–1901', *A History of the County of Middlesex*, vol. II (Victoria County History, London, 1911), p. 112.
7. Elie Halévy, *England in 1815* (New York: Barnes and Noble, 1961), p. 150.
8. Unknown writer quoted in Elie Halévy, *England in 1815* (New York: Barnes and Noble, 1961), p. 151.
9. *Bath Chronicle and Weekly Gazette*, 27 March 1806.
10. *Morning Chronicle*, 10 July 1802.
11. *Morning Chronicle*, 10 July 1802.
12. *Morning Post*, 14 July 1802.
13. *Morning Post*, 14 July 1802.
14. *Morning Post*, 14 July 1802.

15. *Morning Post*, 14 July 1802.
16. Tom Scriven, 'The Electoral Politics of the English Jacobins and Its Legacy, 1796–1807', *Journal of British Studies*, 60 (CUP, October 2021): 890–918. doi:10.1017/jbr.2021.66.
17. *Morning Post*, 14 July 1802.
18. *Morning Post*, 14 July 1802.
19. *Morning Post*, 17 July 1802.
20. *Morning Post*, 17 July 1802.
21. *Morning Post*, 28 July 1802.
22. *Morning Post*, 28 July 1802.
23. 'Sir Francis Burdett', in [Anon.] *Public Characters of 1802–1803* (London: Richard Phillips, 1803), p. 496.
24. *The Sun*, 28 July 1902.
25. Quoted in Melville W. Patterson, *Sir Francis Burdett and His Times, 1770–1844* (London: Macmillan, 1931), vol. I, p. 139.
26. *Morning Post*, 3 August 1802.
27. *Morning Post*, 3 August 1802.
28. *Morning Post*, 3 August 1802.
29. *Morning Herald*, 2 Oct 1802.
30. William Mainwaring, 'To the Gentlemen, Clergy, and Freeholders of the County of Middlesex', 29 July 1802, in the *Oracle and Daily Advertiser*, 31 July 1802.
31. Pitt to Addington, 29 July 1802. Quoted in George Pellew, *The Life and Correspondence of the Right Honourable Henry Addington, First Viscount Sidmouth* (London: Murray, 1847), vol. II, p. 72.
32. See Emma Vincent, '"The Real Grounds of the Present War": John Bowles and the French Revolutionary Wars, 1792–1802', *History*, 78 (1993), pp. 394–5.
33. John Bowles, *Thoughts on the Late General Election, as Demonstrative of the Progress of Jacobinism* (London: Rivington, 1802), p. 1.
34. John Bowles, *Thoughts on the Late General Election, as Demonstrative of the Progress of Jacobinism* (London: Rivington, 1802), p. 16.
35. John Bowles, *Thoughts on the Late General Election, as Demonstrative of the Progress of Jacobinism* (London: Rivington, 1802), p. 17.
36. *Morning Post*, 30 July 1803.
37. *Morning Post*, 30 July 1803.
38. *Hampshire Telegraph*, 14 November 1803.
39. See *The British Press*, 10 July 1804.
40. See London Metropolitan Archives, Middlesex Sessions, MJ/OC, orders of court bks., 5 July 1804, 1 December 1814, 6 April 1815, 7, 21, 27 March, 18 April 1822.
41. *Morning Chronicle*, 20 July 1804.
42. *British Press*, 7 August 1804.
43. Melville W. Patterson, *Sir Francis Burdett and His Times, 1770–1844* (London: Macmillan, 1931), vol. I, p. 150.
44. *Morning Post*, 1 August 1803.
45. *Morning Post*, 9 August 1804.
46. *Morning Chronicle*, 10 August 1804.
47. *Morning Chronicle*, 10 August 1804.

48. *Cobbett's Weekly Political Register*, 25 August 1804.
49. *Morning Chronicle*, 10 August 1804.
50. *Cobbett's Weekly Political Register*, 25 August 1804.
51. *Cobbett's Weekly Political Register*, 25 August 1804.
52. Melville W. Patterson, *Sir Francis Burdett and His Times, 1770–1844* (London: Macmillan, 1931), vol. I, p. 151.
53. Burdett to Thomas Creevey, 18 August [1804], in Sir Herbert Maxwell (ed.), *The Creevey Papers: A Selection from the Correspondence and Diaries of the Late Thomas Creevey, MP* (London: Murray, 1904), vol. I, pp.3–4.
54. Melville W. Patterson, *Sir Francis Burdett and His Times, 1770–1844* (London: Macmillan, 1931), vol. I, p. 78.
55. Michael Ignatieff, *A Just Measure of Pain: The Penitentiary in the Industrial Revolution, 1750–1850* (London: Macmillan, 1978), p. 139.

11. 'He Never Did Feel Shame': The Fall of Thomas Aris

1. London Metropolitan Archives, Middlesex Sessions, General Orders of the Court, SM/GO, 13 September 1798. London Lives ref. LMSMGO556110220.
2. Unknown source, quoted in Melville W. Patterson, *Sir Francis Burdett and His Times (1770–1844)* (London: Macmillan, 1931), vol. I, p. 71.
3. *Morning Post*, 16 May 1801.
4. *Morning Post*, 16 May 1801.
5. *Morning Chronicle*, 16 May 1801.
6. London Metropolitan Archives, Middlesex Sessions, General Orders of the Court, SM/GO, 18 September 1800. London Lives ref. LMSMGO556110488.
7. London Metropolitan Archives, Middlesex Sessions, General Orders of the Court, SM/GO, 18 September 1800. London Lives ref. LMSMGO556110488.
8. London Metropolitan Archives, Middlesex Sessions, General Orders of the Court, SM/GO, 18 September 1800. London Lives ref. LMSMGO556110488.
9. London Metropolitan Archives, Middlesex Sessions, General Orders of the Court, SM/GO, 18 September 1800. London Lives ref. LMSMGO556110488.
10. *The Times*, 22 December 1798.
11. See *Morning Post*, 30 July and 3 August 1802.
12. Dickie's bankruptcy dated to at least February 1802. See *Bury and Norwich Post*, 24 February 1802.
13. *The Trial between Thomas Aris, Governor of the House of Correction for the County of Middlesex, Plaintiff, and William Dickie, Defendant, in an Action for Slander* (London: Stratford, 1803), pp. 2–3.
14. *The Trial between Thomas Aris, Governor of the House of Correction for the County of Middlesex, Plaintiff, and William Dickie, Defendant, in an Action for Slander* (London: Stratford, 1803), p. 22.
15. *Morning Post*, 10 February 1803.
16. *The Trial between Thomas Aris, Governor of the House of Correction for the County of Middlesex, Plaintiff, and William Dickie, Defendant, in an Action for Slander* (London: Stratford, 1803), p. 55.

17. See 'Ellenborough, Edward Law, 1st Baron' in *The Encyclopaedia Britannica*, vol. IX, eleventh edition (1911).
18. *Morning Chronicle*, 31 August 1804.
19. Charles Dickens, *The Posthumous Papers of the Pickwick Club* (London: Chapman and Hall, 1837), pp. 435–40.
20. *The Times*, 26 September 1808.
21. *Morning Post*, 24 January 1801.
22. George Bryan, *Chelsea in the Olden and Present Times* (London: published by the author, 1869), p. 76.
23. *The Examiner*, 21 February 1808.
24. *The Examiner*, 21 February 1808.
25. Sir George Onesiphorus Paul to Sir Richard Phillips, 15 January 1808. Quoted in Richard Phillips, *A Letter to the Livery of London: Relative to the Views of the Writer in Executing the Office of Sheriff* (London: Phillips, 1808), p. 241.
26. *Report from the Commissioners on the Coldbath Fields Prison* (House of Commons, 19 May 1809), p. 4.
27. *Report from the Commissioners on the Coldbath Fields Prison* (House of Commons, 19 May 1809), p. 7.
28. *Report from the Commissioners on the Coldbath Fields Prison* (House of Commons, 19 May 1809), p. 10.
29. *Report from the Commissioners on the Coldbath Fields Prison* (House of Commons, 19 May 1809), p. 22.
30. *Report from the Commissioners on the Coldbath Fields Prison* (House of Commons, 19 May 1809), pp. 10–11.
31. *Report from the Commissioners on the Coldbath Fields Prison* (House of Commons, 19 May 1809), p. 22.
32. For details of St Luke's Hospital I am indebted to Nick Black, 'The Lost Hospitals of St Luke's', *Journal of the Royal Society of Medicine*, 100, 3 (2007), pp.125–9. doi: 10.1177/014107680710000310. PMID: 17339307; PMCID: PMC1809165.
33. *Report from the Commissioners on the Coldbath Fields Prison* (House of Commons, 19 May 1809), p. 5.
34. *Report from the Commissioners on the Coldbath Fields Prison* (House of Commons, 19 May 1809), p. 11.
35. *Report from the Commissioners on the Coldbath Fields Prison* (House of Commons, 19 May 1809), p. 11.
36. John Howard, *The State of the Prisons in England and Wales, with Preliminary Observations, and an Account of Some Foreign Prisons* (Warrington: William Eyres, 1777), p. 69.
37. *Report from the Commissioners on the Coldbath Fields Prison* (House of Commons, 19 May 1809), pp. 38–9.
38. *Report from the Commissioners on the Coldbath Fields Prison* (House of Commons, 19 May 1809), p. 39.
39. *Report from the Commissioners on the Coldbath Fields Prison* (House of Commons, 19 May 1809), p. 12.
40. *Report from the Commissioners on the Coldbath Fields Prison* (House of Commons, 19 May 1809), p. 12.

Notes

41. *Report from the Commissioners on the Coldbath Fields Prison* (House of Commons, 19 May 1809), p. 19.
42. *Bury and Norwich Post*, 5 September 1810.
43. Kellow Chesney, *The Victorian Underworld* (London: Penguin, 1979), p. 300.
44. *The Times*, 31 August 1810.
45. *The Times*, 1 September 1810.
46. *The Times*, 8 September 1810.
47. *The Times*, 4 September 1810.
48. *Caledonian Mercury*, 8 September 1810.
49. *The Times*, 8 September 1810.
50. *Caledonian Mercury*, 8 September 1810.
51. Thomas Aris to the Middlesex magistrates, 22 October 1810. Quoted in *The Times*, 30 October 1810.
52. *Morning Post*, 11 October 1810.
53. *Morning Post*, 11 October 1810.
54. *Morning Post*, 11 October 1810.
55. *Morning Post*, 11 October 1810.
56. *The Times*, 11 October 1810.
57. *Morning Advertiser*, 22 September 1810.
58. *Ipswich Journal*, 10 November 1810.
59. *Morning Advertiser*, 22 September 1810.
60. *The Times*, 4 October 1810.
61. *Morning Post*, 11 October 1810.
62. *The Times*, 2 October 1810.
63. *Morning Post*, 1 October 1810.
64. Old Bailey Proceedings Online (www.oldbaileyonline.org, version 9.0) September 1811. Trial of Robert Roberts (t18110918-3).
65. Freshfields Papers relating to Bank staff: Richard Armitage, Clerk – convicted of forging dividend warrants; hanged with Charles Thomas, 24 July 1811, on evidence by Robert Roberts. Bank of England Archive, ref. F6/53.
66. Trial of Charles Thomas for feloniously forging, on the 9th of August, a certain receipt for money, with intention to defraud the Governor and Company of the Bank of England. www.oldbaileyonline.org/record/18110529.
67. George Laval Chesterton, *Revelations of Prison Life; with an Enquiry into Prison Discipline and Secondary Punishments* (London: Hurst and Blackett, 1856), vol. I, p. 19.
68. Old Bailey Proceedings Online (www.oldbaileyonline.org, version 8.0) April 1813. Trial of Sarah Evans (t18130407-23).
69. Old Bailey Proceedings Online (www.oldbaileyonline.org, version 8.0) April 1813. Trial of Sarah Evans (t18130407-23).
70. Old Bailey Proceedings Online (www.oldbaileyonline.org, version 8.0) April 1813. Trial of Sarah Evans (t18130407-23).
71. Old Bailey Proceedings Online (www.oldbaileyonline.org, version 8.0) April 1813. Trial of Sarah Evans (t18130407-23).
72. *The Examiner*, 18 April 1813.
73. *The Examiner*, 18 April 1813.

74. *The Examiner*, 2 May 1813.
75. *The Examiner*, 2 May 1813.
76. *The Times*, 20 April 1840. Aris also received alms the previous year; see *The Standard*, 29 March 1839.

12. After Aris

1. See *Gentleman's Magazine*, September 1840, p. 326; also George Laval Chesterton, *Revelations of Prison Life; with an Enquiry into Prison Discipline and Secondary Punishments* (London: Hurst and Blackett, 1856), vol. I, pp. 34–5.
2. George Laval Chesterton, *Revelations of Prison Life; with an Enquiry into Prison Discipline and Secondary Punishments* (London: Hurst and Blackett, 1856), vol. I, p. 23.
3. James Neild, *State of the Prisons in England, Scotland, and Wales* (London: Nichols, 1812), p. 146.
4. Abstract of William Adkins's evidence to the Select Committee hearing into the policing of the metropolis, *Morning Post*, 9 September 1818.
5. James Neild, *State of the Prisons in England, Scotland, and Wales* (London: Nichols, 1812), p. 145.
6. *The Fourth Report of the Committee of the Society for the Improvement of Prison Discipline, &c.* (London: published by the society, 1822), p. 20.
7. Samuel Bamford, *Passages in the Life of a Radical* (New York: Cosimo Classics, 2005), p. 85.
8. Samuel Bamford, *Passages in the Life of a Radical* (New York: Cosimo Classics, 2005), p. 91.
9. *The Fourth Report of the Committee of the Society for the Improvement of Prison Discipline, &c.* (London: published by the society, 1822), p. 20.
10. *Papers Presented to the House of Commons, Relating to His Majesty's Prison in Cold Bath Fields*, Ordered to be printed 18th December 1800, p. 26.
11. Thomas R. Forbes, 'A Mortality Record for Coldbath Fields Prison, 1795–1829', *Bulletin of the New York Academy of Medicine: Journal of Urban Health*, 53, 7 (1977), p. 668.
12. William Farr's study of 93 English prisons for the years from 1826 to 1831 shows a mean annual mortality rate of 16.3 per 1,000 prisoners, or 1.63 per cent. See Noel A. Humphries (ed.), *Vital Statistics: A Memorial Volume of Selections from the Reports and Writings of William Farr* (London: Offices of the Sanitary Institute, 1885), p. 418.
13. *Bury and Norwich Post*, 1 January 1812.
14. *Morning Chronicle*, 24 February 1823.
15. *London Courier and Evening Gazette*, 28 August 1824.
16. Anne Lister, diary, 28 August 1824, West Yorkshire Archive Service, ref. SH 7/ML/E.
17. William Cubitt, 'Report to the Committee of the Society for the Improvement of Prison Discipline, &c.', September 1819. Quoted in *Northampton Mercury*, 30 December 1820.
18. [Anon.], *Description of the Tread Mill for the Employment of Prisoners with Observations on its Management* (London: published by the Society for the Improvement of Prison Discipline, 1823), p. 5.

19. *Stamford Mercury*, 11 January 1822.
20. *John Bull*, quoted in the *Caledonian Mercury*, 29 July 1822.
21. [John Ivatt Briscoe], *A Letter on the Nature and Effects of the Tread-Wheel, as an Instrument of Prison Labour and Punishment* (London: Hatchard, 1824), p. 9.
22. Sir John Cox Hippisley, *Prison Labour* (London: Nicol, Rivingtons, Hatchard, and Rodwell, 1823), p. 4.
23. *Bury and Norwich Post*, 10 July 1822.
24. *The Examiner*, 7 July 1822.
25. [Anon.], *Description of the Tread Mill for the Employment of Prisoners with Observations on its Management* (London: published by the Society for the Improvement of Prison Discipline, 1823), p. 6.
26. [Anon.], *Description of the Tread Mill for the Employment of Prisoners with Observations on its Management* (London: published by the Society for the Improvement of Prison Discipline, 1823), p. 30.
27. *Morning Chronicle*, 29 September 1823.
28. George Laval Chesterton, *Peace, War, and Adventure: An Autobiographical Memoir* (London: Longman, Brown, Rees, and Longmans, 1853), vol. II, p. 247.
29. Charles Dickens, *American Notes* (London: Chapman and Hall, 1850), p. 35.
30. George Laval Chesterton, *Revelations of Prison Life; with an Enquiry into Prison Discipline and Secondary Punishments* (London: Hurst and Blackett, 1856), vol. I, pp. 302–3.
31. Philip Collins, *Dickens and Crime* (Bloomington: Indiana State University, 1968), pp. 58-9.
32. *The Standard*, 20 November 1885.

Bibliography

Manuscript Sources

Bank of England Archive, London
Bodleian Library, Oxford
London Metropolitan Archives, Clerkenwell
Parliamentary Archives, London
The National Archives, Kew
The Royal Society Archives, London
West Yorkshire Archive Service, Leeds

Printed Books and Pamphlets

[Anon.], *A Further Account (Being Part II) of the Cruelties Discovered in the Cold-Bath Fields Prison* (London: Jordon [1800])
[Anon.], *An Impartial Statement of the Inhuman Cruelties Discovered! in the Coldbath-Fields Prison, by the Grand and Traverse Juries for the County of Middlesex, and Reported in the House of Commons on Friday 11th June 1800 by Sir Francis Burdett, Bart.* (London: J.S. Jordan [1800])
[Anon.], *Declaration of those Rights of the Commonalty of Great Britain, Without which they cannot be FREE* (Printed and distributed gratis by the Society for Constitutional Information; undated, but c. 1790)
[Anon.], *Description of the Tread Mill for the Employment of Prisoners with Observations on its Management* (London: published by the Society for the Improvement of Prison Discipline, 1823)
[Anon.], *First Report from the Committee of Secrecy, Ordered to be printed 17th May 1794* (London: Debrett, 1794)

Bibliography

[Anon.], *Narrative of the Proceedings at a General Meeting of the London Corresponding Society* (no publisher, 1795)

[Anon.], *Plan of the Finsbury Dispensary, St John's Square, Clerkenwell, for Administering Advice and Medicines to the Poor* (London: no publisher, n.d.)

[Anon.], *Prospectus of the Society for Constitutional Information* (Printed and distributed gratis by the Society for Constitutional Information; undated, but c. 1790)

[Anon.], *Public Characters of 1802–1803* (London: Richard Phillips, 1803)

[Anon.], *Reasons Offered for the Reformation of the House of Correction in Clerkenwell* (London: J. Scott, 1757)

[Anon.], *Regulations and Instructions Relating to His Majesty's Service at Sea* (London, 1790)

[Anon.], *The Annual Register, or a View of the History, Politics, and Literature, for the Year 1797* (London: Rivington, 1797)

[Anon.], *The Correspondence of the Revolution Society in London, with the National Assembly, and with Various Societies of the Friends of Liberty in France and England* (London: no publisher, 1792)

[Anon.], *The London Corresponding Society to the Nation at Large* (no publisher, 1792)

[Anon.], *The Parliamentary History of England, From the Earliest Period to the Year 1803* (London: Longman, Hurst, Rees et al., 1819)

[Anon.], *The Trial between Thomas Aris, Governor of the House of Correction for the County of Middlesex, Plaintiff, and William Dickie, Defendant, in an Action for Slander* (London: Stratford, 1803)

[Anon.], *Thoughts on Prison Labour, &c &c by a Student of the Inner Temple* (London: Rodwell and Martin, 1824)

[Anon.], *Truth and Treason! Or a Narrative of the Royal Procession to the House of Peers, October the 29th, 1795* (no place of publication, or publisher, 1795)

Archer, Thomas, *The Pauper, The Thief and the Convict: Sketches of Some of their Homes, Haunts, and Habits* (London: Groombridge, 1865)

Arnold, Catharine, *Bedlam: London and its Mad* (London: Pocket Books, 2009)

Babington, Anthony, *A House in Bow Street: Crime and the Magistracy, London 1740–1881* (London: Macdonald, 1969)

Bamford, Samuel, *Passages in the Life of a Radical* (New York: Cosimo Classics, 2005)

Bannantine, James, *Memoirs of Edward Marcus Despard* (London: Ridgway, 1799)

Barclay, Katie and Milka, Amy (eds.), *Cultural Histories of Law, Media and Emotion: Public Justice* (Abingdon: Routledge, 2023)

Beaumont, Matthew, *Night Walking: A Nocturnal History of London* (London: Verso, 2015)

Bickerton, John, *A Concise Account of the Fall and Rise of the Family of the Bickertons, of Maiden Castle in Cheshire, to which is annexed, The Gracious Dealings of God in the Life and Conversion of the Rev. John Bickerton, of the Same Family* (London: Trapp, 1777)

Bickley, Francis (ed.), *The Diaries of Sylvester Douglas (Lord Glenbervie)* (London: Constable, 1928)

Blackstone, William, *Commentaries on the Laws of England* (Oxford: Clarendon Press, 1768)

[Bone, John], *Reformers no Rioters* (London: LCS, c. 1794)
Bowles, John, *Thoughts on the Late General Election, as Demonstrative of the Progress of Jacobinism* (London: Rivington, 1802)
[Briscoe, John Ivatt], *A Letter on the Nature and Effects of the Tread-Wheel, as an Instrument of Prison Labour and Punishment* (London: Hatchard, 1824)
Brooke, John, *King George III* (London: Constable, 1972)
Brunsman, Denver, *The Evil Necessity: British Naval Impressment in the Eighteenth-Century Atlantic World* (Charlottesville and London: University of Virginia Press, 2013)
Bryan, George, *Chelsea in the Olden and Present Times* (London: published by author, 1869)
Burke, Edmund, *Reflections on the Revolution in France, and on the Proceedings in Certain Societies in London Relative to the Event in a Letter Intended to Have Been Sent to a Gentleman in Paris* (London: Dodsley, 1790)
Burn, Richard, *The Justice of the Peace, and Parish Officer* (The Savoy: Lintot, 1766)
Campbell, John, *The Lives of the Chief Justices of England* (London: Murray, 1874)
Chesney, Kellow, *The Victorian Underworld* (London: Penguin, 1979)
Chesterton, George Laval, *Peace, War, and Adventure: An Autobiographical Memoir* (London: Longman, Brown, Rees, and Longmans, 1853)
Chesterton, George Laval, *Revelations of Prison Life; with an Enquiry into Prison Discipline and Secondary Punishments* (London: Hurst and Blackett, 1856)
Cockburn, Henry, *Memorials of His Time* (New York: Appleton, 1856)
Coghan [sic], Thomas, *The Haven of Health* (London: Roger Ball, 1636)
Collins, Philip, *Dickens and Crime* (Bloomington: Indiana State University, 1968)
Conner, Clifford D., *Colonel Despard: The Life and Times of an Anglo-Irish Rebel* (Pennsylvania: Combined Publishing, 2000)
Courtenay, John, *Philosophical Reflections on the Late Revolution in France, and the Conduct of the Dissenters in England, in a Letter to the Rev. Dr Priestley* (London: Becket, 1790)
Cromwell, Thomas, *History and Description of the Parish of Clerkenwell* (London: J. & H.S. Storer, 1828)
Davis, Michael T. (ed.), *The London Corresponding Society, 1792–1795* (London: Routledge, 2002)
Dickens, Charles, *American Notes* (London: Chapman and Hall, 1850)
Dickens, Charles, *Oliver Twist* (London: Penguin, 1988)
Dickens, Charles, *Our Mutual Friend* (London: Chapman and Hall, 1865)
Dickens, Charles, *The Posthumous Papers of the Pickwick Club* (Oxford: Oxford University Press, 2008)
Diprose, John, *Some Account of the Parish of Saint Clement Danes (Westminster) Past and Present* (London: Diprose and Bateman, 1868)
Dixon, William Hepworth, *The London Prisons, with an account of the more distinguished persons who have been confined in them: to which is added a description of the chief provincial prisons* (London: Jackson and Walford, 1850)
Douthwaite, William Ralph, *Gray's Inn: Notes Illustrative of Its History and Antiquities* (London: privately printed, 1876)
Fitzgerald, Percy, *Chronicles of Bow Street Police-Office. With an Account of the Magistrates, 'Runners', and Police* (London: Chapman & Hall, 1888)
Gill, Conrad, *The Naval Mutinies of 1797* (Manchester: University Press, 1913)

Bibliography

Glasse, Samuel, *The Sinner Encouraged to Repentance: A Sermon, Preached at the Opening of the Chapel of the New House of Correction, for the County of Middlesex* (London: Rivington, Robinson and Gardner, 1794)

Grant, William, *An Essay on the Pestilential Fever of Sydenham, Commonly Called the Gaol, Hospital, Ship, and Camp-Fever* (London: Cadell, 1775)

Grego, Joseph, *A History of Parliamentary Elections and Electioneering in the Old Days* (London: Chatto and Windus, 1886)

Haddelsey, Stephen, *Poor Bickerton: A Journey to the Dark Heart of Georgian England* (Cheltenham: The History Press, 2024)

Hague, William, *William Pitt the Younger* (London: HarperCollins, 2004)

Hague, William, *William Wilberforce: The Life of the Great Anti-Slave Campaigner* (London: HarperPress, 2007)

Halévy, Elie, *England in 1815* (New York: Barnes and Noble, 1961)

Hall, Edward, *Hall's Chronicle; Containing the History of England* (London: Johnson, Rivington, Payne et al., 1809)

Hathaway, W.S. (ed.), *The Speeches of the Right Honourable William Pitt in the House of Commons* (London: Longman, Hurst, Rees, et al., 1817)

Hippisley, Sir John Cox, *Prison Labour* (London: Nicol, Rivingtons, Hatchard, and Rodwell, 1823)

Hodder, George, *Sketches of Life and Character Taken at the Police Court, Bow Street* (London: Sherwood and Bowyer, 1845)

Holinshed, Raphael, *Holinshed's Chronicles of England, Scotland, and Ireland* (London: Johnson, Rivington, Payne et al., 1808)

Hostettler, John, *Thomas Erskine and Trial by Jury* (Chichester Barry Rose Law Publishers Ltd, 1996)

Howard, John, *The State of the Prisons in England and Wales, with Preliminary Observations, and an Account of Some Foreign Prisons* (Warrington: William Eyres, 1777)

Howell, Thomas Jones, *A Complete Collection of State Trials and Proceedings for High Treason and Other Crimes and Misdemeanors from the Earliest Period to the Year 1783* (London: Longman et al., 1817)

Humphries, Noel A. (ed.), *Vital Statistics: A Memorial Volume of Selections from the Reports and Writings of William Farr* (London: Offices of the Sanitary Institute, 1885)

Ignatieff, Michael, *A Just Measure of Pain: The Penitentiary in the Industrial Revolution, 1750–1850* (London: Macmillan, 1978)

Impey, John, *The Practice of the Office of Sheriff and Under-Sheriff* (London: Clarke, 1835)

Jay, Mike, *The Unfortunate Colonel Despard* (London: Bantam Books, 2004)

Jones, William, *The Works of the Right Reverend George Horne, DD, Late Lord Bishop of Norwich; to which are Prefixed Memoirs of his Life, Studies, and Writings* (New York: Onderdonk, 1846)

King, Richard (ed.), *The Modern London Spy* (London: Hogg, 1781)

Kingsford, Charles Lethbridge (ed.), *A Survey of London by John Stowe, Reprinted from the Text of 1603* (Oxford: The Clarendon Press, 1908)

Kingsford, Charles Lethbridge (ed.), *Chronicles of London* (Dursley: Alan Sutton, 1977)

Lambard, William, *Archeion, or a Discourse Upon the High Courts of Justice in England* (London: Seile, 1635)

Lawless, Valentine, *Personal Recollections of the Life and Times, with Extracts from the Correspondence of Valentine Lord Cloncurry* (Dublin: McGlashan, 1849)

Leslie-Manville, R., *The Life and Work of Sir John Fielding* (London: Lincoln Williams, 1934)

[Mainwaring, William], *The Secrets of the Bastille Disclosed* (London: Rivington, 1799)

Manwaring, George E. and Dobrée, Bonamy, *The Floating Republic: An Account of the Mutinies at Spithead and the Nore in 1797* (London: Penguin Books, 1937)

Maxwell, Herbert (ed.), *The Creevey Papers: A Selection from the Correspondence and Diaries of the Late Thomas Creevey, MP* (London: Murray, 1904)

Mayhew, Henry and Binny, John, *The Criminal Prisons of London: And Scenes of Prison Life* (London: Griffin, Bohn and Co., 1862)

Morpurgo, J.E. (ed.), *The Autobiography of Leigh Hunt* (London: The Cresset Press, 1949)

Moseley, Benjamin, *A Treatise on Tropical Diseases; On Military Operations; and On the Climate of the West-Indies* (London: Cadell, 1792)

Namier, Lewis and Brooke, John (ed.), *The History of Parliament: The House of Commons 1754–1790* (Oxford: History of Parliament Trust, 1964)

Neild, James, *State of the Prisons in England, Scotland, and Wales* (London: John Nichols, 1812)

Nelson, Horatio, *The Despatches and Letters of Vice Admiral Lord Viscount Nelson with Notes by Sir Nicholas Harris Nicolas* (London: Chatham Publishing, 1997)

Nichols, John, *Literary Anecdotes of the Eighteenth Century* (London: Nichols, 1812)

Oman, Charles, *The Unfortunate Colonel Despard and Other Studies* (London: Arnold, 1922)

Paine, Thomas, *Rights of Man* (London: Jordan, 1791)

Parolin, Christina, *Radical Spaces: Venues of Popular Politics in London, 1790–c. 1845* (Canberra: ANU E Press, 2010)

Patmore, Peter G., *My Friends and Acquaintance: Being Memorials, Mind-Portraits, and Personal Recollections of Deceased Celebrities of the Nineteenth Century* (London: Saunders and Otley, 1854)

Patterson, Melville W., *Sir Francis Burdett and His Times (1770–1844)* (London: Macmillan, 1931)

Paul, George O., *Considerations on the Defects of Prisons, and Their Present System of Regulation* (London: Cadell, 1784)

Pellew, George, *The Life and Correspondence of the Right Honourable Henry Addington, First Viscount Sidmouth* (London: Murray, 1847)

Phillips, Richard Sir, *A Letter to the Livery of London, Relative to the Views of the Writer in Executing the Office of Sheriff* (London: Phillips, 1808)

Pinks, William J., *The History of Clerkenwell*, second edition (London: Charles Herbert, 1881)

Pope, Alexander, *The Dunciad with Notes Variorum, and the Prolegomena of Scriblerus* (London: Lawton Gulliver, 1729)

Porter, Roy, *Mind-Forg'd Manacles: A History of Madness in England from the Restoration to the Regency* (London: The Athlone Press, 1987)

Price, Cecil (ed.), *The Letters of Richard Brinsley Sheridan* (Oxford: Clarendon Press, 1966)

Pringle, John, *Observations on the Diseases of the Army* (London: Strahan, Rivington, Johnston et al., 1775)

[Reeves, John], *Thoughts on the English Constitution. Addressed to the Quiet Good Sense of the People of England in a Series of Letters. Letter the First* (London: Owen, 1795)

Ritchie, James Ewing, *Days and Nights in London: Studies in Black and Gray* (London: Tinsley Brothers, 1880)

Roberton, John, *A Treatise on Medical Police, and on Diet, Regimen, &c.* (London: Thomas Bryce and John Murray, 1809)

Rudé, George, *Hanoverian London 1714–1808* (Stroud: Sutton Publishing, 1971)

Sheppard, Edgar, *Memorials of St James's Palace* (London: Longmans, Green and Co., 1894)

Sinclair, John, *Memoirs of the Life and Works of the Late Right Honourable Sir John Sinclair, Bart.* (London: Blackwood and Sons, 1837)

Stirling, Anna M.W., *A Painter of Dreams and Other Biographical Studies* (London: Lane, 1916)

Temple, Philip (ed.), 'West of Farringdon Road', in *Survey of London: Volume 47, Northern Clerkenwell and Pentonville* (London, 2008)

Thale, Mary (ed.), *The Autobiography of Francis Place* (New York: Cambridge University Press, 1972)

Thelwall, John, *Poems Written in Close Confinement in the Tower and Newgate under a Charge of High Treason* (London: printed for the author, 1795)

Thornbury, Walter, *Old and New London* (London, 1878)

Tooke, John Horne, ἔπεα πτερόεντα, *or The Diversions of Purley* (London: J.W. Jackson, 1840)

Wade, John, *A Treatise on the Police and Crimes of the Metropolis* (London: Longman, Rees, Orme, Brown and Green, 1829)

Walford, Edward, *Old & New London: A Narrative of its History, Its People & Its Places – Westminster & The Western Suburbs*, vol. IV (London: Cassell, no date)

White, Jerry, *London in the Eighteenth Century: A Great and Monstrous Thing* (London: The Bodley Head, 2012)

White, Jerry, *London in the Nineteenth Century: 'A Human Awful Wonder of God'* (London: Jonathan Cape, 2007)

White, Jerry, *Mansions of Misery: A Biography of the Marshalsea Debtors' Prison* (London: The Bodley Head, 2016)

Wight, John, *Mornings at Bow Street: A Selection of the Most Humorous and Entertaining Reports which Have Appeared in the Morning Herald* (London: Charles Baldwyn, 1824)

Wilkinson, George T., *The Newgate Calendar Improved; Being Interesting Memoirs of Notorious Characters, Who have been Convicted of Offences against the Laws of England* (London: Thomas Kelly, n.d.)

Wraxall, Nathaniel W., *Historical Memoirs of his Own Time* (London: Bentley, 1836)

Wright, John (ed.), *The Speeches of the Right Honourable Charles James Fox, in the House of Commons* (London: Longman, Hurst, Rees et al., 1815)

Academic Journals and Papers

Alpaugh, Micah, 'The British Origins of the French Jacobins: Radical Sociability and the Development of the Political Club Networks, 1787–1793', *European History Quarterly*, 44, 4 (2014)

Black, Nick, 'The Lost Hospitals of St Luke's', *Journal of the Royal Society of Medicine*, 100, 3 (2007)

Brunsman, Denver, 'Men of War: British Sailors and the Impressment Paradox', *Journal of Early Modern History*, 14 (1–2)

Cox, David, '"A Certain Share of Low Cunning" – The Provincial Use and Activities of Bow Street "Runners" 1792–1839', *Eras Journal* (University of Monash), 5 (November 2003)

Devereux, Simon, 'The Making of the Penitentiary Act, 1775–1779', *The Historical Journal*, 42, 2 (1999)

Emerichs, Mary Beth, 'Getting Away with Murder? Homicide and the Coroners in Nineteenth Century London', *Social Science History*, 25, 1, Special Issue: Bloody Murder (Spring, 2001), pp. 93–100

Finn, Margot, 'Being in Debt in Dickens' London: Fact, Fictional Representation and the Nineteenth-Century Prison', *Journal of Victorian Culture*, 1, 2 (Autumn 1996)

Forbes, Thomas R., 'A Mortality Record for Coldbath Fields Prison, 1795–1829', *Bulletin of the New York Academy of Medicine: Journal of Urban Health*, 53, 7 (1977)

Hardman, Philippa, *The Origins of Late Eighteenth-Century Prison Reform in England*. Unpublished PhD thesis (2007), Department of History, University of Sheffield

Johnston, Kenneth R., 'The First and Last British Convention', *Romanticism*, 13, 2 (2007)

King Fisher, Yvonne, *Coroners in London and Middlesex, c. 1820–1888: A Study of Medicalization and Professionalization*. Unpublished PhD thesis (2019), The Open University, Open Research Online

Lincecum, A.L., 'Typhus Fever', *Buffalo Medical Journal*, 74, 2, September 1918

Moran, Richard, 'The Origin of Insanity as a Special Verdict: The Trial for Treason of James Hadfield (1800)', *Law and Society Review*, 19, 3 (1985), pp. 487–519

Norwood East, W., 'Crime and Insanity', *The Post-Graduate Medical Journal*, IV, 48 (September 1929), p. 202

Scriven, Tom, 'The Electoral Politics of the English Jacobins and Its Legacy, 1796–1807', *Journal of British Studies*, 60 (CUP, October 2021)

Trahey, E.M., *Free Women and the Making of Colonial Jamaican Economy and Society 1760–1834*. Unpublished PhD thesis (2018), University of Cambridge

Vincent, Emma, '"The Real Grounds of the Present War": John Bowles and the French Revolutionary Wars, 1792–1802', *History*, 78 (1993)

Wood, Andy, 'In Debt and Incarcerated: The Tyranny of Debtors' Prisons', *The Gazette* (www.thegazette.co.uk/all-notices/content/100938)

Newspapers and Periodicals

Albion & Evening Advertiser
Bath Chronicle and Weekly Gazette
Bell's Weekly Messenger
British Press
Bury and Norwich Post
Caledonian Mercury

Bibliography

Cobbett's Weekly Political Register
Courier
Evening Mail
Examiner
Ipswich Journal
Jackson's Oxford Journal
Johnson's British Gazette and Sunday Monitor
London Chronicle
London Packet or New Evening Post
Medical Times and Gazette
Mirror of the Times
Morning Chronicle
Morning Herald
Morning Post
Observer
Oracle
Post Boy
Public Advertiser
St James's Chronicle
Star and Evening Advertiser
The Atlantic Monthly
The Gentleman's Magazine
The London Gazette
The Mirror of Literature, Amusement and Instruction
The Standard
The Sun
The Times
The World
True Briton
Whitehall Evening Post

Acknowledgements

In the twenty-five years that have passed since I began my first book, a quiet revolution has occurred in the realms of historical research. The revolutionaries are the nameless bands of archivists and digitisers who, year on year, decade after decade, have gradually copied and published a mind-boggling array of books and documents, making them immediately accessible to researchers and writers the world over. To them, I should like to acknowledge my own very considerable debt: without their work this book might still have been written, but the process would have been infinitely more laborious.

As always, the staff of many institutions have been of enormous help to me, and I should like to mention, in particular, the librarians and archivists of the following: the Bank of England, London; the Bodleian Library, Oxford; the Howard League for Penal Reform, London; the London Metropolitan Archives, Clerkenwell; the Parliamentary Archives, London; the National Archives, Kew; the Royal College of Surgeons, London; the Royal Society, London; the West Yorkshire Archive Service, Leeds; and the Worshipful Society of Apothecaries, London.

At a personal level, I should like to offer my sincere thanks to Lord Ken Macdonald, KC, for his generous foreword; and to Jerry White, Emeritus Professor of Modern London History, Birkbeck, University of London, who has always been willing to answer my questions, despite the considerable demands of his own research and writing.

Last, but by no means least, I must thank my wife, Caroline, and my son, George, for their love, support and good humour as I have carried them with me from cell to cell.

Stephen Haddelsey
Halam, Nottinghamshire

Index

Act for Preserving the Health of Prisoners in Gaol (1774) 23
Addington, Henry 108, 159, 162
Adkins, William 183, 189–91, 194
Aliens Act (1793) 175
Amiens, Treaty of (1802) 155
Amos, Thomas 179, 180
Aris, Charles (son) 180
Aris, Daniel (son) 180, 181, 184
Aris, Priscilla (second wife) 43, 47
Aris, Samuel (son) 43
Aris, Sarah (first wife) 42–3
Aris, Thomas 10
   appointment as gaoler 40–1, 46
   early life 42
   establishes bakery in Clerkenwell 43
   marriages 43
   additional appointments 44
   appointed as baker to the prison and Bridewell 44–5
   accused of assault 46–7, 72, 126, 150, 169, 171
   on prison discipline 72
   describes Burdett's third visit 71, 89
   defended by Mainwaring 103, 155
   accusations of corruption 113, 129, 135–6, 144, 180–1
   caricatured by Gillray 124
   defends squalid conditions 130
   neglect of duties 144, 146
   prosecutes William Dickie 170–3
   treatment of de Blin 175–7
   employment of female prisoners 177–9, 186
   dismissal 181–5
   murder of George Evans 186–7
   last years 188
Aris, Thomas (son) 177–8
Ashhurst, Sir William 50–1
Auburn Prison, New York State 196

Babington, Anthony 48
Bacon, Sir Francis 10
Bagnigge House 29
Bagnigge Wells 29
Baker, Sir Robert 137
Baker, William 139
Ballard, Joseph 143
Bamford, Samuel 190
Bantry Bay 82
Bastille Saint-Antoine (French fortress) 13, 73, 101
Baynard, Dr Edward 29
Baynes, Walter 29, 34

Bethlem Royal Hospital for the Insane 176
Bickerton, John 53–4
Binns, John 80
Bird, William Wilberforce 113
Blackburn, William 31–2, 139
Blackstone, William 47, 48
Bleamire, William 32, 33
Bone, John 89–91 *passim*
Bosville, 'Colonel' William ('Billy') 56–9 *passim*, 70, 99, 101, 109, 135
Bowles, John *Thoughts on the Late General Election, as Demonstrative of the Progress of Jacobinism* 160, 165
Braxfield, Lord 77
Breton, William 156
Bridport, Admiral (Alexander Hood) 61–2
Briscoe, John Ivatt 194
Brown, Lancelot 'Capability' 35
Buller, Sir Francis 81
Burdett, Sir Francis
  background 57
  on marriage 57
  first election to the Commons 57
  motivations 57
  character 57, 58
  visits to Coldbath Fields 9–11, 70–3, 88–9, 135
  meets Edward Despard 99
  speeches in Parliament 103–4, 107, 112–13, 127–132, 148–9
  accusations of misconduct 109–110, 147
  caricatured by Gillray 124
  reaction to Royal Commission 147
  Middlesex elections 152–167 *passim*
Burdon, Rowland 103, 106–11 *passim*
Burke, Edmund *Reflections on the Revolution in France* (1790) 73, 74
Burland, John Berkeley 139
Buxton, Robert John 139
Byng, George 154–5
Byrne, Nicholas 163–4
Byrne, William Pitt 163

Canning, George 107–8
Chesney, Kellow 179
Chesterton, Captain George Laval 185, 195–8
  Revelations of Prison Life 197
Clarence, William, Duke of 168
Clerkenwell Bridewell, Corporation Row 24, 27, 28, 29, 33, 36, 37, 40, 42, 44, 45, 46, 137
Coigly, James 80–1, 98–9
Coldbath Fields House of Correction
  appearance and design 10, 37
  selection of site 27, 29–31
  specifications 28, 31–3
  costs of construction 34–6
  construction 34–6
  opening 37
  prisoners' impressions 37–8, 190
  escape of mutineers 67–70
  treatment of radical prisoners 86–7, 90–1, 100–07, 112, 125
  vagrants' wards 127, 130, 142–3
  mortality rates 141–2, 191
  overcrowding 144, 190
  introduction of the treadmill 194
  introduction of the Silent System 197
  closure 198
Coldbath Square 10
Coleridge, Samuel Taylor 124
Collins, Philip 197
Combe, Alderman Harvey 156
Convention of London (1786) 95
Courtenay, John 58–9, 70, 99, 100–2 *passim*, 104, 106–7, 109, 125, 132, 135, 154
Coutts, Thomas 57, 153
Cox, Robert Albion 161
Creevey, Thomas 166
Cubitt, William 192, 195
Curtis, Sir William 165

Davis, John 67, 68, 71, 72
de Blin, Chevalier Charles 175–7
de Blin, Thérèse 176, 177
Dell, William 124, 125, 129

Index

Despard, Catherine (née Gordon) 97, 98, 99, 104–7 *passim*
Despard, Colonel Edward Marcus 90
  early life 91
  character 92, 98, 162
  Nicaragua campaign 92–4
  Black River campaign 94
  Superintendent of Bay of Honduras 95–7
  campaign for reinstatement 97
  joins LCS 97
  marriage to Catherine Gordon 97
  sympathy with United Englishmen 98
  arrest 99, 100
  treatment in Coldbath Fields 100–1, 105–6, 110
  contradiction of wife's claims 106, 109, 111
  support for United Irishmen 162
  charged with High Treason 162
  trial 162
  execution 162
Despard, General John (brother) 99
Devonshire, Georgiana, Duchess of 158
Dickens, Charles *The Posthumous Papers of the Pickwick Club* 172, 196
Dickie, William 123, 125, 127, 169–73
Diprose, John 82
Discharged Prisoners Act (1774) 23
Dobrée, Bonamy 66
Dumouriez, General Charles-François du Périer 175
Dundas, Henry (Viscount Melville) 65, 81, 83, 97, 101, 102, 104
Dundas, William 110, 111, 131, 136, 148

Eardley, Luke *see* Early, Luke
Early, Luke 133–4, 136, 148, 168,
Eastern State Penitentiary, Philadelphia 196
Elford, Sir William 150
Elizabeth I, Queen 10
Ellenborough, Edward Law, Baron 170–2, 188
Ellison, Richard 110
Erskine, Thomas 78, 164, 171

Evans, George 185–7
Evans, Sarah 185–7
Evans, Thomas 83, 90

Finsbury Dispensary 44, 46
Fleet Prison 137, 172–3
Fleet, River 29, 30, 34
Flitcroft, Henry 9
Folkard, William 184
Forbes, Thomas R. 191
Ford, Sir Richard 53–4, 108
Fox, Charles James 59, 78, 80, 103, 158
Foy, John 184
French Revolution 54, 59, 65, 73, 74, 75, 76, 105, 160, 175, 197

Gainer, George 67
Gaol Distemper *see* Typhus
Gaol Fever *see* Typhus
Gaols Act (1823) 196
Gardiner's Field Clerkenwell 30, 35, 38, 42
Garrow, William 169–71 *passim*, 173
General Conventions (1792 and 1793) 77
Gentleman's Magazine 34, 184
George III, King 38, 53, 65, 79, 153, 176, 178, 194, 197
George IV, King 189
Gerrald, Joseph 77
Gillray, James 124
Glasse, Rev. Samuel 38–41 *passim*
  The Sinner Encouraged to Repentance (1794) 39, 103
Glorious Revolution (1688) 74–5
Goodluck, Thomas 85, 90
Gordon Riots 137
Gray's Inn 10
Gray's Inn Lane 10, 186
Greenwich, Royal Naval Hospital 60, 62
Griffiths, John 67
Gurney, John 52
Gwynne, Nell 29

Habeas Corpus Act (1679) 54, 78
  suspension of 73, 78, 99, 100, 102, 104, 123, 139, 155, 160–3 *passim*, 167, 173

237

Hague, William 78
Halévy, Elie, *History of the English People in the Nineteenth Century* 154
Hardy, Thomas 77–8, 164
Harper (alias Smith, prisoner) 179, 181, 182
Harwood, John 40
Hawkins (prisoner) 133
Heron, Joseph 169
Higgles, Obaker 89, 110, 112, 135, 136, 169
Hippisley, John Cox 194
Hobhouse, Benjamin 150
Hoche, Louis Lazare 66
Hockley-in-the-Hole 29
Hogarth, William, *Humours of an Election* 154
Holland, Henry 35
Hone, William 172
Hook, Theodore 193–4
Hooper, William 67
Horsemonger Lane Gaol 37, 162
Howard, John
  early life 9
  capture and imprisonment 13–4
  appointment as High Sheriff of Bedfordshire 14
  researches into prison conditions 15–17, 19–21
  presents findings to Parliament 21–3
  The State of Prisons in England and Wales (1777) 23
  recommendations 23–4
  visits Clerkenwell Bridewell 24
  advocates site at Mount Pleasant 30
  death 107
Hudson, Joseph 149–50
Hunger in gaols 19–20
Hunt, James Henry Leigh 37, 188
Hunt, John 37
Hurst, Aaron Henry 29, 31, 139

Ignatieff, Michael 166
Iliff, John, *A Summary of the Duties of Citizenship!* 70

Impey, John 134
Insolvent Debtors Relief Act 172

James II, King 74
Jervoise, Jervoise Clarke 30, 34
Johnston, James 135–6, 138, 145, 148, 169
Johnston, Kenneth R. 77
Jones, James 67, 72, 126, 149

Kean, Edmund 161
Keir, Robert 85, 90
Kenyon, Lloyd (Lord Chief Justice) 50, 101, 169
Kerr, John 49–51
Kew, Elizabeth 177–8, 186
King's Bench Prison 32, 48, 49. 97, 170, 186, 187
Kirby, John 87–8
Knowlys, Newman 164–5

Lambard, William 47
Lawless, Valentine 104–5
Le Fevre, Charles Shaw 139
Leroux, Jacob 29, 32–4 *passim*
Lever, George 169
Lincoln's Inn 9, 162
Lister, Anne 192
London Corresponding Society (LCS) 73, 75–85 *passim*, 91, 97–8, 163
London Metropolitan Archives 68
London West India Committee 153
Louis XVI, King 76
Lowrie, John 48–9

Mainwaring, George Boulton 162–6 *passim*
Mainwaring, William 38, 39, 69, 103, 128, 129, 131, 132, 140, 146, 153, 154, 155–62 *passim*, 170, 181
Manwaring, George E. 66
Margarot, Maurice 77
Marshalsea Prison 13, 16
Marsham, Charles, Viscount 161
Martin, James 150
Matthews, PC John 187

Index

McNamara, Michael 180, 181
Millar, Thomas 49–51
Mitford, Sir John 129, 131, 132
Monro, Dr Thomas 176
Mordaunt, Sir John 110
Morning Chronicle 36, 52, 85, 155, 164, 195
Morning Post 78, 105, 139, 149, 155, 157, 158–9, 163, 182
Moseley, Dr John 93
Mount Pleasant, Clerkenwell 30, 123, 198
Muir, Thomas 77

Neagle (prisoner) 85, 90
Neild, James 88, 189
Nelson, Abraham 67
Nelson, Horatio (Viscount Nelson) 59, 92–4 *passim*, 162
Newgate Prison 13, 16, 36, 49, 85–8 *passim*, 91, 108, 109, 137, 161, 169, 184
Nicholson, John 137–8
Nicholson, Thomas 90, 109
Nore, Mutiny at the 59, 62–6, 80, 82
North, Frederick (Lord North) 58–9

Office for National Statistics 153
Oldcastle, Sir John 29
Oxford's 'Black Assizes' 16

Page, Edward 169
Paine, Thomas 66
    Rights of Man (1791) 73, 74, 105
Paris, Treaty of (1783) 95
Parker, Richard 63, 65, 66
Paul, Sir George Onesiphorus 135, 141, 145
    Consideration of the Defects of Prisons (1784) 146, 147, 174, 191
Paull (prison watchman) 180
Pearse, John 184, 185
Pearson, Michael 152–3, 157
Peel, Sir Robert 193, 194
Pelham, Thomas, Lord 159
Penitentiary Act (1779) 27, 31

Phillips, Sir Richard *Letter to the Livery of London* (1808) 86
Pierrepont, Evelyn 150
Pinks, William J. 29, 30, 43
Pitt, William 65, 66, 77, 78, 79, 81, 86, 90, 96, 102, 108, 111, 131, 133, 147, 150, 159, 162, 163, 174, 197
Pitt, William Morton 139, 174
Place, Francis 83, 85, 87, 88, 89, 98
Plumer, Thomas 165
Polson, Major John 92, 94
Pope, Alexander 30, 59
Portland, Duke of 53, 54, 69, 87, 91, 105, 108, 109, 139, 148, 150
Preston, Christopher 30
Price, William 134
Prisons Act (1835) 196
Prisons Act (1877) 198

Quakers' Society for the Improvement of Prison Discipline 189, 190
Quakers' workhouse, Clerkenwell 27–9 *passim*

Ratcliff Highway murders 191
Rawlins, Sir William 161
Read, James 176, 177
Redfern, William 148
Reeves, John 104–6, 160
Revolution Society of London 74–5, 80, 152
Rich, Mary 123–6, 129–30, 157, 169
Roberts, Robert ('Bob') 179–85
Robespierre, Maximilien 156
Rogers, Thomas 35, 36
Rosoman, Thomas 42–3
Rudé, George 127
Russell, Lord William 158

Saint Bartholomew's Hospital 136
St Giles 9
Saint Luke's Hospital for Lunatics 176
Scott, Sir John 102, 104, 106, 109
Seditious Meetings Act (1795) 79
Separate System 38–9, 196–7

Sheppard, Jack 82
Sheridan, Richard Brinsley 113, 128–9, 131–2, 167, 173–4
Silent System 196–7
Simpson, Mrs 187
Skirving, William 77
Smith, John 70
  Impartial Statement of the Inhuman Cruelties Discovered! in the Coldbath-Fields Prison 135, 138
Society for Constitutional Information (SCI) 74–5, 156
Society for the Improvement of Prison Discipline 192, 194, 195
Society of the Friends of the People 156
Spithead, Mutiny at 61–4 *passim*, 66, 80, 82
Spranger, John 139
Stephens, Alexander 173, 174, 177
Stone, Thomas 47, 171
Stuart, Daniel 163

Taylor, John 182–4 *passim*
Thelwall, John 78
  Poems Written in Close Confinement in the Tower and Newgate 86, 164
Thomas, Ann 191
Tierney, George 102, 125, 129, 131
Times, The 136, 138, 151, 183
Titchfield, Marquess of 109
Tone, Wolfe 66, 98
Tooke, John Horne 78
  Diversions of Purley 152, 160, 164, 173
Tooke, William 152–3, 157
Tothill Fields Bridewell 85, 109
Townshend, George (1st Marquess Townshend) 58
Townshend, Thomas (Viscount Sydney) 94–5

Transportation 20, 27
Treadmill 192–5
Treasonable and Seditious Practices Act (1795) 79
Treatment of the insane 21
True Britons, Society of 88
Tyburn, River 9
Typhus 16–19, 86, 142

United Englishmen 80, 83, 88, 98
United Irishmen, Society of 66, 80, 98, 104, 162

Vere Street Coterie 51–3
Vickery, John 189, 191
Victoria, Queen 188

Waddington, Samuel 'Little' 191
Wakefield Prison 197
Walter, Edward 112, 135
Webb, John 89
Webbe, Dr Thomas 109, 127, 130, 133–5, 140, 142, 148, 150, 176, 179, 191–2
Wellington, Arthur Wellesley, Duke of 195
Wells, John 67
Whitbread, Samuel 22, 30
Wilberforce, William 103, 106, 110, 126, 136, 152
Wilkes, John 152
William III, King 31, 74
Williams, John 191
Willoughby, Sir Christopher 139
Wood Street Compter 87

Young, Sir William 113–4

The destination for history
www.thehistorypress.co.uk